GLENN ELLIOTT

A Ranger's Ranger

BY

GLENN ELLIOTT

WITH
ROBERT NIEMAN

First Edition — April, 1999
Second Edition — June, 1999
Third Edition — November, 1999

Library of Congress Catalog Card Number
99-93014

ISBN 0-87244-122-9

Printed
by

Texian Press
Waco, Texas

TABLE OF CONTENTS

DEDICATION

I would like to dedicate this book to my wife and children: Catherine, Diane, and Dennis. They are the faithful ones who made the sacrifices in order for me to do the job that I was truly dedicated to. My entire career was never an eight to five job. To the contrary, it was long days and nights, and always on call, with little or no time left to spend with the ones who truly needed it. This meant many meals, family gatherings, church and school affairs, and ball games without a husband or father. They did these things and yet always supported my efforts one hundred percent, never expecting an explanation as to what I was working on, how many had been killed in a traffic accident, or who shot John. At best they might read about it in the tomorrow's newspaper or hear part of my telephone conversations while talking with the press, insurance adjusters or others.

Mention should also be made of those officers I was associated with early in my career: Lloyd Webb, Guy Smith, Sam Guynes, Pat Spier, Jim Riddle, Jim Ray, Lewis Rigler, Red Arnold, and others—seasoned men who gave encouragement to a rookie country officer. Their advice and guidance were instrumental in any success I may have had in my tenure.

The friends I met and made along the way played an important part in my career. They were always ready to help in some way to make my job easier, to show community support, do jury service, and offer words of encouragement. Letters in my personnel file at DPS headquarters in Austin are appreciated beyond words. Equally as important was hearing personally and through others from the citizens I was sworn to protect was particularly uplifting.

To you and all the officers I worked with daily throughout my career, I say thanks.

Glenn Elliott

ASSOCIATE'S THANKS

I met Glenn Elliott twice. The first time was in 1978. My family and I had just moved to Texas from Batesville, Arkansas, and we were living on a ranch just east of Hallsville across the street from a ranch operated by a German immigrant named Rudy Meeser. Shortly after we moved there a man tried to swindle Rudy out of tens of thousands of dollars worth of cattle, and when Rudy caught him red-handed—the man murdered Rudy.

The night of his murder Rudy's ranch home was swarming with police and bystanders, of which I was one. I remember when I got home I told my wife, Donna, that I had met a real Texas Ranger. I was so excited that looking back I don't think I even asked him his name.

Even though I had no way of knowing it at the time, the second time I met Glenn was an extremely important date in my life—February 7, 1994.

Throughout my life my hobby has been my passion—history. We had not lived in Longview long before I realized I was sitting on top of a gold mine of history, what with many old-timers still around from the fabulous 1930s Great East Texas Oil Field boom days. In 1993 I had taken to videotaping many of these veterans of the Great Oil Boom days. Two veteran Texas Rangers who were in Kilgore during those years fascinated me, Lone Wolf Gonzaullas and Bob Goss—and Glenn knew them both well. A friend of mine, Bill Utsman, knew of Glenn and sat up a meeting with him.

I started off on the wrong foot with Glenn. I was late for our interview. Those who know Glenn know this is a monstrous no-no. But fortunately for me there is only one thing that Glenn loves more than the Rangers—family. When he learned why I was late he was quick to forgive.

Little did I know that the very day that Glenn entered my life, my father was leaving it. The night before I had sat up all night with Daddy. It was the first of many nights. Over the next two and a half years, my dad, Robert, Sr., or Senior as most everyone in Longview who knew him called him, suffered terribly before passing away.

Glenn reminds me of my father. They were both the first at work and the last to leave. Captain Jim Ray once described Glenn as so active that he wore out his clothes from the inside out. He could just as easily have been describing my father. Glenn only got to know Dad slightly. I wish they could have known one another better. They would have been great friends.

One day Glenn and I were having coffee at my office when he asked if I would write down some of his recollections for his children and grandchildren to have. I was flattered, but my first thought was "no". I hadn't written anything since getting out of the University of Tennessee at Martin in 1968, and even then the writing I had done was history theme papers. But by this time Glenn had become more to me than just a friend. I don't know of anything I could ever say no to this man about. So I said yes, but requested that since we were going to have to put in the work, let's expand to more than just a paper for Diane and Dennis (Glenn's daughter and son). Let's do a whole book. He reluctantly agreed. For me, it's been an effort of pure enjoyment. But looking back, if Glenn had realized how much I would be pestering him over the next several years, I am not sure he would have agreed.

I want to make this point extremely clear. Glenn gave me a completely free hand in choosing the cases related in this book. In all honesty, I sometimes became a little aggravated with his lack of assistance in choosing cases. He simply said, "Here are my files. You pick out the ones you think people would want to hear about." Later when I would make yet another run at him to pick out a case, his reply was always the same, "You're writing the book." So if there is any shortcoming with this book, it is regretfully the person who put the words on the paper, not the man who wrote the stories during thirty-eight years with the Texas Department of Public Safety.

In truth Glenn had a bigger part in the actual writing of the book than he is likely to ever admit. He meticulously read very page as I finished each chapter making sure that every word and story was correct to the nth degree.

For example, when I first handed him the chapter dealing with the 1968 Lone Star Steel strike I had included a story of a truck driver who had told me that he had received immense pressure from Lone Star Steel to haul its product. He was told in no uncertain terms that once the strike ended if he expected to haul out of Lone Star Steel, he better haul now. Sympathy with the strikers aside, he did not cherish the thought of being shot at like so many other truckers had been. Obviously he felt he was in a catch-22 situation.

When Glenn read this, he said, "Take it out. No one ever said that to me." Pleading my case I said, "But the driver said it to me!" To which Glenn replied, "I don't doubt that it happened, in fact, I'm sure it did, but he did not say it to me. And I am not going to say something in the book was said to me that wasn't."

During the entire preparation of this book, Glenn and I had only one contrasting view—the title of this book. Glenn wanted *Glenn Elliott, Texas Ranger*. While looking through Glenn's scrapbooks I had seen many of his fellow officers and superiors address Glenn as the Rangers Ranger. Without question this described Glenn. I dug in my heels and argued that *Glenn Elliott, A Rangers Ranger* was the prefect title. And furthermore, I reasoned, he was not saying this—his peers were. I don't know whether it was the logic of my reasoning, or he simply tried of my badgering, but he finally consented to *A Rangers Ranger*.

I had not known Glenn long before he became a great puzzlement to me. He never solved a case! It was always Max Womack or Bob Mitchell or Jim Ray or Slick Alford or Red Arnold or Lewis Rigler who solved the case. He just happened to be there. You can imagine my shock when I interviewed Max, Bob, Jim, Slick, and Lewis and found that, like Glenn, they had likewise never solved a case. It had been Glenn or, or, or......... So it came as no surprise that time after time the manuscript would come back with the word "I" crossed out and the word "we" substituted.

Many people, far to many to name them all, helped put these words on paper. Patty Littleton spent countless hours transcribing the forty-one hours of interviews. A special thanks to Marsha Babin who spent what must have seemed like an eternity correcting my poor punctuation. Historians and writers Leon Metz and David Stroud for giving freely of their valuable time reading the raw manuscript and giving valuable suggestions. I also owe a huge thank you to Byron Johnson, Director of The Texas Ranger Hall of Fame and Museum, for his invaluable advise. And especially my wife, Donna, for putting up with me for numberless nights and weekends as I worked on this book.

I can not begin to name all the new friends I made because of their deep love for Glenn Elliott. Because of their feelings for Glenn, anything I asked for, I got. I want to personally say thanks to Howard Alford, Selwin Denson, Bob Mitchell, Jim Ray, Lewis Rigler, Max Womack, James Wright, and many others that I—not Glenn—have overlooked.

Oh yes. After that second "first meeting" Glenn and I became great friends. One day I asked him if he was the Ranger who had worked the Rudy Meeser murder in Hallsville. He didn't remember the case, but by the date he felt sure he did. Later he checked his files and discovered that it was indeed he who had worked the case. Out of the countless cases he had worked during twenty-six years as a Texas Ranger, it had been such a simple case to solve, he did not remember the case offhand. But why was I not surprised when he claimed to have had little or nothing to do with solving Rudy's murder. The offices of the Harrison County District Attorney and Sheriff solved the case. Typical Glenn.

GLENN'S CREED

I think this poem by Elbert Hubbard describes Glenn's attitude toward not only his job, but his life.

Remember This

If you work for a man, in Heaven's name,
Work for him.

If he pays you wages which supply you bread and butter,
Work for him;
Speak well of him;
Stand by him and stand by the institution he represents.

If put to a pinch,
An ounce of loyalty is worth a pound of cleverness.

If you must vilify, condemn and eternally disparage—
Resign you position,
And when you are outside,
Denounce to your heart's content,
But as long as you are part of the institution do not condemn it.

If you do that,
You are loosening the tendrils that are holding you to the institution,
And at the first high wind that comes along,
You will be uprooted and blown away,
And probably will never know the reason why.

GLENN ELLIOTT

A Ranger's Ranger

CHAPTER I
LEGAL'S LEGAL
AND RIGHT'S RIGHT

Sometimes even for a Texas Ranger what's right becomes more important than what's legal. One time I did something that was as wrong as wrong could be—legally. But as far as I was concerned, then and now, morally it was the right thing to do. If faced with the same situation today, I'd do exactly the same thing again.

In the mid- and late-1970s we were constantly receiving intelligence regarding the activities of The Bandidos, a Texas outlaw motorcycle gang. There were several members in my area who tried real hard to live up to their outlaw image. They had gone so far as to open a licensed bar so they could meet and drink beer and do whatever else they felt like, with total immunity—they thought. Though it was licensed as a public bar, they considered it private, with outsiders definitely not welcome.

I didn't approve of their lifestyles, but as long as they didn't break the law I didn't give them much thought. But that changed when one of my oldest and closest friends, not knowing the club's feelings toward outsiders, stopped by one night after work for a beer. No sooner had he entered the bar than four bikers jumped him. He was beaten, stomped, and kicked to the point of unconsciousness. Struggling to keep from passing out, he somehow made his way to his pickup, only to find that while the four goons in the club had been beating him, some of their friends had slashed all four of his tires.

Slashed tires or not, he started driving and kept driving until he reached safety. He received such a bad beating that he could have easily died, but he was too ashamed to let anyone know that he had stopped at a bar, so he refused to file a report with the police or even go to the hospital.

I found out about the beating by accident through a mutual friend. I went to see my injured friend and he was a mess. To say he was beaten badly would be a massive understatement. Not only was he battered and black and blue all over, but a boot print was plainly visible on his chest. Obviously one of the tough guys had tried to stomp his chest in.

1

The following evening at approximately the same time of my friend's beating the previous night, I just happened to be in the area. And since I was in the area and didn't have anything else to do, I decided to checkout the club. I walked in armed with my trusty Colt 45 automatic and 12-gauge shotgun. Not one of the scumbags made a move to whip-up on me. In fact, none of them said a word. They just sat there like the morons they were. I didn't say anything either. I walked behind the counter, reached up and yanked down their beer license. While I was doing this, I asked the cowards if any of them felt like tossing me around the room. There were no takers.

I informed them the place was closed and I walked out the door with their liquor license in my hand. Somehow the license was destroyed, and for some reason the bar closed. Oh, well, good riddance.

Were my actions legal? No, they were not—any shape, form, or fashion—but as far as I am concerned it was the right thing to do. I am not proud of what I did, but neither am I ashamed. And like I said, if I had it to do all over again, I'd handle it exactly the same way—with no apologies.

There is a happy ending to the story. I am glad to say that my friend recovered completely, and to this day he has never stopped off anywhere to have another beer. As for the bar, the last time I drove by where it used to stand is now a vacant lot filled with weeds.

SECTION 1

Early Years

CHAPTER II
WINDOM, TEXAS

My name is Glenn Elliott—no middle name, no middle initial—just plain old Glenn. I was born August 1, 1926, in a box house about three miles south of Windom, Texas, in the Flag Springs community. Windom is on the state map—barely, Flag Springs is not at all. Located near the Texas-Oklahoma border, just south of the Red River, it lies snugly between the Texas towns of Bonham and Honey Grove.

Deep down I think most people enjoy being recognized—at least for the right and honorable reason. Outside of the area where I grew up and worked very few people have ever heard of Glenn Elliott. But the man who was born and grew up right across the road from my birthplace was known worldwide; presidents, kings, prime ministers, rich and poor, the powerful and the weak, all vied for his favor. The tiny community of Flag Springs was the birthplace of the legendary Sam Rayburn—"Mr. Democrat." Of course, Mr. Sam, as he was commonly known, quite probably was the most powerful Speaker of the House of Representatives this country has ever known. I suspect that Tip O'Neil, Jim Wright, and Newt Gingrich all envy the extraordinary power he wielded. A former teacher and lawyer in Bonham, our county seat, he first served as a state legislator from 1907-1913, the last two years as the Speaker of the Texas House of Representatives. In 1912 he ran for the U. S. House of Representatives. He won the election easily. And the next twenty-four times he came up for re-election he continued to win easily. Until his death in 1961, he served in the House of Representatives for forty-eight years, seventeen of them as Speaker.

Though Mr. Sam was sixteen years older than my dad, they were close friends. I can remember many times that my dad and I visited Mr. Rayburn, both before and after he became the legendary "Mr. Sam." I wish I could say that I had numerous personal stories that I could relate about Mr. Rayburn, but I do not. He was already in Washington when I was born and by the time I

5

was old enough to know to be in awe of him, I seldom, if ever, saw him except when I was with Dad. Also, he did not live across the road from us anymore by the time I came along. He had moved to Bonham, twelve miles west of Windom, about the time he went into politics.

As a youngster growing up in Windom I thought it was surely the quietest town in all of Texas. It may have been small, but it was a thriving and enormously proud little farm town with four grocery stores, two cotton gins, a bank, a school, the post office, and five churches. Over the years Windom has seen many sad changes. It still has a bank and post office, but the school, the cotton gins, three of the stores, and two of the churches are but fond memories. You may not be able to buy gasoline in Windom today, but one thing will never change—its pride.

I was the second child of Dewey and Edith Elliott. My brother, Dewey, Jr., who has always been called D. L., is four years older than me. Doctor H. H. Leeman of Windom brought my brother and me into this world. My grandparents, James and Minnie Elliott, rode a train from Alcorn County, Mississippi, to Fannin County, Texas. I never knew exactly what year they came to Texas. All I know for sure is that they got off the train at Dodd City, a tiny community near Windom, in the late 1800s. Arriving with a son and daughter and all their other earthly possessions, they settled in the Flag Springs community close to other relatives who had arrived in the area earlier. By 1898, when Dad was born, two more daughters had been added to the family brood. Another brother and two more sisters were born after Dad. I would give anything to have known my grandpa, but that was not meant to be. He died in 1912. Grandma lived until 1931. I was only five when she died, but I have some memory of her, and for that I am thankful.

My maternal grandfather, Robert Winchester, also came to Windom from North Carolina in the late 1800s. My grandmother, Mary DeSpain Winchester, was born in Grayson County, Texas, near Van Alstyne. After marrying, Grandpa and Grandma settled north of Windom in the Spring Hill area. In 1902 my mother was born. She grew up and attended school in Spring Hill.

With four years difference in their ages, Mother and Dad did not run around together growing up, but Windom was such a small community that they knew one another. By 1921, they knew one another well enough to have fallen in love, and Mother decided that Dad had sown all the wild oats that he needed to sow. Later that year they married and sat up housekeeping in a small house they rented in Windom. In 1922, my only sibling, D. L., was born.

By the time I came along four years later, they had moved from Windom into a small box house in the Flag Springs community. I may have been young, but I remember that house well. I should. I was born and lived the first five years of my life in that little house. It was a little square, plain house that offered few comforts. About the only protection it afforded from the

6

elements was the studs with one-by-twelve planks nailed to the outside. There was no inside covering on the studs. Sitting inside the house you got a good look at the studs and the one-by-twelve's. Believe me, those thin pieces of plank were all that stood between those of us on the inside and the freezing north wind. It seemed like there was hardly any difference between the temperature inside the house and the temperature outside. Most Texans will tell you we have two seasons in Texas, summer and February, and no in-between. It's blistering hot in the summer and bone chilling cold in the winter. Dad used to say that the only thing that stood between Windom and the North Pole was a barbed wire fence. Years later someone moved the house into Windom where it still stands today. I suppose that someone put some kind of interior covering on the inside studs.

We lived in that house until Grandma Elliott died in 1931. Dad had always loved the homeplace and he and Mother wanted to make it their home. After buying out all of his brothers and sisters, we moved onto the old homeplace north of Windom. Years later when I left the farm I swore I would never live there again. Never say never. Today I still own that farm and I love it more than anything in the world. One day my children will own it.

Like most people in those years, Mother and Dad worked like dogs making a living for my brother and me. When D. L. was born, Dad and my uncle, Billy Head, ran a combination meat market, ice house, and cafe in Windom. Not long ago I was at a Cowboy football game in Dallas. A major grocery chain had hired an airplane to fly around the stadium, pulling a giant banner that proclaimed to the world that they made home deliveries. Back in the early 1920s, Dad and Uncle Billy were doing that from the back of a buggy. I guess modern day grocery stores are finally catching up to them.

By the time I came along, Dad had gotten out of the mercantile business and was farming. To bring in hard cash we always had a truck garden. During the Great Depression, bartering and growing crops for personal use was as common as the exchange of cash. For instance, grain crops like corn and wheat were often ground into meal and flour. After taking what was needed for personal use, the meal or flour was often traded at the local mercantile store for farm equipment, clothes, etc. Likewise, truck garden products like cabbage, watermelons, beans, etc., could usually be sold to people for cash, much like local farmers sell their garden products alongside a highway today.

Believe me, back in the 1930s, greenbacks were mighty hard to come by. We raised other cash crops like corn, cotton, and grain. And yes, I picked cotton; but so did everyone. We raised a few head of cows, hogs, mules, chickens and lots of turkeys. All of us, especially Mother, worked our butts off on that old farm. Besides doing the normal housework that all women did, Mom could often be found riding a mule-drawn cultivator in the fields with Dad. Until I was big enough to work, Mom would make a pallet in the shade

7

of the cornstalks on the edge of the field. My brother's assignment was to watch me while Mom and Dad worked the field.

"Innovative" was the word that best described Dad when it came to making a living. We would sell a couple of hundred turkeys every year. He also sold and traded mules, and cut grain for other farmers in the area. During the off season the County Judge, Choice Moore, would sometimes hire Dad to rework some of the roads in his jurisdiction. Remember that was before the motorized road-grader. This grader was operated behind four mules. It was not that big of a deal; it was the best method available at the time. As if this was not enough work, we milked cows and sold the milk to the Kraft Cheese Plant in Bonham. There was one thing I really learned to hate about cows— they never, ever, take a day off. We milked twice a day, seven days a week, three hundred sixty-five days a year. For those of you who have never milked cows, when I say twice a day, I mean four o'clock in the morning, and six o'clock in the afternoon. Not about elevenish or so. Four o'clock—rain, sleet, snow, or anything in between.

My childhood was pretty normal for a farm kid in the 1920s and 1930s. True, we all worked hard, but don't think we didn't have any time for fun; we did. Sometimes we went to Bonham to the movies; and no, at that time I had no desire to be a Texas Ranger. I loved Laurel and Hardy, Tom Mix, Hoot Gibson, and Douglas Fairbanks, Sr., as did most of America. Our family was one of the few who had a radio, and we would gather around to listen to shows like *The Lone Ranger, Walter Winchell, Amos and Andy*, and a few others. We did not get to listen as much as we wanted. The old radio was battery-powered, and it took forever to recharge the batteries. Naturally, if we failed just once to recharge them, we would be right in the middle of a program we really wanted to hear and the batteries would go dead. Of course, there was no such thing as television.

Almost every Sunday after church (we attended the Windom Methodist Church), the whole family would meet over at Grandpa and Grandma Winchester's. After everyone had filled their stomachs, we boys would get up a sandlot baseball game. If I do say so myself, I was a pretty fair country third baseman. Today, my son Dennis is a good ball player. We get it naturally. Dad was an outstanding baseball player. After finishing school he played professionally for awhile in the old Texas League for the Wichita Falls Spudders.[1]

---

[1] The Spudders actually started out in 1905 in the old Texas-Oklahoma League as the Cremos—they were sponsored by The Cremo Cigar Company. In 1919 they transferred to the Texas League and continued there until 1932. Being the smallest city in the Texas League, they simply could not draw the attendance they needed to remain in business. In 1932 the franchise transferred to Longview, in the heart of the fabulous East Texas Oil Boom. In Longview they became known as the Cannibals.

In September, 1931, even though I was only five years old, I started school. Unlike most country schools, little old Windom, with a population of about three hundred, had a nice brick school building, which was pretty fancy stuff in those days. In the 1930s most country schools were little better than the box house in which I was born. Sixty-five years later, I can still remember every one of my teachers.[2]

Little did I realize that one teacher, Elmer Riddle, would have an extremely profound influence on my life. Besides being my math and study hall teacher, he was also the baseball and basketball coach, and a darn good one, too! We really had a good baseball team at Windom, and the biggest reason was Coach Riddle. Coach played ball the old-fashioned way, one base at a time. He stressed the fundamentals. Babe Ruth notwithstanding, he could not have cared less about the home run. His philosophy was: make contact with the ball, and then only if the ball was in the strike zone. He developed an ingenious way of encouraging his players to make that contact. Every time we swung at a ball, and missed, we got a lick from his paddle. Believe me, we quickly learned to discipline ourselves to swing only at strikes, and we learned to make contact. Can you see a coach doing that today, and getting by with it? Throughout my life, I feel that my self-discipline and my belief in the fundamentals have been two of my strongest traits. Coach was not the only one I learned this from—Mother and Dad believed the same thing—but unquestionably he played a major role in my life. I am not one to get on a bandbox, but I would like to make one very important statement: teachers, as long as one of your students is alive, your influence never stops.

Later, Coach Riddle would drop his middle name and go by his first name, Jim. He left the teaching profession in 1941 and went into law enforcement, a great loss to the education field, and a great gain for the law. Serving first as a highway patrolman, later a Texas Ranger, and finally a Ranger Captain, he went to the top of the ladder. I am proud to say that in 1997 Jim Riddle became only the twenty-ninth Texas Ranger in history to be inducted in the Texas Ranger Hall of Fame in Waco, Texas. To this day, if you meet a Ranger who served under Jim Riddle he will proudly tell you that he was a "Riddle Ranger." I will talk more about him later, but Coach Riddle is the man who got me into law enforcement.

I graduated from Windom High School with twenty-six others in 1942, having not yet turned sixteen. I'm not implying that because I was only sixteen when I graduated, I was an outstanding academic student. I graduated at the same age as most of the rest of my class. Until 1943 school consisted of

---

[2] My teachers were: Adran Burtrum, Elizabeth Council, W. D. George, Mrs. Leola Jacks, Mrs. Iris Lightsy, Jess Moxley, Elmer Riddle, Mrs. John I. Wheeler, and Mrs. Max Wheeler.

only eleven grades in Texas. I was not a bad student, but neither was I a great one. All in all, "normal," I think, would best describe my academic endeavors. However, I was extremely active in school and I have very fond memories of Windom High. I participated in baseball, basketball, and acting, to name a few of the outside curriculums I enjoyed in high school. I even managed to win ten dollars writing a newspaper jingle for a flour company whose name I forgot years ago.

Old friends will probably find this hard to believe, but I was on the stage. My speech teacher, Iris Lightsy, was in charge of the school play, *The Henpecked Husband,* one year and she wanted me to play the leading role. Not me! I was, in today's terminology, too "macho" for any of that sissy stuff. But there was one thing I failed to take into consideration—Miss Iris had ways of getting things done. She went to see Superintendent W. D. George. After Miss Iris' talk with the Superintendent, he and I had a little talk. Funny, but for the life of me, I cannot remember saying much, but the next thing I knew, I was on the stage of Windom High School playing the henpecked husband. I had trouble admitting it to myself, let alone to my buddies, but I enjoyed my stage debut so much I could hardly wait to perform for the next play. When Miss Iris put on the next play, there I was, right in the middle of the stage playing the lead in *The Absent-Minded Professor.*

When I graduated in 1942 I had one of the greatest honors an American can have bestowed upon him. I received an appointment to West Point. Rest assured the appointment was not because of my brilliance in the classroom. It was due to Dad's close relationship with Mr. Sam. I never used the appointment. First of all, I couldn't, because at fifteen I was too young to go to The Point. Second, by the time I was old enough, I did not want to go. World War II was in full swing, and like thousands of other boys my age, I was afraid that if I took any time out to go to school I would miss the whole war. And third, by the time I got out of the Army in 1945 I was married, and married men were not accepted at West Point, so my appointment was revoked. Let me be clear about one thing: without a moment's hesitation, I have never regretted for one minute not going to West Point. It is one of the greatest institutions of higher learning in the world, but it was not for me.

When I graduated I really wanted to see what the country looked like away from Windom—the farther away, the better. Unfortunately, traveling takes money, and I did not have any. I have always heard that if there is a will, there is a way. My way was a neighbor, Bert Chandler. Bert and several other men from around Windom were going to the state of Washington for the wheat harvest. Bert had an old '39 Chevrolet truck and for ten dollars he would let

AGPR-M 201 Elliott, Glenn
(4 Nov 44) JHL-jrb-4446   4 November 1944.

        Honorable Sam Rayburn,

            House of Representatives.

    My dear Mr. Rayburn:

            Information has been received in this office that
    Mr. Glenn Elliott, your first alternate candidate for the
    United States Military Academy, is married.

            The regulations governing the appointment and ad-
    mission of cadets to West Point prescribes that no married
    person or person who has been married shall be admitted as
    a cadet. Accordingly, the appointment issued to Mr. Elliott
    on 26 September 1944 from the fourth Congressional district
    of Texas has been canceled on the records of the War Depart-
    ment and he has been so advised.

            A nomination form is inclosed for your use in naming
    another candidate if you so desire.

                                Sincerely yours,

                                    ROBERT H. DUNLOP,
                                    Brigadier General,
                                    Acting The Adjutant General.

        1 Incl.

    DISTRIBUTION:
            Mr. Glenn Elliott,
                Windom, Texas.

11

me ride to Washington with him. Our crops were in and I wanted to go. It didn't matter to Bert that I was years younger than any of the other men—I would not turn sixteen until we reached Washington—as far as he was concerned, if I had ten dollars, I was old enough.

I figured that after paying Bert ten dollars, another twenty-five dollars should carry me until I got to Washington, found a job, and received my first check. I went to my parents and asked for the money, but Dad and Mother did not want me to go, and they would not give or loan the money to me. I may have been only fifteen, but I already had an independent streak a mile wide and I was determined that I was going to Washington. I wanted adventure, to meet new people, and to see new sights.

Not to be outdone by my parent's refusal to give or loan the twenty-five dollars to me, I went to see the local banker, Carl Wright, and asked for a fifty-dollar loan. For collateral I offered some hogs I had raised. But with every farmer and his brother in the area raising hogs, Mr. Wright was not overly thrilled with my collateral. Mr. Wright was a no-nonsense banker and in no uncertain terms he informed me that he did not loan money to young boys to gallivant around the country. However, with the hogs as collateral and if Dad would co-sign the note, he might consider loaning me thirty-five dollars. I told him Dad was not keen on my going to Washington, and he would not cosign the note. "All right, get your grandpa to sign the note, and you can have the money," he countered. Like I said, even then I had a real stubborn streak, and I was not going to ask for Grandpa's help either. I didn't know how, but one way or another when Bert and the boys left for Washington, I would be with them.

Fate was on my side. There happened to be a man in town buying livestock on the hoof—still alive. With hogs being so plentiful, he had no intention of giving fifty dollars for my small herd, but I had no intention of going below thirty-five dollars. After a little bickering we struck a deal. He had my hogs and I had thirty-five dollars. I paid Bert ten dollars and was off to the farming metropolis—at least it was to me—of Lacrosse, Washington. Thank goodness I held out for thirty-five dollars. When we arrived in Lacrosse, I had ninety-seven cents in my pocket.

I will never forget that trip as long as I live! It took us a week to get there. Lacrosse, our destination, was a couple of hundred miles south of the Canadian border, right where the neck of Idaho goes up beside Washington. The best I can remember, there were about ten of us in that old truck. I cannot remember all of their names now,[3] but besides Bert Chandler, I well remember Woodrow Crossland. Over the years Woodrow and I have stayed in touch

---

[3] Some of the names I can remember are: Bert Chandler, Woodrow Crossland, Peck Keel, Bill Hicks, and John Nickols.

and today he lives comfortably retired in Sherman, Texas.

But back to the trip. We threw a homemade tarpaulin made of old cotton sacks over the bed of the truck to provide some protection from the elements. It did all right providing shade, but every time it rained—and it rained often— it just as well not have been there. We got soaking wet. Someone had the foresight to throw an old mattress in the back of the truck. Even though we had to sleep in shifts, at least we did not have to lie on the hard wooden floor of the truck bed.

By the time we reached Pocatello, Idaho, we were so filthy that none of us could stand ourselves, let alone one another. We decided that half of us would check into an old three-story, second-rate hotel, while the other half slept in the truck, but all of us would take a bath. It had been so long since any of us had slept in a bed, or been able to clean up, that even a night in a second-rate hotel was as good as the best Hilton.

Eating was sparse, to say the least. None of us had any spare money to spend foolishly in a restaurant. We stopped at local grocery stores along the way and bought bologna, cheese and crackers. It is a good thing I liked bologna; I think that is all we ate the whole way to Lacrosse. Looking back almost fifty-five years, that was some of the best eating I have ever had.

The trip was memorable for one other reason: I had my first encounter with the police in Amarillo. We ran into one of those rainstorms that only the Texas Panhandle is capable of having. In Amarillo we found ourselves in a downpour. Seeking someplace dry, we pulled under the canopy of a service station. We had been there a short time when a police officer came along and told us that rain or no rain we were on private property and had to move on. Having never spent any time around city boys back then, I couldn't speak for what they might do, but arguing with the police never entered the minds of us country boys. We moved on and got thoroughly soaked. Even though we were wet, we were not to be deterred from our objective.

We arrived in Lacrosse on a Saturday night. We did not waste time sightseeing; we did not have any money for such niceties. We needed work, and quickly. Woodrow Crossland and I found jobs right away with a German family named Kleinsmith. Things were swell for two weeks. Then Mr. Kleinsmith told us that he felt he could get by with just one hired hand during the harvest. He did not care which one of us stayed and which one went— Woodrow and I could decide that between ourselves. That was a no-brainer as far as I was concerned. With the harvest season in full bloom, I knew it would be no problem to find another job. Anyway, I had not come to Washington only to work; I wanted to see all the country I could. With two pay-checks in my pocket, I could take a little time looking for another job, so I told Mr. Kleinsmith I would be the one to move on.

There was one other thing that was definitely a factor in my decision to move on. Mr. Kleinsmith was getting ready to bag his grain and I really did not want any part of that if I could keep from it. I only weighed about one hundred twenty pounds at the time and the sacks weighed anywhere from one hundred to one hundred fifty pounds per bag. It didn't take a mathematical genius to figure that one out.

I was sitting in the pool hall in Lacrosse when a man named Holliday walked in. He was from the little town of Benge, about thirty miles northwest of Lacrosse. Like most towns in the United States in the 1940s—in mind as well as in reality—Benge was a farming town. Mr. Holliday was looking for a harvest hand to help gather the wheat. I told him I was available and he hired me on the spot. It took only a few minutes to gather my belongings and throw them in the back of Mr. Holliday's 1940 Chevrolet. Then I was on my way to Benge.

By the time we arrived at the Holliday home in Benge it was very late in the evening. Mr. Holliday showed me to a room in the basement that would be mine. He said Mrs. Holliday had already gone to bed and that I would meet her at breakfast. I wish I could remember their first names, but for the life of me, I cannot. One thing is for sure: two nicer people never lived than the Hollidays.

During the trip from Lacrosse to Benge, Mr. Holliday asked me if I knew how to milk a cow. I told him I had been milking since I was five years old. At breakfast that first morning, he told his wife I would be milking Old Betsy that day, but after that, she would have to do the milking. I would be too busy in the fields gathering wheat from then on.

The mountains around that part of Washington are high and steep—so steep that the tractors of that day were not strong enough to pull combines up and down the rugged slopes. It was a common sight to see a Caterpillar pulling a combine up, down, and around the mountain.

My first job was to drive the grain truck from the field to the elevator in Benge, six miles away. I had not been there but a few days when Mr. Holliday's son, who normally drove the Caterpillar, came down with a terrible case of hay fever. Mr. Holliday asked me, "Are you afraid to drive the Caterpillar?" I answered, "I'm not afraid to drive, if you are not afraid to ride behind me." The mountains in the Benge area are so steep that in addition to the driver of the tractor, someone had to ride the combine to adjust the cutter-head[4] to the terrain. Since the combine had its own power source to operate the cutting heads, they could be adjusted up to forty-five degrees to enable it to cut the hillside. Clearly, whoever rode the combine had it much tougher than the person driving the Caterpillar.

I worked with Mr. Holliday twenty-three days in the fields, making

---

[4] This was the giant scythe on the front of the combine that actually cut the grain.

twenty-five dollars a day, plus room and board. Remember, those were 1942 dollars—real money. Not long ago a friend of mine gave me a copy of the Department of Labor's index of the purchasing power of the dollar from 1913 through today. Twenty-five dollars in 1942 would be equal to one hundred fifty dollars today. Until then I had never made more than a dollar a day. It was certainly not bad for a boy who had just turned sixteen. We had to work from daylight until dark, but so what—we worked like that back on the farm in Windom. I thought everyone worked that way.

The Hollidays really took a liking to me. When we finished the harvest they tried to get me to stay on and work full-time. Seldom have I ever had a more wonderful compliment paid to me than when they told me I was the kind of boy they would like to have in their family. If I would stay, they would pay me one hundred twenty-five dollars a month, plus room and board. During the harvest season they would pay me an additional twenty-five dollars per day bonus. And as an added incentive, since it was farm work, I could get a deferment from military service, but that was the last thing in the world that I wanted.

I do have to admit that it was tempting. I knew it would be impossible to make that kind of money in Texas, and with the Hollidays being the nicest people in the world, it was not easy to say no, but I was ready to move on. After saying my good-byes to the Hollidays, I went back to Lacrosse with my pockets full of money.

The first thing I did was to get five hundred dollars in cashier's checks and send the money home. Then I started looking for any of the other guys I had traveled with. I learned that Bert had sold the old truck, and he and most of the others had already taken a train back to Texas. The only homeboy I could find was Peck Keel. Peck liked to play cards, and when the others left, he was on a hot streak. All gamblers will tell you that when they are on a hot streak, wild horses could not pull them away from the game. Needless to say, Peck was not going anywhere. Cards may be red hot one moment, but the next they can be ice cold. Shortly after I arrived in town, that's what happened to Peck. The cards turned against him.

But before they did, I lounged around while Peck played. I heard they were picking apples within a couple of hundred miles of Lacrosse. When Peck realized his luck had run out, I told him we could make almost as much money picking apples as we had in the wheat fields. Despite my best efforts, Peck was finished with Washington; he was ready to go home. Honestly, he was not the only one. I had been away from home a long time, and frankly I was a little bit homesick. I was ready for Texas, and Catherine Cooper.

We caught a train in Lacrosse and rode it all the way to Wichita Falls, Texas. From there we had to take a bus to Windom. I got off the bus in Windom at 12:30 at night and even in the darkest of night, Windom looked mighty fine. Having mailed most of my money home, when I got on the bus in Wichita Falls all I had was twenty-seven silver dollars that I had rolled up in some clothes and stuffed into an old metal suitcase. When I got off the bus in Windom, my suitcase did not. The bus was crammed with people, and to be honest with you I did not even think of the suitcase until the bus was pulling out. "Well, kiss the suitcase and the twenty-seven dollars good-bye," I thought to myself. But I was not really that upset. The only thing in the suitcase of any value was the money. I do not know everywhere the suitcase went, but the next morning it was back at the bus station in Windom, with the twenty-seven silver dollars right where I had left them.

I don't think anything could have upset me that night—I was back in Windom and going home. I had not told Dad and Mother that I was coming home; I wanted to surprise them. The sidewalks in Windom had been rolled up[5] for hours and there was no taxi. I would not have spent the money on it if there had been one—it was only about a mile to the house. I started walking. It took me about thirty minutes to walk from Windom to the house. Normally it would not have taken that long. I would have cut through the fields and woods. But having no flashlight and not having seen the fields in several months, I stayed on the road. At one o'clock in the morning, I knew that Dad and Mother had been asleep for a long time and I did not want to awaken them. I just eased into the oh-so-familiar house and started up the stairs to my room—back in those days people did not lock their houses. When I was about halfway up the stairs, I heard the most wonderful sound in the world, Mother's voice "Is that you, Glenn?" Mother had no way of knowing it was me. D. L. was in the Army Air Service, so it could just as easily have been him instead of me. But like mothers in the past, present, and future, she just knew which one of her flock had come home. Mother and Dad got up and we had a family reunion right there. They scolded me for not letting them know I was coming in so that they could have picked me up. It's true, there is no place like home.

The next day I beat a path to the Cooper's home in Windom. Catherine was born in Dodd City, a small community about five miles from Windom. While in the second grade, her parents, Virgil and Florence, and four sisters— Geraldine, Mutt, Ruth, and Mary—left Dodd City and moved to Windom. Catherine and I went through school together, but it was not until the tenth grade that we really started dating. From then on there was never really any question about our future together. On Christmas Day, 1943, we were married.

I wish I could say that we had a big church wedding and everyone in

---

[5] In country terminology this means that every business in town had closed for the night and the streets were deserted.

Windom attended. The truth is that we eloped to Durant, Oklahoma. Because of our youth, Catherine's parents were not too thrilled about the idea of us getting married, but they knew they could not stop us. My parents were dead set against me getting married to anyone and refused to sign consent papers. Unlike the Coopers, they thought they could prevent us from getting married. Who knows? If we had not lived so close to Oklahoma maybe they would have been successful, but I doubt it. At that time Texas had a law that said people under eighteen were considered too young to get married without the consent of their parents. Oklahoma did not have such a law and some our friends had recently gone there to get married. They said all you had to have to get married was a five-dollar license and a preacher. We told Catherine's parents where we were going, but not mine, and on Christmas Day, 1943, we were off to Durant, Oklahoma.

Man, it was cold on our wedding day, bitterly cold. Christmas Day, 1943, in Durant, Oklahoma, had to have been one of the coldest Christmas' on record. Cold or not, we arrived in Durant, found a clerk, and purchased a marriage license. He helped us find a preacher and we were married in the preacher's home. Looking back, one part of the marriage ceremony was almost comical. I was a Methodist; Catherine belonged to the Church of Christ; and the preacher was a Presbyterian.

We spent the night in Durant before heading back to Windom the next day to sit up housekeeping. Needless to say, I was not looking forward to facing my parents, but things worked out well. Mother and Dad realized that further resistance was futile and reluctantly accepted our marriage.

In 1942 we were at war and the military was building facilities all over the country. I remember Mr. Sam came home to Bonham late in 1942 and sent word that he wanted to see Dad. Dad was very active in politics. In fact he was a "yellow dog Democrat";[6] he would have voted for a "yellow dog" before he would have a Republican. Since Mr. Sam and Dad had always been good friends, Mr. Sam told Dad that the Army was going to build two air bases around Bonham, and at least forty houses would be built on the bases. If Dad was interested, he would see to it that he got the job building those houses. All Dad would need to do was go to the bank and borrow ten thousand dollars. That would be no problem; the project was a cost-plus contract. With a government contract and Mr. Sam letting it be known he wanted it done, any bank in Texas would have been more than willing to loan Dad the money. But Dad was old-fashioned and a man of the Great Depression, and like most who survived the 30s he believed in paying as you go. Borrowing money went against the grain with him. After giving it a lot of thought, he thanked Mr. Sam, but refused his kind offer. Many people made a lot of

---

[6] This term came about during the 1930s and the Franklin Roosevelt era.

money out of this project, but Dad never regretted his decision.

They built the bases and by 1943 they were in operation. This presented opportunities for me. I wanted more than anything to join the service—every red-blooded American male wanted in the service—but I was only seventeen years old, and that meant I would have to get my parents to sign a consent form.

Again they refused to sign the dastardly consent form, and this time it would do me no good to run off to Durant, Oklahoma. Added to this, I did not have only my parents and Catherine's to fight, but they had plenty of help in the form of Catherine herself. I would have to wait to serve my country.

So I did the next best thing. In December I got a job at one of the bases, Jones Field in Bonham, working on the flight line. I had to be at work by four in the morning. Let me tell you, December in Bonham, Texas, at four o'clock in the morning, can be mighty cold. December, 1943, was no exception. It was cold. Fortunately they furnished us with fleece-lined clothes like the pilots wore, so the cold was bearable. My job was to make sure that all the hatches on all the planes were closed. Then I would crank one plane and taxi it up and down the runway until the oil pressure warmed to the required temperature. Then I would park the plane, get another, and do the same thing over again. Being in an airplane, if only taxing it around the airport, was great fun for a seventeen-year-old boy fresh off the farm.

Unfortunately it did not last long. The military discovered they had overbuilt, and had too many people doing too few jobs—some things in the government never change. They closed one of the bases, mine, and combined the two into one. My employment was no longer needed.

They may not have needed me, but I still had a wife to support, so I could not waste any time moping. I went in search of a job. I have never had trouble finding a job, and I did not this time. Knowing that as soon as I turned eighteen I would be going into the service, I did not want to commit myself to anything long-term. The best place to find the type of short-term work I was looking for was in Dallas. Other than the one time while I was still in school, when they had loaded us up on a school bus for a quick visit to the State Fair, I had never been to Dallas. So I had no idea where I was going to find a job when I got to Dallas. Nor was there any question but that Catherine would stay in Windom. We did not have the money to rent a place big enough for the two of us.

I went to Dallas knowing it would be a snap to get a job in the defense industry. I was in for a rude awakening. I was still only seventeen years old, and guess what I had to have before anyone would hire me—a consent form. I was really beginning to have serious problems with consent forms. I explained that I was married, and that Catherine and I did not live with either one of our folks, but in a house we rented in Windom. I saw no reason why I needed to have Dad sign a consent. My pleas fell upon deaf ears. No signed consent form—no job.

It was a dejected Glenn Elliott who headed for the Continental Bus station on Jackson Street. For one of the few times in my life, I felt defeated. I think if I had taken too big a step I would have stepped on my bottom lip. But it is funny how things seem to work out. Walking down Akard Street heading for the bus station, I ran into Neal Parish, an old acquaintance from Windom. Neal was the doorman at the Baker Hotel. A blind man could have seen my spirits were dragging bottom, and Neal was certainly not blind.

Directly across the street from the Baker Hotel was the old R & D Cafe. He said, "It's time for me to take a break. Let's go over to the R & D for a cup of coffee." Once seated he asked why I had such a long face. After relating my story, he told me I could go to work that very afternoon as a bellboy at the Baker. There was one hitch in the get-along. I would have to pay the Baker Hotel fifty cents for every six hour shift that I worked! I was flabbergasted. Imagine, having to pay to work. Neal told me not to worry; I would make more money than I had ever made in my life. He was almost right. I did not make quite as much as I had in the wheat harvesting fields in Washington, but I did all right.

Imagine, if you can, Glenn Elliott in a white bellboy uniform. Today, even I have trouble imagining that sight, but there I was. I do not think a week went by that I did not make at least a hundred dollars. Things were great, or least they were until I sprained my ankle.

Back in those days, Dallas's Baker Hotel was a beehive of activity. We used every elevator in the hotel, regular and service, carrying luggage to and from people's rooms. I have always been a little impatient, and I did not like taking the time to wait for an elevator, so I used the staircase. I had a rather unique way of going down the stairs. By holding onto the handrail and leaping, I could take a whole flight of steps in two bounds. One day I came charging down the stairs in my customary way, but this time I landed wrong and twisted my ankle badly. I did not need a doctor to tell me that my ankle was seriously injured. Instinctively I knew it would be a long time before I would be able to do any bellhopping. My bellhopping days were over. I knew that by the time my ankle healed I would be old enough to go into the service—without anyone having to sign a consent form. So I quit my job at the Baker and headed for Windom.

After my ankle healed, I worked around the grain elevator in Windom until my eighteenth birthday. Both my dad and Mr. Cooper wanted me to get a deferment and stay home; after all, I did have a family. By this time Catherine was pregnant with the first of our two children—Diane was the first; Dennis was born in 1954. I wanted no part of a deferment. I was afraid the war would be over before I could get into it.

19

I turned eighteen on August 1, 1944. By September, I was in the Army. Dad and Mr. Cooper drove me to Bonham where at four o'clock in the morning I caught a bus to Dallas to be sworn in. I admit that the Army was not my first choice. I wanted to be in the Army Air Corps like my brother, D. L., but I flunked the color chart, so I had to make another choice. At the induction station the recruiter asked what branch of the service I preferred. I told the recruiter my first choice was the Navy, then the Marines. As I live and breathe, he stamped my induction papers "Army."

CHAPTER III
FROM THE MP'S
TO THE HIGHWAY PATROL

They swore us in and marched us down Commerce Street right through downtown Dallas to the train station. Two things I remember about that train ride. First, it was dark—I think all troop trains must surely move at night. Second, we had absolutely no idea where we were going—the Army never told us where they were sending us. After the initial excitement died down I went to sleep and the next thing I knew I awoke in San Antonio. We stayed in San Antonio only long enough to get all our shots and other things they like to do to recruits during induction. Then it was back to the train station for another unknown journey. This time it was to Fort Hood, near Killeen, Texas. We unloaded and began our basic training. Basic, for me, was no different than for hundreds of thousands of others during World War II. Sure, it was tough, but I did not mind. Hard work never bothered me then—or now. I knew that it would be a lot tougher in Europe, China, the Pacific, or wherever they sent me.

After completing basic I was ordered to Fort Mead, Maryland. Like most of the men, I looked for every opportunity to go home. Fort Hood, Texas, to Fort Mead, Maryland, via Windom, was not much out of the way and Lady Luck was smiling on me. I do not know why, but my group received "delay in route" orders. Unlike most of the men, I was able to spend my week's delay at home.

There may have been a war going on, but when I arrived at Fort Mead, they had very little for us to do. One of the greatest causes of low morale in the military, or any profession for that matter, is boredom. Obviously, the military powers-to-be also knew this and wanted to avoid sinking morale at all costs. One of the methods they hit on could not have suited me better—a base boxing match. In boxing there are several weight divisions, and the winner of each division was to receive a three-day pass to New York City. I mentioned earlier that I was very active in sports in high school. Besides baseball, basketball, and acting, I had also done a little boxing. And these old

21

boys did not look any tougher to me than the boys in Windom. I entered the tournament and won the one hundred forty-five weight class.

With the exception of the trip to Washington State and the train ride to Fort Mead, I had never been anywhere outside Texas. Naturally, I had heard of and seen pictures of New York City all my life, so I was really looking forward to seeing the great city. Before leaving we were given one bit of advice—watch your money while in the Big Apple. You will find people who have more ways to take your money than you can possibly imagine. That was no lie. We didn't stay three days. After two days and one night, with most of our ready cash gone, we returned to Fort Mead. Albeit we were definitely richer in experience, but we were also flat broke.

As for military training, we still had not been doing much of anything up to this time. But it didn't take me long to realize there is one thing in life you can count on: in the Army, you will not be allowed to remain idle for long. Sure enough, they loaded us on a train and sent us to Newport News, Virginia, were we practiced boarding and disembarking a ship. There were perfectly good gangplanks extending from the ship to the dock, but do you think they let us use them? No. We climbed up and down cargo nets. Up and down, up and down. I have no earthly idea how many times we climbed those nets, but I know it was more than I care to remember. Obviously, some of the guys were less than enthused. To their way of thinking, they had not joined the Army to climb up and down stupid ropes. Just as clearly, the Army brass could not have cared less what we—I mean, they—thought. To make a short story even shorter, we just kept on climbing up and down those cargo nets.

One evening after a hard day of exercises, I was lying in my bunk daydreaming of home. I do not believe in psychics, or anything like that, but I was dreaming that it would be great if they would station me at Camp Maxey in Paris, Texas. Paris is only about thirty miles from home.

One day we were ordered to fall in. Everyone under twenty-five years of age was ordered to turn in all heavy wool clothes for khakis and mosquito nets—that was a dead giveaway that we would not be going to Europe. Completing our equipment change, they put us on a train. As usual, we didn't have a clue as to our destination. All we knew for sure was that we were on a train headed west, and of course since it was a military troop train, it was in the dark of night.

Believe me, there is not a whole lot to do on a troop train, except play cards and trade stories. I have never been much of a card player, and by the third day some of the tales were making their second and third trips around the train. Even in those days I bored easily, and I quickly got bored doing nothing. I had already investigated the rest of the train and the other parts were as boring as ours. So I gave up and went to bed. The next thing I knew it was morning and a voice was yelling, "Gather up your equipment, and get off the train." "Shocked" is putting it too mildly when I stepped off the train and found myself at Camp Maxey—Paris, Texas! I felt like pinching myself, my luck could not be this good!

I thought it surely could not get any better than this. We were supposed to train at Camp Maxey for six weeks. We ended up being there only two weeks, but I did get home both weekends.

The Army had built a small man-made island right in the middle of the camp. We were told that it was identical to the one we would be attacking in the Pacific. For two weeks we practiced slipping in close to the island from a make-believe submarine. We would row to shore in a rubber dinghy, and destroyed anything on the island that might have been of use to the enemy. Completing our mission of destruction, we would escape back to the imaginary submarine.

After only two weeks of training, we packed up and shipped out for San Francisco—I guess our group was so good we didn't need the customary six weeks. We all looked forward to enjoying the city by the Golden Gate. Once more the Army did not take our feelings into consideration. We barely slowed as we passed through the city on our way to the merchant marine ship, *USS Dashing Wave*, where we found ourselves in the company of twenty-five hundred other soldiers, all bound for New Guinea. There are three things that stand out in my mind about that trip. It was hot, it took us twenty-nine days, and I got seasick. I still get seasick easily. You have never seen a man more ready to get off of a boat than me.

New Guinea looked liked a nice place, but unfortunately we didn't get to stay there long enough to find out. With all the commando-type training they put us through at Camp Maxey, a blind man could see we would be put in a commando unit. It may have been evident to us, but not the Army. We became the Army's newest searchlight unit headed for Manila in the Philippines.

This was in April or May of 1945. The Japanese Air Force was pretty well on its last leg and the powers-that-be in all their infinite wisdom decided they had made a mistake. They really had no need for another searchlight unit after all. What they really needed was an additional Military Police unit. So they put MP armbands on us, and assigned us to the 520th Military Police. Just like that, I was a lawman. Until that moment, I had never had a thought in my life about being in law enforcement. While pulling that armband on, little did I dream that for the better part of the next forty-three years I would be a lawman. I have been asked if being in the Military Police later influenced me to make law enforcement my career. Not one bit. Looking back, I cannot think of any branch I had rather have been in. Considering my future career on the highway patrol and with the Texas Rangers, it was purely coincidental that I ended up in the Military Police.

We were in Manila only a short time before being ordered to Baguio to support our invasion force. Baguio is centrally located on the west side of the island of Luzon. I did not see any combat during the invasion. That was not the Military Police's job. Our foremost duty was to keep traffic flowing smoothly. This is an extremely important job and I am proud to say that we did our job.

During the Battle of the Bulge, the Germans understood the importance of traffic control. They found some men who could speak English fluently, put them in American uniforms, and sent them behind our lines. One of their main responsibilities was to change the road signs and really mess up our traffic. Remember the scene in the movie, *Patton,* when George C. Scott, as Patton, had to personally unsnarl a huge traffic jam caused by the crossing up of the road signs by the German spies.[1]

I said that I did not see any combat on Baguio, but I was shot at and darned near hit. We were on an extremely slow-moving troop train headed for Baguio. The train consisted of old coal cars. Since there were still a lot of Japanese snipers in the area, the officers ordered all the men to sit down where they would be completely protected by the heavy steel sides of the coal car. MP's were stationed as guards at the end of each car. Unlike the men, we had to stand up, thus leaving ourselves totally exposed. Everything went along smoothly until the stock of my rifle literally exploded in my hand. I do not know if I moved just as the sniper fired, or if he was a bad shot. Either way, the only damage he did was to ruin a perfectly good rifle and gash my right hand between the thumb and index finger, leaving a sizable scar.[2]

It was not long before we had things in shape in Baguio and we started training for the invasion of the Japanese mainland itself. Fortunately, Truman ordered that the bombs be dropped on Hiroshima and Nagasaki, and the Japanese surrendered before that surefire bloodbath started. I still went to Japan, but at least not under combat conditions.

In September, 1945, we landed at Kobe, Japan. Kobe, located near Osaka, sits on Osaka Bay. Since it was one of the largest bays in Japan, it was vital to the Japanese war effort. Because of this significance, our bombers had really given it a blasting. We made camp just outside the city and the Provost Marshall ordered me and two other men to go into town to find a building that could be used for company headquarters. As I said, our bombers had flattened most of the city, so there were not many buildings from which to choose. But we found an ideal building. It was a large three-story building made out of huge eighteen-inch reinforced concrete blocks. Other than a few windows being

---

[1] In 1944 my associate's father, Robert Nieman, Sr., was in the traffic jam that Patton straightened out.

[2] While compiling this book, I was asked if I received the Purple Heart. No. The wound was so slight it barely required medical attention.

knocked out, our bombers had not hurt the building.

In 1995, a major earthquake leveled Kobe and naturally my interest was a little more than normal. Would you believe, right there on the television screen was that same great big old concrete building? Neither bombs nor earthquakes could bring that fortress down. That was, and is, one tough old building.

I can think of only one outstanding thing that happened to me while at Kobe. Most of my time was spent keeping soldiers, sailors, and Marines in order. Except when a couple of officers thought they were something special, and that no snot-nosed, punk MP was going to order them around,[3] we never had any trouble. When the men realized who we were, they usually became pretty orderly. Other than keeping the drunks straight, about the only thing we did was carry classified memos and orders between the generals. And as has every MP in history, we had to deal with the black market. Every war has its black market and World War II was no different. We worked against the black market quite a bit, but I do not remember anything out of the ordinary happening.

There is one thing I remember above all others about my days in the Army. I made friends with a great bunch of guys. Rarely did I meet anyone who wasn't great. But one guy from Birmingham, Alabama—Louie Tillman— was better than great. Fortune has smiled on me throughout my life with the many tremendous friends I have been blessed with. And I want to say right here, I liked Louie Tillman as well as anyone I have ever known.

It's funny what you remember about people. Louie had this thing about Shirley Temple. Back in the 30s and 40s there was no star in Hollywood bigger than Shirley Temple. Her fame was worldwide, and she had no bigger fan than Louie Tillman. Whenever a new issue of *The Stars and Stripes* arrived, Louie would go through it with a fine-toothed comb looking for anything about Shirley Temple. The most trivial bit of information would rivet his complete attention. Mention Shirley Temple, and Louie became a truly inspired GI. Unfortunately for Louie, Shirley was not always mentioned. The way Louie looked at it, it was not his fault if some dumb editor failed to devote great quantities of space to his beloved Shirley. He would just have to make up for their obvious lack of taste. And then his imagination would go into overdrive, with no boundaries allowed. He told Shirley Temple stories that boggled the mind. I bet a lot of the people, who did not know Louie and his fixation with Shirley, were astounded to learn that somehow Louie had "scooped" every reporter on the planet Earth when he announced that Shirley had just gotten married. (I always wondered why those who didn't know Louie never questioned why his "scoops" always started and ended with Shirley

---

[3] This only happened a couple of times. Even these guys did not give us any serious trouble; they were too drunk.

Temple.) Another time he professed to all, far and near, the astounding news that she had just given birth. To some he reported she had given birth to a beautiful girl; to others he said it was a boy. (I never said he could keep his stories straight.) It was always "Shirley this," or "Shirley that." The man's fantasy was limitless on almost any subject, but when it came to Shirley, it went into the stratosphere.

Anytime a new person came into the unit, we naturally wanted to know who he was, where he was from, and what he did in civilian life. Of course, I always looked for someone from Texas in general and northeast Texas in particular. A lot of good it did to look. I never found anyone who had heard of Windom. But I didn't discourage easily, I told them not to worry; all they had to remember was that Windom was right next to Honey Grove, the sweetest town in all of Texas.

That bit of advice paid off one day in the early 90s. An old Army buddy of mine named Miller[4] was driving from his home in Arkansas to California to visit his kids. As luck would have it, he happened to stop for lunch at the Dairy Queen in Honey Grove. Something in his mind clicked, ". . . Honey Grove, the sweetest town in all of Texas." It was quiet in the Dairy Queen that day and as he was paying his check he turned and asked everyone sitting in the restaurant, "Does anyone know Glenn Elliott? He was raised around here somewhere." John Bomer, an old friend, spoke up and said that he knew me. He told Miller I had been raised in Windom, five miles west of Honey Grove. Coincidentally he had seen me in Windom at Oliver's Store picking up supplies that very morning. It is one hundred twenty-six miles from my home in Longview to Windom, so I do not make it up to the farm as much as I would like. Luck was with me that day.

I was out in the yard working when a car drove up. Take my word for it, if anyone drives up to my farm in Windom they have to be coming to my house. Anyway, a man got out of the car, called me by my first name, and started talking to me. The longer he talked, the more mystified I became. After a while I said, "Partner, it's obvious you know me, but I don't have any idea who you are." Miller already knew that and was having a big laugh at my expense.

Early in 1946, we had shipped out of Kobe together, headed back for the States—and yes, near the Alaskan coast I got seasick again. The last time we had seen each other was when we disembarked in Seattle. Our visit brought back many wonderful memories that only service buddies have.

After parting company with Miller in Seattle, I found myself on yet another troop train, this time headed in the general direction of San Antonio, Texas. Once the train arrived in San Antonio, I stayed only long enough to

---

[4] I have tried, but I cannot remember Miller's first name.

secure a leave. Even though I was only going to visit for a few days, the minute I had my pass in my hand, I headed for Windom. After an all-too-brief visit with Catherine, our daughter Diane, Mother and Dad, and a few friends, I had to return to San Antonio to have minor surgery performed; then I was mustered out.

In Kobe, I had been burned on the right side of my face, and a growth had developed on my right eye. Before leaving the Army I wanted to make sure this was corrected. It was a simple operation and I was as good as new. But even then the government was looking for ways to give away the taxpayers' money. I was told I could draw a small pension. This was preposterous. Why, I asked, should I draw a pension? I was perfectly capable of working. As far as I was concerned, that would have been like stealing. I didn't deserve the money and I didn't want it. I did tell them that if I ever lost the sight in that eye, I would come back for my pension. In April of 1946 I was discharged, and I never went back for any pension, partial or otherwise.

I want to say before leaving my Army life behind that one of the great regrets I have in my life is that I did not keep in touch with Louie and my other Army buddies after I got out of the service. I meant to, but somehow time just got away.

Out of the Army and back in Windom, the first thing I had to do was find a place for my family to live, then find a job. The first was pretty easy. When I went into the Army we gave up the house we were renting and Catherine and Diane moved back in with her parents. Luckily, the old Methodist parsonage was available and we rented it for ten dollars a month. It was a huge old house with three bedrooms, a kitchen, library, dining room, living room, and a few others I have probably forgotten.

Before the war, Windom's Methodist Church had enough in attendance to justify a full-time pastor. But so many people left during the war that it caused attendance to dwindle to such a point, that the church could only afford to pay a student from Southern Methodist University in Dallas to come to Windom every other weekend to hold services. On that weekend we had to share the house with the pastor and do his cooking and washing. Catherine and I figured this was a small price to pay for a nice home. And, as an added bonus, we truly enjoyed the student's company.

The next problem, finding a job, was not as easy to solve. By the time I got out of the Army in late 1946, most of the jobs were taken. I had no choice but to join the *52-20 Club*. Members of the *52-20 Club* were returning veterans who received twenty dollars per week for fifty-two weeks while looking for a job.

This is the only time in my life I have ever taken a government handout.

Among the many positive things about living in the country is that even on twenty dollars a week you will not starve. I helped Dad milk and work around the farm, while looking for a job. Between the garden, the chickens, the hogs, and the cows I milked, we always had plenty of fresh eggs, milk, pork, and vegetables.

After the war the government had given Jones Field—where I had worked briefly before joining the Army—to the city of Bonham. The Jaques Power and Saw Company of Denison, Texas, manufactured augers that were used to drill holes for utility poles. The owner of the company, Mr. Jaques,[5] had an idea for a new type of tractor he wanted to build. He agreed to construct his plant in Bonham if the city would sell him Jones Field. The city agreed and sold him the Jones Field facility for one dollar. The Jaques Tractor plant was quickly built and began taking applications for jobs.

Since it was the only job opening in the area, I applied. When I arrived at Jones Field, there must have been three hundred people standing in line applying for the few available jobs. Needless to say, my hopes were not very high. When it was finally my time to interview, I was asked if I had any specialized training that would help me with the job. I told the interviewer that I had no specific training in anything they were doing, but if he would hire me I would be the best hand they had at whatever they put me to doing. I did not care what the job was, sweeping floors or cleaning the toilets. I needed a job. I told him, "If I don't make you a good hand, run me off." He looked me straight in the eye and said, "Young man, that's just the attitude we are looking for. Can you go to work Monday morning? The job pays seventy-five cents an hour." On Monday morning I was there when they opened the doors.

Mr. Jaques' tractor was a good product, but it had one major problem. It was so heavy that it took all of its power just to pull itself. After about a year and a half of trying to improve the tractor, Mr. Jaques realized that the competition was too strong for a newcomer, so he shut the plant down.

Three others and I were asked to transfer to the main plant in Denison. By now my pay was a dollar and twenty-five cents per hour. I asked how much more I would make. They said they were sorry, but they could raise me only an additional ten cents per hour. I knew I needed a larger raise than ten cents an hour to justify the move. There were a lot of things to consider: I could not possibly hope to find a house in Denison for ten dollars per month and I would have to buy a car. There had been no need for one in Windom. With all the people in Windom working in Bonham, it was no problem catching a ride. Besides, if needed, I could always use Dad's or my in-laws' car, so transportation had never presented a problem. Also, the grocery bill would go up. No store could match the price of the milk, eggs, and other farm

[5] I do not remember his first name.

products we got from Mother and Dad. I told them I appreciated their offer, and I understood their position, but I hoped they understood that I simply could not move to Denison for a dime an hour.

They understood, but they really did not want to lose me, and I did not want to lose them, so we reached a compromise. They had an old International truck that they would let me drive back and forth between Bonham and Denison. I could pick up a load of equipment every morning in Bonham, drive to Denison, work around the plant while it was being unloaded, then go back to Bonham and do the same thing again the following day. Doing this, it would take several months to move all the equipment. Would I agree to this plan? I jumped at it.

Instead of several months it took only about a month before the move was completed. Then it was time to look for another job.

During the month of February, 1949, there was a huge ice storm across northwest Texas. Power lines were down everywhere, but living inside the city limits of Windom we did not go without electricity for long. The same could not be said for Mother and Dad. Living in the country, they were on REA (Rural Electric Association), and it was weeks before they had their electricity restored.

The storm had knocked all the electric and telephone poles down and I found a job helping an independent telephone contractor, a Mr. Dorris, restore phone service around the area. I knew this job would not last long. Luckily, it didn't have to.

In Windom, Catherine and I lived right across the street from the parents of my old high school coach, Elmer Riddle. Many an afternoon I would come home and find Mr. and Mrs. Riddle sitting on their front porch. I always tried to take time to visit them for a few minutes.

In 1941, for the want of twenty-five dollars per month in pay, the Texas school systems lost a lot of good men to the Department of Public Safety. One was Elmer Riddle. Once he joined the DPS, he dropped the Elmer, and became Jim.

In those days, when someone died, the body was brought home where family and friends would sit up all night with the deceased. When Jim's father died, I sat up all night with the family, as I did when his mother died in 1948.

After his mother's funeral, Jim and I were sitting on his parents' front porch talking. He asked what I was doing, and I told him. He asked if I had ever given any thought to joining the DPS and becoming a highway patrolman.

Since I didn't have any college I told him that I did not think I was qualified. The closest I had ever come to police service was as an MP in the Army and I knew that did not mean much to the Department of Public Safety.

"No," he said. "You're qualified. We need men like you."

When he told me it paid two hundred dollars a month, plus a car and clothes,

29

I did not need to know anything else. I was definitely interested. At that time Catherine and I did not even have a car. As an added bonus they provided clothes to boot! What else did I need to know other than where to sign up?

I wish it had been that easy. It was not.

Jim told me that I would have to write the DPS in Austin to request an application, then take a test. He did not know if it would help me or not, but I was welcome to use him for a reference. I knew it would.

I sent in my application and shortly received word that one of the testing sites would be in Dallas.[6] They had forty openings to fill and in the eight testing locations throughout the state there must have been three or four thousand people there to take the test.

In September, 1948, I took the test, and was rejected. They told me there would be another test in about six months, and if I wanted, I could retest then. Now that my back was up, I really wanted to be a highway patrolman. Realizing how unprepared I was for the first test I started studying, and studying hard, for the next examination. I was determined I would not fail again! I learned from the first test that the Department of Public Safety was big on current events and statistical information. Armed with this knowledge, I studied the Dallas newspapers and the *Texas Almanac*. When it came time for the next testing, which was held in Fort Worth, I was ready. I thought I had done well, but you never know.

At ten minutes before noon, on Saturday, April 1, 1949, I was sitting on top of a telephone pole four or five miles north of Windom, hooking up a farmhouse. We were still using the old crank-type phones then, and I remember I had just completed the outside work. I climbed the pole and called the operator to check the line. Mrs. Dorris[7] was the operator, and when I completed the line check she told me that W. J. Elliott,[8] Chief of the Highway Patrol, had been trying to reach me. She told me to stay right there and she would connect me. Sitting on top of a telephone pole, I called the Chief in Austin. I told Chief Elliott that I was sorry I had not been available when he called, but I was working. He told me, ". . . never apologize for working. A man who will work is exactly the kind of man I need on the highway patrol. Can you be in Austin Monday morning at six o'clock to start highway patrol training?"

Could I? Wild horses could not have kept me away!

On April 3, 1949, I would start training at Camp Mabry in Austin. Eleven weeks later, I would be a Texas Highway Patrolman.

---

[6] Testing sites were located in every major city in Texas. All the tests were given the same day.

[7] Once again I am sorry to say that I do not remember either of the Dorris' first names.

[8] Chief Elliott was no relation to me.

SECTION 2

Texas Highway Patrolman

CHAPTER IV
I BECOME A HIGHWAY PATROLMAN

From noon Saturday until six o'clock Monday morning left me with but a few hours to get my affairs in order before reporting to Camp Mabry. Leaving my old job was no problem. Knowing I had applied to the DPS, Mr. Dorris had hired me as temporary help. There is one thing to be said about not having anything: you have very little to get in order.

Sunday following church Catherine, Diane, Mother, and Dad drove me to the bus station in Bonham. No sooner had we arrived than State Senator Jones,[1] who represented Windom, came strolling into the station. Like a good politician, he was glad-handing everyone within reach. With Dad being so active in politics, he and Mr. Jones were good friends.

Asking what the Elliott clan was doing in the bus station, Daddy told him that I was on my way to Austin to start highway patrol school. No sooner were the words out of his mouth than the Senator turned to the bus station attendant and told him to tear up my recently purchased ticket to Austin and reissue one only as far as Sherman. I was not asked—I was informed he would accompany me to Sherman on the bus. In Sherman a fellow Senator[2] from Gainesville would meet us in his car and from there we would complete the trip to Austin in the Senator's car. Needless to say, riding to Austin in a car instead of a bus really appealed to me. What happened after we arrived in Austin did not appeal to me. It was my worst nightmare come true.

Jim Riddle had warned me to stay clear of politics. They had no use for politics in the DPS. We arrived in Austin about eight o'clock that night, and I thought they would simply drop me off at the DPS School at Camp Mabry and that would be the end of it. Wrong, wrong, wrong! Not only did they not just let me out at the door, but they also insisted on going inside " . . . to make sure I got the proper introduction."

Sam Guynes was the monitor on duty that Sunday night. Senator Jones proceeded to tell Sam what a wonderful person I was, and how I was going to

---

[1] I do not remember Senator Jones' first name.

[2] I do not know this man's name.

33

be an enormous credit to the highway patrol. According to the Senator, the DPS was about the luckiest agency in Texas to have landed a prize catch like me! As hard as I tried, I could not find a rock, rug, or anything else to crawl under. I was horrified! One thought kept racing through my mind: "Glenn, there's no need to even unpack. They're going to throw me out of here so fast, I won't even remember being here."[3] Later Sam Guynes and I became great friends, but that was still in the future. After Senator Jones finally left—and it seemed like an eternity—I figured that at best I would get a dressing down that would make the toughest Marine DI turn green with envy.

I did not give Sam a chance to tear into me. Before he gave me the boot I wanted him to know my side of the story. I told him that Jim Riddle had already told me how the DPS felt about politicians, and I certainly agreed. Today had been the first time I had ever met Senator Jones. As far as the other Senator was concerned, I had never heard of him before today.

Finally finding a chance to get a word in, Sam said, "Whether we like it or not, all of us have to use a little politics every once in a while. There may come a time when we have need for a Senator who is a friend of the highway patrol. Don't forget the way to Senator Jones' door; you may have to knock on it someday." I never had to knock on Senator Jones' door, but if I had needed to, I would not have hesitated. Over the years Senator Jones proved to be a true friend of law enforcement in general, and the highway patrol in particular.

Later, after Sam and I became friends, he told me I was the most pitiful sight he had ever seen standing there beside the Senators. Later I could laugh about it, but at the time it was happening, it was anything but funny.

They did not throw me out and the next morning at six o'clock sharp we started training. I did not have any trouble with the physical training. We did some boxing. Fortunately I had not lost anything from my Army days and I was still a pretty fair country boxer. I had no problem on the firing range. I was not a great shot, but I was good enough. And then there were the motorcycles. Naturally I had ridden bicycles as a kid, but I had never been on a motorcycle in my life. They put us on an old '36 Harley and a slightly newer '37 Indian. Learning to ride a motorcycle was quite an experience, but I handled it without any problem. Having driven since I was old enough to reach the foot petals, driving was probably the easiest part of school. We did a lot of running. No problem, I was in as good a physical shape as I ever have been in my life.

Then there were the books, and that was a problem. I had been out of school since 1942, and I regret that reading has never been one of my strong

---

[3] Co-author's note: There are a lot of crooks in prison who wish that Glenn had been thrown out.

suits. I just never had the patience to sit down and read a book—I still find it difficult. I think I have spent my whole life trying to catch up. I simply cannot sit still for an hour at a time.[4] I had to work doubly hard on the books. Never in my life have I been afraid of hard work, so I doubled up on the bookwork and passed all the tests.

There were many men in the spring class of '49 that I would be inter-twined with for the better part of my career. G. W. Burks would become the Captain of Ranger Company B, and also be my Commanding Officer. Butch Albers likewise became a Ranger Captain in Waco over Company F. Johnny Krumnoe became a fellow Ranger stationed in Waco. And Leo Gosset would go farther than any of us; he retired as the top lawman in the State of Texas—the Director of Public Safety.

During the eleven weeks of school, they brought in various people from different branches of the DPS to speak to us. In 1949 the farthest thing from my mind was to become a Texas Ranger, but I was extremely impressed when-ever one of the Rangers spoke. What red-blooded Texan would not have been? These were Texas Rangers, the very symbol of Texas! I started at the top of the mountain when I met my first Ranger, Captain M. T. "Lone Wolf" Gonzaullas. I had only seen one other Ranger in my life, but right there in front of us was the "Lone Wolf." Three of my uncles[5] had worked in Kilgore during the boom years in the early 1930s. I had heard them tell how rough and tough it had been in those early years of the oil boom, and I had heard them talk about Lone Wolf Gonzaullas. More than anyone, Gonzaullas and his partner, Bob Goss, had tamed the wild and woolly East Texas Oil Field. I do not remember the subject he spoke on, but even if I had not become good friends with him later,[6] he was the type of man you could never forget. Try to imagine, if you will, what a Texas Ranger should look like. How should he dress? How should he walk, talk, and act? What you will be imagining is the legendary "Lone Wolf."

Selwin Denson, another Ranger, also spoke to us. Until Gonzaullas, Selwin was the only Ranger I had ever seen. Dad was on a first-name basis with the Sheriff and other lawmen in Fannin County. One day, shortly after I had gotten out of the Army, I was at the courthouse in Bonham with Dad when he pointed to this man and said, "That's Selwin Denson. He's a Texas Ranger." No one had to tell me Selwin was a Ranger. I could tell by the way he carried himself that he was somebody special. Like Gonzaullas, after I

---

[4] Co-author's note: Captain Jim Ray says that Glenn is so active that he wears out his clothes from the inside out.

[5] Three of my mother's brothers—Leon, Luther, and Eugene Winchester—worked in the East Texas Oil Field in and around Kilgore during the boom years of the 1930s.

[6] At his funeral, Glenn would serve as one of Gonzaullas' pallbearers.

became a Ranger, Selwin and I became truly great friends.

May 25, 1949, was one of the greatest days of my life. I became a Texas Highway Patrolman. Catherine, Mother, and Dad came to Austin for graduation. I suppose the other guys were as proud as I was, but I do not see how. The commander of the Department of Public Safety, Colonel Homer Garrison, was the keynote speaker. Garrison is to Texas law enforcement what J. Edgar Hoover is to the FBI. I will have more to say about him later, but the Colonel deserves every honor bestowed upon him, and there have been many.

Two weeks before graduation we were told where our duty station would be. Before that none of us knew what town we would be assigned. None, that is, except me. They had asked us what District[7] we preferred. Of course, there was no guarantee we would get the District we chose, but at least they asked. Scuttlebutt[8] had it that there were openings in Amarillo, Corpus Christi, and El Paso. It did not take a brain surgeon to figure out that any of these cities is a long way from Windom. Originally I had hoped for Dallas, but I knew I was going to Longview.

As my good friend Paul Harvey says, "Now, the rest of the story." One of my DPS school monitors was Sergeant A. E. Jones from the Waco District. The other was the already-mentioned Sergeant Sam Guynes, from the Tyler District. One night Sergeant Guynes came to me and said, "I need to talk to you." I figured that I must have done something wrong, though I could not think of what it might have been. Monitors[9] did not need much of an excuse to hammer us; they stayed on us pretty well all the time.

Sam told me right up front not to say anything to anyone about our conversation. Our conversation was ". . .strictly off the record. You know I'm not supposed to do this, but next Monday you're going to have to make a choice where you go. I don't know whether you've thought about it or not— I'm sure you have—but I've got a place for you in my District in Longview. I'd like to have you as one of my men. And I've got just the man for you to work with—Lloyd Webb."

Later that same day Sergeant Jones came up to me and said he needed to talk to me "off the record." He asked me to go to Waco. I would have been flattered if only one of my monitors had asked me, "off the record," to join his command. Words cannot describe how honored I felt that both asked me.

I had only passed through Waco going to and from San Antonio and Fort

---

[7] Later the State was broken up into Regions. Each Region had so many Districts. In 1949 they were called Highway Patrol Districts.

[8] On the sailing ships of the early US Navy, the water barrel was known as the "scuttlebutt." It was around the scuttlebutt barrel that sailors would exchange the latest rumors; thus rumored information became known as scuttlebutt.

[9] In the Service they would have been called DI's. I suppose the DPS felt they were monitoring us, not drilling us.

HOMER GARRISON, JR.
Director

JOE S. FLETCHER
Asst. Director

TEXAS DEPARTMENT OF PUBLIC SAFETY
CAMP MABRY,
AUSTIN

Commission
GEORGE PRENDERGAST
Chairman
J. PRICE MADDOX
HOXIE H. THOMPSON
Commissioners

May 16, 1949

Mr. Glenn Elliott
Student-Patrolman
Texas Highway Patrol Training School
Camp Mabry
Austin, Texas

Dear Sir:

Effective June 1, 1949, your station will be Longview, which place will be your headquarters until further advised.

Captain Guy Smith, whose headquarters is at Tyler, will be your commanding officer, and you should report to him for further instructions.

Your salary will be $230.00 a month, effective June 1, 1949.

Your attention is called to Regulation 20 (f), Page 29, Texas Highway Patrol Manual, which provides a penalty of dismissal for failure to report a change of address or telephone number within twenty-four hours to your Chief, and Captain under whom you are working.

Yours very truly

Homer Garrison, Jr.
Director

By: W. J. Elliott, Chief
Texas Highway Patrol

WJE/br
dc - Captain Guy Smith
cc - Accounting Division
cc - Headquarters Division
cc - Personnel Clerk

Hood when I was in the Army. As for Longview, the closest I had ever come to it was when I went to Tyler after the war looking for a job with the Flure Construction Company.

Longview is closer to Windom than Waco. Both Catherine and my folks still lived in Windom, so distance was an important factor. My three uncles had worked in Kilgore back in the 1930s, and I had heard them talk about the Longview area. That was not a major influence, but I had been intrigued with their stories about the oil field. Most importantly, I had already told Sam Guynes that I would ask for the Tyler District, but I could not tell Sergeant Jones that I had already talked to Sam Guynes. I told Sergeant Jones that I had already talked it over with Catherine, which I had, and we had decided that Tyler would be our first selection. However, I would request Waco as my second choice, with Dallas third on the list.

I was accepted into the Tyler District.

I graduated on May 25, 1949. That gave Catherine and me one week to find a place to move to in Longview. Our first home away from Windom was in the western half of a duplex on 110 East Marshall Avenue in Longview.

Having lived all of our lives in Windom, you would think Catherine and I would have trouble leaving. Not so. Catherine had more foresight than I. After initially talking to Jim Riddle, I told Catherine I wanted to apply for the highway patrol, but if I was accepted we would undoubtedly have to leave Windom. The idea thrilled her. She knew that if we remained in Windom it was a dead-end street for us. The best we could ever hope for in Windom was a future either in a factory, of which there were very few, or working on a farm. There is nothing wrong with either profession, but I am much too restless to do the same thing day after day. Catherine knew me better than I knew myself; she realized I would not have lasted long in either job.

For most people, a week would not have given them enough time to move all their earthly possessions. With so little to move, it was ample time for us. The State was no help. Their philosophy was simple—if you wanted the job, you had to figure out how to get there. That was why they gave new officers a whole week before reporting for duty.

I asked my uncle, Claude Elliott, if I could borrow his old '41 Ford two-ton cattle truck to use to move our things. Believe me, a moving company was never considered. Then I asked Kenneth Oliver[10] if he would help us. We loaded everything we owned on Uncle Claude's little truck and away we

---

[10] Kenneth was later elected Constable in Fannin County. His grandson, Brad Oliver, at the time of this writing, is a member of the DPS Narcotics Division.

went. A few hours later we were in Longview unloading our few belongings into our little duplex.

We were moved, but it would be two weeks before we sat up housekeeping. My partner, Lloyd Webb, was on vacation when I graduated from highway patrol school, and I had been ordered to spend my first two weeks training in Tyler before taking up my permanent duty station in Longview. Not wanting to spend two weeks alone in a new town, Catherine and Diane went back to Windom until I could join them permanently.

This was our first home away from Windom and I will never forget our little duplex. For anyone not familiar with Longview, Marshall Avenue is better known as Highway 80. Interstate 20 was still a long way off, thus making Highway 80 the main east-west traffic artery through town. I believe every vehicle going from Florida to California passed within a few feet of our bedroom window. Sometimes I thought every vehicle that went up and down Marshall Avenue either backfired or had no muffler. But eventually we became like the people who live beside a railroad track; we were aware of the traffic noise, but did not hear it.

The street noise was pretty much the only negative thing about living next to the highway. There were far more pluses than minuses. Since we didn't own a car,[11] the main advantage was its close proximity to the downtown area, and in those days the downtown area was still the center of a town's life. Within a block of the house was a grocery store, a drug store, a cafe, and a service station. Anything that Catherine needed, as far as the day-to-day operations of the house were concerned, was within a two-minute walk. Not only were stores close by, but just as important, so was our church.

Catherine was raised Church of Christ. There's one thing about people who are Church of Christ—every time the doors are open, they are there. Catherine was no exception. In 1949 the Church of Christ was at Second and Whaley, only a few blocks from our home. I usually had to work on Wednesdays and Sundays nights, so Sunday morning was about the only time I was able to go to church. Catherine and Diane usually walked to church and someone from church would always bring them home.

As a child, Mother and Dad had taught me three things above all others: fear the Lord, respect my elders, and work hard. All three lessons are still with me. I attend church, with enthusiasm, every Sunday if I am in town. To this day I love to be around old people. If I am at home, my day is a little bit empty if I do not make my morning coffee round with my friends at the nursing home just down the street from my house. They seem to enjoy my company, and I dearly love their fellowship. As for the third lesson in life, I have many faults, but I have never been accused of not working hard.

---

[11] We did not buy our first car until 1950.

I was raised a Methodist. One of my proudest moments was when I was elected to be a Steward of the Windom Methodist Church. Catherine and I had not been married long when I started going to the Church of Christ with her. Even though I regularly attended the Church of Christ for the next twenty plus years, I was, officially, a member of the Windom Methodist Church.

On July 16, 1965, a wonderful friend of mine, Justice of the Peace William M. "Mack" Harrison died. As I listened to the preacher eulogizing Mack during the funeral service I got to thinking about my own religion and what would happen if I died on my way home. Mother and Dad would naturally want me buried as a Methodist, and why not? I still belonged to the Methodist Church. Just as naturally Catherine would want me buried as a member of the Church of Christ, and why not? I had been attending the Church of Christ for more than two decades. I realized I would be putting my family in a terrible position. This was a decision I needed to make.

The people at the Church of Christ were wonderful. I believed as they believed. Inside, I knew I had made my decision a long time ago. Sitting there at Mack's funeral I knew it was time to quit procrastinating. It was time to act.

As is customary at the end of the service, the preacher, Boyd Fannin, offered the invitation to join the church. I don't know why, but I had not said anything to anybody about my decision. I simply stood up, stepped into the aisle, and walked down front. I am sure this surprised a lot of people. After attending the same church for eighteen years, most people assumed I was already a member.

I had no more than sat down when one of the proudest, and happiest, moments in my life occurred. My son, Dennis, walked down front and sat down beside me. I wish I had a good enough vocabulary to tell you how good this made me feel. Dennis and I were baptized together. As a child I remember being sprinkled in the Methodist Church. The Church of Christ believes in submersion, and then not until you are old enough to fully understand the meaning of baptism. Never in my life have I felt cleaner than I did on July 18, 1965, when Brother Fannin lifted me out of the water. I honestly believe that the only way to ever feel that clean and that good again would be to redo my baptism, something I do believe would help everyone.

We continued to live in our little duplex for two years. In 1951 we built our current home on Ruthlyn Drive in north Longview. Since my partner, Lloyd Webb, lived in north Longview, we looked for property in the same area. In 1951, highway patrolmen were really on duty twenty-four hours a day. Since we were called out at all hours of the day and night, it only made sense to build in the general area where Webb lived.

When we bought our property on Ruthlyn it was actually in the country. We may have been alone in the early 50s, but today we are in the middle of

Longview. In 1951, we had very few neighbors, but we had one couple like no other—D. C. and Blanc Ellerd. Mr. Ellerd has been gone a long time, but Blanc,[12] now in her mid-80s, is going as strong as ever. Sit down and write out your idea of the perfect neighbor. When you get done, you will have described Blanc.

On Tuesday night, May 31, 1949, I arrived in Tyler, ready to report for duty the following morning. I was twenty-two years old, and would be making the big bucks—$230 per month. In 1949 that was good pay.

As a courtesy Captain Guy Smith met me at the bus station and we visited for about two hours. During the entire two hours he did not give me any special instructions. He just tried to make me feel comfortable. In my thirty-eight plus years with the DPS I served under six captains, but none were any better than J. Guy Smith. In my book, he was as good as they came. He was under no obligation to spend any time with me, let alone two hours, but he did. I remember feeling I was on cloud nine when the Captain and I parted later that night. I knew I belonged.

There were two cots upstairs in the DPS office and the Captain let me stay there for two weeks. The only drawback was that I had to walk one and one-half blocks to the fire station to take a shower. Only in hindsight was it a disadvantage. At the time I remember thinking, "You've hit another lucky break. No hotel bills for old Glenn."

Radio communications for the whole area was based in Tyler and with all he had going on, the Captain had forgotten the operator was on vacation. To Captain Smith's way of thinking that was no problem. He wanted his men as diversified as possible, so my first two weeks as a bona fide highway patrolman was spent as a radio dispatcher. Captain Smith worked the first day with me until noon showing me how to operate the radio, two phones, and the teletype. From that first day until the day I retired in August, 1987, I have had nothing but admiration and respect for the people who handle the radios.

There is more to running a communications room than meets the eye. Let's say that a patrolman has stopped a car from Illinois and the license plate needs to be run. Unlike today where they get an almost instant response through the NCIC[13] system, in 1949 it was a little different. There was a

---

[12] On March 18, 1937, the New London School blew up, killing over three hundred people. All but a handful were children. Young Blanc McCord was the telephone operator on duty in nearby Overton. She got word to the outside world of the tragedy.

[13] Today every modern law enforcement office is hooked into the NCIC (National Crime Information Center) computer system. Any agency on it can gain immediate access to license numbers, warrants and arrests, etc.

teletype in each state capitol and the first thing I had to do was get a chart that showed the teletype number for the state of Illinois. Finding the number I would dial it up, then sit down at my teletype machine and type out the information I wanted. My counterpart in Illinois had to look up the information I wanted and teletype it back to me. All this does not happen instantly, so while I am waiting for a reply, another patrolman radios in wanting some kind of information from Florida. We had two teletypes, so while waiting for the reply from Illinois, I go through the same procedure with Florida. While all of this is going on, calls are coming in via the radio that have to be answered. As if this is not enough, the phone is ringing. It could be the sheriff's office or a local city police department and they too need something checked. In those days we did not just handle the highway patrol, but any of the local law enforcement bodies.

Looking back, the two week stint in the radio room was some of the most valuable training I could have received as a green rookie. Later, when I would radio in and not get an immediate response, I would lay my microphone down in the car seat and wait. I knew that as soon as the dispatcher could, he would respond. I have always felt, and still feel, that every field officer should spend a few weeks in communications. It would make them better officers.

It seemed I had hardly started when the two weeks were over and Lloyd Webb was back from vacation. It was time to go to Longview and hit the streets.

CHAPTER V
STATE TROOPER

It was mid-June, 1949, and I was finally ready to assume my duties as a Texas Highway Patrolman. That weekend Catherine and Diane made the final move from Windom to Longview.

I have been blessed throughout my life. I have had wonderful parents, family, and friends. I had a great friend in the service named Louie Tillman. My first captain, J. Guy Smith, was marvelous. As for my partner, over the next five and one-half years I would spend an average of eighty hours a week with Lloyd Webb. It doesn't get any better than Lloyd. Not only was he my partner, he was my best friend. Many a time on our day off we would go fishing or play dominoes. We simply enjoyed one another's company.

I first met Lloyd in Gregg County Sheriff Noble Crawford's office the last week of May, 1949. While Catherine and I were in Longview looking for a place to live, I went by the Sheriff's office to introduce myself, and there was Lloyd. We hit it off from the start.

Lloyd was born in Houston and lived there until he was twelve-years old; then his family moved to Harrison County. By the time I partnered up with Lloyd, he was already a twelve year veteran, having joined the DPS in 1937. Things were a lot different in 1949 than they are now. Only four patrolmen had all of Gregg County. Lloyd and I were in Longview and two other patrolmen were stationed in Gladewater.[1] Lloyd and I normally worked from two in the afternoon until two in the morning, six days a week. On Friday and Saturday nights it was usually three or four o'clock before we were able to call it a night. We didn't think anything about the hours; every highway patrolman in the State of Texas worked the same hours.

In 1949 we didn't have radar, computers, and a whole host of other things that officers now take for granted. One of the largest changes has been the car. Not only did they not have air conditioning; they did not

---

[1] Pat Spier, from Gilmer, Texas, was one of the patrolmen assigned to Gladewater. Later Pat would become succeed Homer Garrison and become Colonel Pat Spier, Director of the Department of Public Safety.

even have a heater. It wasn't that they didn't put heaters in cars in 1949; they did. But the State was not going to spring for the twenty-five or so dollars on such a luxury. I think they really believed that old joke—Texas has only two seasons, summer and February. That's a funny story to tell to people up north, but we in Texas know better. It can, and does, get cold in the winter. Lloyd and I salvaged a heater from a wrecked car and installed it in our patrol car. I don't believe anyone ever wrecked a car in our area that had an air conditioner that we could fit into our patrol car, so that left us only one way to stay cool in the summer—roll the windows down and drive fast. We stayed cool. No one has ever complained that I obstructed traffic by driving too slow.

I have often been asked to describe my first case. To be honest with you, I don't have a clue what it was. I suppose it was a speeding ticket, or some old drunk. However, I do remember my first major case. It was a murder.

It was about eleven o'clock at night, Wednesday, May 3, 1950. I was hungry, but Lloyd was not, so I dropped him off at his house and headed downtown for the old Hollywood Cafe[2] and something to eat before going home. I had just stopped at the corner of Center and Methvin Streets in downtown Longview waiting for the light to change, when a car came roaring down the street, ran through the red light and stopped right beside me. "There's a man killing another one down on Tyler Street in front of the Elite Cafe,"[3] he yelled.

At that time city, county, and state radios were all on the same frequency.[4] I radioed the city dispatcher and reported what I had been told and asked him to send backup. By the time I finished the message I was at the Elite. What I saw was not a pretty sight. Two men were in the street near the curb in front of the cafe—one was kneeling over the prone body of the other. The man on his knees was striking the other man over and over with what I later found out was a ten and one-half inch boning knife. Blood was everywhere, and it was obvious that the man in the street was already dead.

I could see the kneeling man had something in his hand, but I could not tell exactly what it was. When he saw me he turned and headed up the stairs towards the living quarters above the Elite. Still not knowing for sure what he had in his hand, I drew my .38 Special, but did not fire. I started after him and yelled for him to stop. He ignored me and kept running. I caught him at about the third or fourth step and tackled him. As he went down, the killer fell,

<hr>

[29] The old Hollywood Cafe was a twenty-four hour cafe. It was located on Tyler Street about where the entrance to Bank One is located today.

[30] Texas Furniture is now at the Elite Cafe's location. The extreme east end of the two story part of Texas Furniture was where the stairway was located. The stairway has since been removed, and the outside entrance eliminated.

[31] Frequency 37.260.

stabbing himself in the chest.[5]   Even with a serious chest wound, he kept fighting. By this time I had seen the knife, and I wasn't about to give him a chance to use it on me. Throughout my struggle with the assailant I had managed to keep my grip on my Smith and Wesson, so I gave him a little tap on the side of the head and he got real calm.

While he was still dizzy-headed from my little tap to his head, I hand-cuffed the knifeman and drug him back down on the sidewalk. It was only then that I realized he had stabbed himself when I tackled him. Two Longview City Policemen, Roy Stone[6] and his partner, Sam Burkham, had arrived at the scene just as I had tackled the killer on the stairwell. They took custody of the prisoner.

The killer's work had been repulsive. Nick Georgepul and Mose Swidan had been partners in Nick, The Greek's cafe in Kilgore. As is the case with most partnerships that come to an unsatisfactory end, there was a heated argument over money. Nick's was a twenty-four hour operation, with Nick operating the cafe during the daytime, and Mose handling the nighttime business. Since it did the majority of its business during the day shift, it naturally collected the most money during that time. Mose, who allegedly had a serious drinking problem, claimed that Nick was skimming the profits. Although Mose was never able to produce the first shred of evidence to support his accusation, the situation continued to worsen until they finally dissolved their partnership in October, 1949, and closed the cafe. Nick shortly thereafter opened the Elite Cafe in Longview.

During his trial, Swidan testified that he had paid Georgepul twenty-eight hundred dollars for an interest in Nick, The Greek's cafe in Kilgore. He had paid eleven hundred dollars down and given a promissory note, payable at one hundred dollars per month, for the remaining seventeen hundred dollars.

Swidan claimed that Georgepul refused to sell the restaurant equipment and pay him his interest, which he claimed came to eight hundred dollars. Instead he took the equipment and opened the Elite. During the ensuing months, Swidan had approached Georgepul on nine different occasions demanding the money due him, each time with the same negative results.

During the ninth and final confrontation, Swidan decided he was getting nowhere, so he had gone to the restroom on the second floor of the building adjacent to the Elite. As he was leaving the restroom, Georgepul suddenly appeared and the argument between the two men immediately resumed. Tragically, this time the argument grew more heated than usual.

In his testimony, Swidan claimed that Georgepul suddenly attacked him

---

[5] In reflection, I have often wondered if he was not trying to kill himself.
[6] Roy would later serve many years as Longview's Chief of Police.

and kicked him down the flight of stairs. He claimed his memory was blank from that point on, and he did not recall anything after that. He especially did not remember stabbing his former partner.

The story is painfully clear. Swidan was obviously armed. He produced the ten and a half inch boning knife, and proceeded to carve up Georgepul. When he finished, he had stabbed his former partner forty-seven times.

In the ensuing inquest, Justice of the Peace Jeff Richardson ruled that Mose Swidan had caused the death of Nick Georgepul by repeated stab wounds. And even while he lay in the Gregg Memorial Hospital recovering from his self-inflicted wound, R. L. Whitehead, the District Attorney, charged him with murder in the first degree.

During the trial, District Attorney Whitehead in his opening remarks made my head swell about two or three sizes. I had never been in a courtroom before, and I suppose I was like the starry-eyed kid in the candy store, trying to take everything in at once. I have to admit that I was feeling proud of myself. Here I was, fresh out of highway patrol school, and I had apprehended a killer. No one had to tell me—I knew I had done something good, but I also knew I had done only what I was being paid to do.

Anyway, right in the middle of his statement to the jury, Whitehead pointed to me and said, " . . . that highway patrolman sitting right there on the second row could have tried this man in that hallway that night, but he brought him here to you and he wants the citizens of this county to say what kind of punishment he gets." Proud. That doesn't begin to describe it. The District Attorney pointing me out for praise for just doing my job—I know my hat size expanded about three sizes right then and there.

The trial went quickly. There really was not a lot to debate. On Thursday, August 28, 1950, the jury, after deliberating three hours on Wednesday and one hour on Thursday, handed down its verdict—guilty. Guilty of murder with malice, with a recommendation of a twenty-five year prison sentence.

While in prison Mose died of natural causes—a sad conclusion to what had once been a good friendship.

I have been asked many times if I ever gave any thought to shooting Nick. In all honesty, I have to answer that with a yes and no. I knew that whatever he had in his hand—and with the blood in the street there was little doubt that it was a knife—as long as his back was to me, he couldn't hurt me with it. I am almost as afraid, or possibly more afraid, of a knife than I am of a gun, so there is absolutely no doubt in my mind that if he had turned and faced me with that knife in his hand, and I thought it was either him or me, I would have shot him dead.

I suspect every patrolman in the country would dispute this, but I believe that Lloyd and I had to have worked more drunks than anyone else in the world. But, of course, I may be a little biased. In the 40s and 50s Gregg County was the only official wet county within fifty miles in any direction. I don't know why, but how a drunk responds with the police always seemed to go in cycles. We would go for days without any kind of problem. You stopped the guy, and gave him a ticket or hauled him in without any problem. Then, just like you turned on a switch, they all wanted to run or fight. I never could figure it out.

I have to admit, the fighting didn't bother me too much. It's not that I wanted them to fight, but if they insisted, that was okay too. If they wanted to run, well, I was young, and I didn't mind an occasional car chase. In 1950 we got our first Ford with an interceptor engine. It irritated Lloyd to no end for someone to "rabbit" when I was driving—he liked the chase as much as I did and he wanted to do the driving. At this writing I am in my seventies and I still do not let any "grass grow under my feet" when I am behind the wheel. Some things never change; even now it seems I am always in a hurry.

Highway 80 between Longview and Greggton seems quiet enough today. Greggton has long been incorporated into Longview and it is one continuous city today. In the 40s and 50s the area between the two communities was open country, except for the honky-tonks and beer halls. When Highway 80 was built, it was only two lanes. After World War II the stretch between Longview and Greggton was widened to four lanes. This put most of the buildings, including the beer joints, right up on the highway—so close that in 1948 nine people were killed when they staggered out of a joint onto the highway and were run down. This was just the number of people who were killed. I have no idea how many were seriously injured or permanently lamed. It was nothing unusual for Webb and I to arrest as many as thirty people in one night!

The tragedy becomes even more misfortunate when you realize that the Greggton strip is only one small area in the county. Most of Gregg County was wet and there were beer joints and honky-tonks scattered all over the county. Pat Spier and his partner were working just as many drunks over in Gladewater. Kilgore had more honky-tonks than anywhere in the county, but there were no patrolmen stationed there. Needless to say, disregarding all other crimes, Gregg County law enforcement officers had more than their hands full just working the drunks.

Thank goodness, not all the drunks were on the highway. One day we were on ordinary patrol between Longview and Kilgore when we came upon Blanch Stewart's[7] old club on Highway 31. Everyone was standing outside and obviously very excited about something. With experience you get to where you have a pretty good idea what's going on by the actions of the crowd. It had the look of a fight in progress. We were almost right. There had been a fight, but it was already over.

Blanch's Club had a well-deserved reputation as one of the toughest clubs in the county. This particular evening Blanch had hired a band, and sometime during the evening the drummer had become irate over some infraction, imaged or otherwise. When we drove up he was standing in the doorway challenging any and all. He was a medium sized man, but with the chair leg he had in his hand, he looked huge. He had cleaned the club out—bouncers, patrons and his fellow band members. There had been some big old boys in the club, but nobody wanted any part of him. I can't say that I blamed them. After all, he had already whipped everybody in the club.

It has never been my style to needlessly antagonize a person I am going to arrest. I always tried to put myself in the other person's shoes—"Glenn, how would you want this officer to treat you, if you were in his position?" You know the old saying, "You can lead a person easier than you can push him." Easing up to him[8] I said, "What's the problem, Partner?" He said that he was sick and tired of people taking advantage of his good nature. I listened patiently as he rambled on and on.

One thing you always have to remember about a wanna'-be tough guy: they want everyone to know how tough they are. When he paused for breath I told him that I could not rightly remember having seen anyone tougher than he. I kept on talking to him, bragging on him. He really liked being told how tough I thought he was. All the time that I was bragging on him, I was also telling him that I was sure he could understand the predicament he had put me in. He knew that I was going to have to arrest him and take him downtown. Continuing as calmly as possible, I explained that my partner and I did not want to fight, and I would really appreciate it if he would come along peacefully. After several minutes of talking he said he understood our situation and

---

[7] I do not remember the exact name of Blanch's club, but it was located between the railroad tracks and the highway across from where the Con-Way truck terminal is located today. At that time Highway 31 was Highway 26 and was a two lane road.

[8] I do not remember this man's name, but I remember him well.

would go with us quietly.

We got him in the car and everything continued going along nicely until we got to the jail. All the way from Blanch's Club to the courthouse he whined and complained. That particular day had been a really rough one on Lloyd and I. Everybody we stopped wanted to fight. I guess even through the whisky he realized that he was getting on Lloyd's nerves. When we arrived at the courthouse, he decided he wanted to fight Lloyd. Between Lloyd and I, it did not take long to subdue the prisoner and get him upstairs for booking.

All the time we were booking him, his whining continued. Just before we put him in a cell we had taken the cuffs off. Everything was still going as well as could be expected under the circumstances. It was going well, that is, until we got to the cell block. He turned around to mouth off once more. As I said, Lloyd and I had, had a real hard day, and Lloyd told him where to get off.

That did it. The fight was on. I can see why he cleared out that old honky-tonk. This was no wanna'-be tough guy—he was the genuine article. My old boxing days came in handy. I got a clean shot and popped him in the jaw with a solid right cross. He went down like a rock. Sleeping peacefully, we got him up and into his cell. As we were leaving he awoke and turned on me again, saying, "We went around tonight, but I haven't had enough of you yet." I told him to go ahead and sleep it off and if he wanted any more of me, I would be around tomorrow. I knew that after he sobered up that would the last I ever saw of him. Sure enough, the following day they let him out and I have never seen him again.

In 1949 or '50, John Ben Shepherd from Gladewater was the Texas Secretary of State. On this particular day, Lloyd and I had picked him up at the local airport and taken him to Longview to speak to a civic group. While we were driving into town he told us he had pressing business in Austin and as soon as he finished the speech he needed to head back for the airport as quickly as possible. Following his instructions, as soon as he completed his speech we quickly escorted him back to our car and headed for the airport.

Seconds before we reached the intersection of highways 322 and 149, a propane truck's brakes failed just as he came into the intersection. Highway 322 dead-ends into 149, so the driver had no choice but to try and turn onto 149, but his speed was too great. The truck flipped over and was lying upside down on the shoulder of 149 just a few feet north of the intersection.

Because of the vast amount of gas and oil being transported in East Texas, we had received special training in knowing what to expect and how to handle this kind of accident. I knew that the tank's pressure valve should let off enough pressure to keep the tank from exploding.

What I had not counted on was fire. When the truck overturned it broke a gas[9] line near the engine's carburetor. There was a spark, then flames. Quicker than I can tell this, the flames spread forward to the cab, and rearward toward the back of the truck and to the spewing propane from the pop-off valve. The heat was so intense that it ignited the truck's tires.

As I said, the fire had spread into the truck cab. I pray that the driver was knocked at least semi-unconscious when the truck turned over. He was groaning weakly, and was on fire. Lloyd and I, plus a passerby whose name I regretfully do not remember, pulled the burning driver out of the cab and threw dirt on him until we extinguished the fire. Then we carried him across the road to the shoulder on the west side of Highway 149, safely away from the burning truck.

We radioed for an ambulance and a fire truck. Clearly the driver was severely burned. Since we were only a couple of miles from the airport, Lloyd told me to direct traffic while he ran Secretary Shepherd to the airport. There was nothing the Secretary could do to help us, so I was in total agreement. Lloyd was gone no more than five minutes before returning.

After making the driver as comfortable as I could, I went to direct traffic. I could hear the fire trucks coming. People then were no different than they are now; they loved to rubberneck and bottle up traffic. I had to clear a way for the emergency vehicles to get to the injured driver and the burning truck.

The pressure valve from the propane tank was blowing gas out, exactly as it was designed to do. If it hadn't been for the fire, everything would have been fine. The heat from the fire was so hot that it caused more pressure to build up than the pop-off valve could let out. The rapidly expanding gas sought out the weakest point in the tank, a welded seam. Unfortunately the weak point was on the side nearest me.

I was about fifty feet from the burning truck still directing traffic when the tank exploded. The only thing that saved my life from the flame-thrower-like sheet of fire was the steel-plated quarter-fender on the truck. It formed a "u" over the tires, and when the flames hit the quarter-fender, it diverted the flames upward and away from me. As it was, it still created enough heat that it burned the hide off my neck and the back of my ears, and blistered my back except where my Sam Brown belt[10] crossed my back. I guess the heavy wool pants I had on were thick enough to absorb enough of the heat that my legs

---

[9] Unfortunately this was a gasoline engine instead of a diesel. A diesel would have been much less likely to have caught fire.

[10] In the Texas DPS, a Sam Brown belt ran from the waist belt, front and rear, over the left shoulder. It was standard Army uniform issue from before World War I until World War II. It was named after it's inventor, Sam Brown.

were not blistered. The force of the blast knocked me face down into the highway pavement, but caused only minor scratches and bruises. Thinking back on it from today's perspective, I remember every detail in slow motion. Of course, from the moment the tank blew, until I was knocked into the pavement was only a split second.

It's funny what you remember about such terrible moments. The driver's billfold was so hot that when I tried to go through it looking for identification, I could hardly touch it. I don't remember if I was able to identify him then, or if it was later.

As for myself, I had to go to the doctor. Besides the burns from the explosion, I had received burns on my hands and arms when pulling the driver from the truck, and also while smothering the flames on his body. Fortunately my injuries were minor and I soon recovered. I wish I could say the same for the driver. He never recovered from his burns, and died from his injuries.

From 1931 to the time of this writing,[11] twenty highway patrolmen have been shot in the line of duty. In the early 50s, I almost became number twenty-one.

I don't remember if Lloyd was sick or had just taken a day off, but for whatever reason, I was alone as I patrolled Highway 80 just west of Longview. It was a Sunday night about eight o'clock and I was near where the Longview Christian Fellowship School is located today. I was heading east toward Longview when I met a Mercury swerving all over the road. I turned around and got in behind him. As soon as he saw me, he pulled over to the side of the road.

When I approached the car I saw there were three men in the car, and unmistakably all had been drinking heavily. After stopping the car I told the driver to get out and the two passengers to stay in the car. Everyone did as instructed. So far, so good. I ordered the driver, Harold Bowman, to the customary right rear of his car away from passing traffic. I had Bowman's driver's license in the clip of my clipboard. He was so drunk he had no business being a passenger in a car, let alone driving one.

I said, "I think you've had a little too much to drink and I'm going to have to place you in the custody of the Sheriff. Now come on around here and get in my car."

I reached and got Bowman by the arm, and when I did, he swung at me. I saw the blow coming and dodged quickly enough so that he barely touched

---

[11] 1998.

me. My old boxing days came back in a hurry, and I swung. I didn't just barely touch him; I nailed him dead solid. He went down like a poled mule. He was lying there on the ground sleeping as pretty as a picture.

With Bowman sleeping soundly I turned my attention to his partners and ordered them out of the car. Like Bowman, they had been drinking, but were not in nearly as bad a shape as was the would-be Joe Louis. I checked them out to make sure they were not armed. Satisfied that they were unarmed, I locked their car and ordered them to help me get the still sleeping Bowman into my patrol car. Bowman stood about 6'4", weighed about 220 pounds, and had the biggest feet I had ever seen. Even with three of us working, it was a job getting him into the front seat of the car. He was still unconscious, so I did not bother to handcuff him—huge mistake on my part. Once we finally got him in the car, I ordered the other two into the backseat of my car.

Both of our cars were on the shoulder of the westbound lane. As I pulled back onto the highway to make a U-turn to head for Longview, I dropped off of about a five-inch curb that ran down both sides of the road. Crossing to the other side of the road to complete the U-turn, I hit the other curb. When I hit the second curb, the bump started bringing Bowman to life.

He started rubbing his head and face. When he brought his hands over his face, he discovered a little blood where I had hit him. Seeing the blood, the fun started. He swung around in the seat with his back against his door, drew those gigantic feet and legs up, and kicked me in the side. If I had not known better, I would have thought he hit me with a baseball bat.

I knew that I could not fight him in the front seat. I managed to pull onto the shoulder, shut the car off, pull my keys out of the ignition, and get out of the car. While I was busy doing that, Bowman was whaling away at me with those skis he called feet. Once I was out of the car I grabbed his feet and held on long enough to drag him out of the car. I did not have a nightstick, and my slapper was hanging on the door handle. With nothing hard available, I popped him with my fist. He started falling back, this time, unfortunately, still conscious.

As he was falling I saw that he had somehow gotten my Colt .38 Special out of my holster and was holding it. To this day I have no idea how he became the first—and only—person to ever get my gun away from me. He had the pistol in the grasp of both hands, pointed in my direction, but without his finger on the trigger. I was thankful that he was still staggering from my fist to his head, but I knew he would not hesitate one second if I gave him a chance to get his finger on the trigger. I jumped on top of him and grasped the four-inch barrel with my right hand. He was holding the pistol between his hands in such a way that he could not get his finger on the trigger. We rolled around right in the middle of Highway 80—this was before I-20—and the traffic was extremely heavy. While we were wrestling I could hear car tires squealing, as drivers tried not to hit us.

Still on top of him and still holding the barrel with my right hand, I was able to get my left thumb on the hammer and my finger on the trigger. I cocked the pistol, shoved it into his right side and through gritted teeth said, "I'm fixing to pull the trigger of this pistol. I am going to get some lead in my hand, but you're going to get a bullet right through your gut if you don't relax right now and throw your hands back behind your head."

It was like Jesus calming the raging sea. Bowman became the calmest man in Texas. Even in his drunken condition I guess he realized where the muzzle of the pistol was pointed that it was highly unlikely he would survive. And he knew unequivocally that I was not bluffing. Anyway, he very, very calmly put his hands behind his head as instructed. This time I handcuffed him securely and hauled all three to jail.

While we were fighting, his two partners stayed in the car. I suppose they thought that since Bowman had started the fight, he could finish it without their help.

Several years later, Bowman got into trouble with the Lone Star, Texas, City Police. During the confrontation, a Lone Star policeman shot him in the chest numerous times with his .38 Special. Each time he shot him, Bowman would scream and cuss at the policeman, then pound his chest and tell the officer to shoot again. It took three shots to finally stop him—not kill him— just stop him.

Still later, he got into a fight in an area between Longview and Gladewater on Highway 80 known as Death Valley.[12] In the fight, someone cut his throat. Two highway patrolmen stationed in Gladewater came on the scene, stopped the fight and carried him to the hospital. During the trip one of the highway patrolmen, held his veins closed so that he would not bleed to death. At the hospital as the doctor was trying to sew him up, he starting cussing and fighting the doctor. The doctor finally had enough and told him, "You're gonna die if you don't hush up and let me sew you up, and I ain't gonna fight to save your life!" Bowman was a real pillar of society.

---

[12] This was an area where numerous honky-tonks were located. Going from Longview toward Gladewater on Highway 80, just before reaching Lake Devernia you descend a long hill. During the oil boom years of the 30s, this strip was known as The Western Front. During the 40s and 50s it became known as Death Valley. Today, radio station KEES is located along that strip.

After five and a half years of serving with the best partner a man could ever hope to have, Lloyd was promoted to sergeant and transferred to San Angelo. Now I was the experienced officer and it was my turn to train a rookie. Lloyd left huge shoes to fill, but he trained me well.

My new partner was a young man named Kenneth Walker. I only hope that I did the job with Kenneth that Lloyd did with me. Regretfully, Kenneth and I worked together for only a year and a half. In 1956 Kenneth transferred to a new station in Daingerfield.

After Kenneth transferred, I was assigned another rookie, Howard "Slick" Alfred. From September 8, 1956, until I became a Ranger on October 8, 1961, Slick and I were partners. Earlier I said that it didn't get any better than Lloyd Webb, and it didn't. But it could, and did, get as good. Slick and I served together for the better part of the next five years. In all that time I can truthfully say that we never had one cross word. Try spending sixty to eighty hours a week in an automobile with a person for the better part of five years without ever getting into an argument. It was remarkable. I became a Ranger in 1961; Howard followed in 1970.[13] To this day I have no closer friend than Howard Alfred.

One of the most exciting and dangerous incidents of my entire career happened with both Lloyd and Howard.

In early September of 1958, Sergeant Harvey Derrick of the Irving[14] City Police responded to a policeman's worst nightmare, a family disturbance. Arriving alone at the disturbance address, he left his car and headed for the residence. He saw a man, who turned out to be Lee Joseph Roe, walking down the street. Sergeant Derrick called out for him to stop. In reply Roe spun around with a pistol in his hand getting the drop on Derrick.

After forcing Sergeant Derrick to surrender his pistol, he made him get into his squad car. In the car, he told Derrick they were going for a ride — all the way to Little Rock, Arkansas. If Derrick offered any resistance, Roe

---

[13] At the time of this writing, 1998, Howard is the sheriff of Henderson County, Texas. (Athens)

[14] Irving, Texas, is a suburb of Dallas. It is best known as the home of the Dallas Cowboys.

54

assured him that he would kill him on the spot.

Roe ordered Derrick to radio his headquarters and inform them that he was being held at gunpoint, and if the roads were not cleared of all police cars he would be killed. Irving Chief of Police C. J. Wirasnik agreed to Roe's demands. Heading east, they went through Irving, Grand Prairie, Dallas, and Mesquite without being bothered.

In Terrell, Texas, they stopped for gas. The attendant of the gas station had no idea anything was wrong until they sped off without bothering to pay. But by this time the highway patrol decided Roe was not going to get a free ride all the way through Texas. In Terrell they tried to stop Roe and the hostaged police officer. When they approached, Roe started shooting, blowing out the windshield of one of the highway patrol cars, showering the officer with glass, but otherwise didn't hurt anything but his pride. With the bullets flying, Derrick was waving desperately to the highway patrolmen to back off.

When they got into the patrol car Roe had confiscated the officer's shotgun and with that shotgun pointed at his head, Derrick roared away from the station continuing east. Even hitting speeds up to 110 miles per hour, the highway patrol stayed nailed to their tail. Occasionally a patrol car would get a little too close and Roe would blaze away. From start to finish, Roe fired about fifteen times, without ever hurting anyone.

Howard and I first heard of the kidnapping and high-speed chase on our patrol car radio when they passed through Mineola about eighty miles from Longview. We listened closely, but didn't give the chase a lot of thought with it being so far away. We continued with our work. We arrested an old drunk who had torn up the Ranch House Club south of Longview on Highway 149. He had given us a nice chase until we ran him to ground in Longview at the corner of Highway 80 and Tyler Street. About the time we got him stopped, a couple of Gregg County Deputies arrived at the scene. Like every police officer in the area, they too had been listening to the hostage situation on their police radio. By this time it had gotten close enough to Longview that they knew Howard and I would shortly be involved in the chase. They volunteered to carry the prisoner to the courthouse and book him. Since the disturbance had happened inside the club and not on the highway, technically the prisoner was really the Gregg County Sheriff Department's responsibility anyway. We turned the prisoner over to the deputies, and headed for Gladewater.

As we headed west on Highway 80 toward Gladewater, Captain Glen Warner[15] contacted us on the radio. He told us that the fugitive was not,

---

[15] By this time Guy Smith had been promoted to Regional Commander and transferred to Dallas. Glen Warner, who had been a sergeant stationed in Dallas, was promoted to Captain and moved to Tyler, replacing Captain Smith.

under any circumstances, to leave his district. That was the sum total of his instructions. What else did we need? We knew our duty. The orders seemed simple, but there were possible problems. The Irving Chief of Police, C. J. Wirasnik, was radioing all up and down Highway 80 to let the car through. We did not bother arguing. Our Captain had given us our orders—Roe was not getting past Howard and me.

By now Roe was leading a regular convoy. Besides a whole host of highway patrol cars, the Rangers were also on his tail. None had been in position to get in front of Roe, so they were forced to follow. Three of the Rangers were destined to have a profound impact on my life: Jim Ray, Red Arnold, and Jay Banks. Jim and Red were simply doing their jobs. Action attracted Jay like honey to a bear.

Since I was the senior officer on site, I was in charge. I chose as a roadblock site an area on Highway 80 west of Gladewater. Actually it was just a few feet east of the main entrance to the Gladewater Rodeo grounds. This was the perfect place. The highway had only two lanes, and there were high banks along both sides of the road. It was about eleven or twelve o'clock at night, so I did not have to worry about much traffic. What little there was we directed into the huge parking lot of the rodeo grounds. The parking lot was large enough that, if needed, we could park hundreds of vehicles there, and since it was a good quarter of a mile from the roadblock, I did not have to worry about any stray gunfire, if there was any.

I stopped two tractor-trailer rigs and asked the drivers if they would help us. They volunteered to do anything they could. I asked them to park with their trailers facing west, the direction that Roe and Derrick were coming. I left only enough room between the trucks to park my patrol car. I wanted there to be enough room to let an ambulance through, if there was a need. With the high banks on each side of the road, there would be no room to drive around the roadblock. I knew from the radio traffic that Roe was making Derrick drive that old Plymouth wide open. Right before the roadblock site there was a little hill, and when they topped the hill they would be running about ninety to one hundred miles per hour, leaving no chance to stop and turn around. They would be boxed in perfectly.

The chase was nearing its climactic end, and by this time Howard and I had been joined by several of our fellow officers: Lloyd Webb,[16] Bob Nolan,

---

[16] Lloyd had made sergeant while in San Angelo and shortly thereafter transferred to the Tyler office. He knew when he went to San Angelo that there would soon be an opening in the Tyler office and he could return to the Longview area. For that reason he had not sold his home in Longview. In 1957 Captain Warner reorganized his command, the Northeast Texas Highway Patrol District, and created five sub-districts. One was headquartered in Longview, and Lloyd was given command of the new sub-district and moved back to Longview.

Johnny Andrews, and John O'Holzappel. I positioned myself in the south ditch, right where I knew they would be stopping—one way or the other. Howard and Nolan stationed themselves atop the bank on the north side of the road, while Andrews and O'Holzappel directed vehicles into the rodeo grounds, safely away from harm's way. Webb was in his vehicle providing communications between the pursuing officers and the roadblock.

Sure enough, Derrick came roaring over the hill with that old Plymouth wide open.[17] When he saw the trucks right in front of him, he shut her down. And I mean right now! He was braking so hard that the front end of the Plymouth dipped down and actually went under the back bumper of one of the semi-trailers. When the car stopped and the front end came up, the bumper of the truck dented the car's hood ornament.

As soon as the car stopped, I ran out of the ditch and yanked the passenger door open. I was armed with an old ten-gauge double-barreled shotgun that Lloyd had given me, and I stuck it right in Roe's face. I was prepared to use whatever force that was necessary. Meanwhile Howard had run up to the car and opened the driver door to get Derrick out. Both Howard and I started yelling at Derrick to get out, but he was frozen at the wheel. He just sat there, with his hands frozen to the wheel, staring at the back of the semi literally inches from his face.

This put me in a terrible predicament. If Roe tried to resist, I couldn't shoot. If I had, I would have hit both Derrick and Howard. Thank God, Roe threw his gun down, threw up his hands, and started crying and pleading, "Please, don't shoot me." A real tough guy. I guess the back end of a semi coming up at you at a hundred ten miles an hour and a ten gauge double-barreled shotgun stuck in your face, will take the fight out of you.

The highway patrol trooper from Terrell had been in the chase ever since Roe shot out his windshield. Running up to Roe, he started to hit him. There were a lot of spectators and press representatives around by this time and I knew we didn't need this kind of publicity. I gently walked the officer away from Roe and calmed him down. I told him I understood his frustration, but all he would do was help Roe and hurt himself if he continued with such foolishness. It took only a few minutes for him to settle down and everything was fine from that point.

We carried Roe to Gladewater's jail. Later Roe told officials that on the day of the kidnapping he had been drinking all day. He had started brooding over his girlfriend who was in Iowa. In his alcohol-filled brain he came to the conclusion that if he had a policeman for a hostage he could go all the way to Iowa. He was in a first-class alcoholic stupor. First he told Sergeant Derrick they were going to Little Rock. That is only about half-way to Iowa. Then he

---

[17] Derrick later reported that he had been running one hundred ten miles per hour.

57

commanded Derrick to head east on Highway 80. The only problem with this was that Highway 80 doesn't come within hundreds of miles of Little Rock, let alone the still more distant Iowa.

Ironically, Sergeant Harvey Derrick of the Irving City Police had worked in the Longview Police Department from 1951 to 1952. Former Longview Chief of Police, Roy Stone, remembers that Derrick was a very good officer, and he had hated it when he left the Longview Police Department to work at the ordinance plant in Karnack. Derrick had not stayed there long, before joining the Irving Police Department.

At the 1997 East Texas Peace Officers Barbecue in Tyler, Texas, Major Glen Warner remembered: "The Derrick kidnapping and the subsequent car chase was one of the worst days of my life. I remember my thoughts as clearly as if it was today. When I ordered that Roe not be allowed to get out of Texas, I wondered if my first major decision as a Captain might very well be sending a lot of men to their deaths. To this day I remember the heavy burden I felt."

Howard Alfred recalls: "I remember looking over at Glenn and that doubled-barreled shotgun. Let me tell you, the double bore of that old ten-gauge looked like twin fruit jars. All I could think of was, 'Jesus, Glenn, if you shoot him, you're going to get me and the hostage, too'."

Earlier I said that an officer's worst nightmare is being called to domestic disturbances. I didn't just dislike them, I hated them. As we have already seen, they get real messy, real quick. Nine times out of ten, the abused spouse will turn on the police officer who is trying to protect her. I know it doesn't make any sense, but it's a fact. The man could have just beaten the woman (and sometimes the reverse) to a pulp. What does the woman do? Not only will she usually refuse to file charges, but she will claim it was all her fault. It happens almost every time police officers answer a domestic disturbance. Like I said, I loathe domestic cases.

I remember one potentially explosive situation that I was able to smooth over by using elementary psychology. It too grew from a domestic squabble.

Many times when you stop a car, for whatever reason, you are faced with a potentially dangerous situation just waiting to happen and, as often as not, it has nothing to do with you. More times than I care to remember I have pulled someone over, only to find myself in the middle of a bitter family argument. In the heat of battle, so to speak, the spouse is actually happy that the companion has been stopped. This only adds to the anger and frustration of the driver, so by the time you get the driver out of the car, they are already mad enough to blow a fuse.

We usually ask the driver to get out of the car and go to the rear passenger side of the patrol car. This is done for two reasons: one, to get as far away as possible from passing vehicles, and two, to separate the family members, creating a cooling-off time. As a rule, after a few minutes, the anger has cooled at least to the point that they are no longer mad at the world. Generally it ends here, but not always.

One day I was driving east on Highway 80 about where ABC Auto Parts is located today, heading into Longview. I came up behind a car that was speeding and weaving all over the road. When I got close behind the car, I could see a man and woman really going at it, and I don't mean figuratively. They were screaming, yelling, and trying to hit one another. So intense was the battle raging in the car that my emergency lights failed to get their attention. Finally the combination of emergency lights and my siren got the driver's attention and he pulled over. When he came out of the car, I knew I had trouble.

The first thing he said was, "Well, you can write that ticket out, but I'm not going to sign it."

I said, "I've got to write it out anyway. May as well go ahead and do it out here."

This guy was really smoking, so I tried to be as understanding and tactful as practical. I knew that if I showed the least bit of aggression on my part, I would have a fight on my hands. Using all my tact, I tried to explain to him that signing the ticket was simply a promise to appear in court, and not a guilty plea.

His reply was, "What are you going to do if I don't sign."

Remaining as calm and polite as I could, I said, "I'm going to take you and place you in the custody of the Sheriff."

I seldom told anyone that I was going to haul their butt to jail. It sounded better and less confrontational to say "in the custody of the Sheriff." Throughout my career I always tried to keep one thing in mind; my job was to be a "peace officer," not a fighter. Anything I could do to avoid confrontation, and still perform my duty, I considered my responsibility to do.

But this time it looked like tact was not going to work. This guy was still smoking, and he was trying to box me into a corner, so that I would have no choice but to fight. He slammed the door closed and said, "I'm not going to sign that ticket, and I'm not going to jail. If you try to put me in jail, you'll wish you hadn't."

That was it; he left me no choice. I looked him straight in the eye and this time not so gently said, "This is a 357 Magnum I've got here in my holster, but I don't want to have to use it. You've got your family in your car, think about it. Now if you don't sign this ticket, you are going to jail—one way or the other. In fact, I've about made up my mind to carry you in whether you sign or not. You've just about let your mouth overload your rearend. Now, you either sign the ticket, or go to jail. If you resist me, I will be forced to use my weapon. Friend, this 357 makes but a little bitty hole going in, but you could drive your car through the hole it makes where it comes out."

You have never seen calmness and reason overcome a person so fast. "Officer, if you'll accept my apology and let me sign that ticket, I promise you will have no more trouble from me."

You hate it when a situation gets to this point, but sometimes it happens. There are two things you always have to remember. First—you have to do your duty; everything else comes after that. Second—give the person every opportunity to get out of the situation without "losing face."

Shortly before I became a Ranger, I got the biggest shock of my entire thirty-eight-year career in law enforcement. I remember it like it was yesterday. It was mid-afternoon and I was patrolling south of Longview on Highway 149. Where Sixteenth Street runs into Highway 149[18] I came upon a terrible auto accident. I did not see the accident, but when I arrived at the scene, the accident was only moments old.

In the late 1950s there was a service station at the intersection. Then, like today, the street was wide, with a fifteen-foot shoulder along each side of the highway. A woman was leaving the station and was in a hurry. Instead of waiting until traffic cleared and it was safe to enter the highway, she took off along the shoulder going south on the northbound side. Evidently she thought she had an opening and could dart in front of the oncoming car, and into the southbound lane. She may have thought she had room, but she didn't. The car coming at her dodged to the right, barely missing her, finally coming to a stop in the service station's parking lot. Unfortunately, there was another car right behind the first car, but in the inside lane. The driver of this car never saw the oncoming racing car, and never stood a chance. The two cars hit head-on.

When the dust settled, both vehicles were smashed and sitting in the roadway. I had been working accidents for more than ten years and I knew a

---

[18] This location today would be the intersection of Martin Luther King Boulevard and Estes Parkway.

bad wreck at first glance, and I knew this was a bad one. Before getting out of my car I called for an ambulance: then I rushed to the car that had been hit. There were three people in the car—one man and two women. The car was still running, the throttle jammed wide open. I was afraid that a gas line might have broken, creating a definite danger of fire. So before checking the victims I switched the motor off.

Looking in the car, it looked like a scene right off a battlefield. There was blood everywhere. The woman in the front seat was about half in and half out of the car. This was long before seat belts and airbags. She had hit the windshield and had literally been scalped. From right above her eyebrows to the back of her head, her scalp was stripped away. The driver also had blood running everywhere, though he had not lost consciousness. He was cut up very seriously and all his front teeth had been knocked out when he hit the steering wheel. I got the driver's door open, and helped the man out.

It was only when I had the man out of the car and on the ground that I realized it was my dad! The woman who was scalped was my mother! I think Dad recognized me before I did him, but I am not sure. Stunned, shocked, scared—none of these words can begin to describe how I felt.

Several years before, Dad and Mother had moved from Windom to Longview. Both had gotten jobs at the Resistol Hat factory. They had just gotten off work and were headed home. Never in my almost forty-year career did I have such a shock as I did that day. I ran back to my squad car and again called for help—this time, I am sure, more frantic than before. It was not long before a city police unit and an ambulance arrived.

They carried my parents to the hospital. Dad was not hurt as bad as it first appeared. After much work, the doctors were able to reattach Mother's scalp. But for months thereafter she picked glass out of her scalp. I am happy to report that after about a week in the hospital they were released and both had a full recovery. The lady riding with them, Emma Varna, was not injured seriously. She was carried to the hospital, treated for minor cuts and bruises, and released.

As for the woman who caused the wreck,[19] she was also hospitalized. I do not know how long, or if, she stayed in the hospital.

A highway patrolman's job is one of the most hazardous occupations in the world. I am not big on statistics, but please consider the following statis-

---

[19] Howard was called out to the wreck site and he conducted the investigation. The woman who caused the accident was filed on for aggravated assault with a motor vehicle.

tics that have been compiled by the DPS since 1931.[20] Troopers[21] killed while on duty: on motorcycles, six; shot to death, twenty-one;[22] struck by a vehicle (this includes vehicles pulled off to the side of the road), sixteen; automobile accident (this includes high-speed pursuits), seventeen; line of duty (not automobile or shooting), two; accidental, two.

Pulling a vehicle off the side of the road can be extremely dangerous, even fatal. As you can see, several officers have been run over and injured or worse, killed—when they had someone stopped. I found this out the hard way—twice.

The first time I was nearly killed by a drunk driver was on Lake Lamond Dam on Lake Lamond Road in Longview.

It was about 10:40 p.m., August 26, 1958. I had been patrolling Highway 80 and was heading south, changing my position to Highway 31.[23] As soon as I turned off Highway 80 onto Lake Lamond Road I saw a car stopped in the middle of the road.

I pulled up beside the car and shined my flashlight into the car. The car's headlights were on, but the motor was not running. A man was slumped over the steering wheel, passed out. When my light hit him, he jerked his head up, and started trying to start his car. The only thing I could do was try to get his car keys before he cranked up and got out on Highway 80. I threw my squad car into neutral[24] and set the emergency brake, jumped out of the car, and ran to the door of the drunk's car. I reached into his car, shut the motor off and withdrew the keys. While I was doing this I heard another car turn off 80 heading toward us. He was skidding his wheels and making a lot of racket. Even though my car was sitting there with its emergency lights on, he didn't realize I was stopped. As soon as he straightened out he gunned his engine.

---

[20] These statistics are from 1931 to the time of this writing, 1998.

[21] In mid-1974 the DPS started referring to uniformed officers as troopers.

[22] Two of these patrolmen were H. D. Murphy and Edward Wheeler. They were shot down in cold-blood on April 1, 1934, by Bonnie Parker and Clyde Barrow. A laughing Bonnie did a jig as she stood over the patrolmen and fired a shotgun into their already dead bodies.

[23] The stretch of highway from Kilgore to Longview has been redesignated twice since this incident happened. In 1958 when this happened it was known as Highway 26. Later it was changed to Highway 259, and at the time of this writing it is known as Highway 31.

[24] At that time our patrol cars had standard shift transmissions.

No sooner had he gunned his engine than he realized I was sitting still and only a short distance away. He slammed on his brakes, but he couldn't stop before sliding into my car. Fortunately I was away from it and in no real danger. He was almost stopped when he hit my car and thus did very little damage, at least to my car. But he banged his up pretty good.

It turned out that the driver was a young Navy man home on leave. He had been celebrating too much and was just driving a bit too fast. Anyway, instead of taking one drunk to jail, I took two.

The second time almost got me killed. It was the night of December 23, 1959. Like today, Highway 149 heading south out of Longview had four lanes, with a fifteen-foot safety shoulder on each side of the road. Just before reaching the Sabine River bridge,[25] the road narrowed to two lanes. Where the road narrowed, I had stopped a man for erratic driving. I pulled in behind him and flipped on my emergency lights. When he saw my lights, he immediately pulled onto the shoulder and stopped, and I dropped in behind him. Even with the fifteen-foot shoulder, both of us pulled over far enough to the right so that we had two wheels off the shoulder of the road.

Walking up to the pickup's passenger door I saw an open bottle of whiskey lying in the seat, and it was obvious the driver was intoxicated. I got him out of the pickup and took him to the customary point between, but off to the right of, our two vehicles. I told him he was under arrest, to stand right where he was and not to wander around. Seeing several Christmas presents in the back of his pickup and not wanting them to be stolen while he was in jail, I told him I would put them in the back of my car. I would check them in at the courthouse and he could pick them up when he got out of jail.

I also intended to retrieve the bottle of whiskey from the pickup's seat for evidence. Just as I opened the door of the truck and reached in to get the bottle, another car with an intoxicated driver hit the back of my car. I have never been sure, and he was too drunk to remember, but I believe he saw the lights of my patrol car, didn't realize it was parked, and decided to follow me across the bridge. So he dropped onto the shoulder and rammed the back of my car. He hit it so hard that it slammed my '59 Ford patrol car right into the back of the pickup. The pickup then caromed into me with such force that it knocked me into the middle of the highway. At that time in the evening there was a lot of traffic. Thank God I didn't get run over.

---

[25] Today this area is know as "Whiskey Bend."

The blow did not knock me out and I instantly jumped up as rapidly as I could under the circumstances, heading for the second drunk. At the time I didn't think I was hurt badly. I had several minor cuts and bruises, and a terrible pain in my side where the pickup had hit me. Just as I was arresting the second driver, Chief Deputy Johnny Spradlin from Panola County came along. He stopped to assist me and called for help. Johnny stayed and directed traffic until deputies from Gregg County arrived.

I did not think I needed it, but to be on the safe side, I went to the Good Shepherd Hospital emergency room. My good friend, Doctor George Tate, was there, and he examined me. Completing his examination he said, "Glenn, I'm going to put you in the hospital tonight. The bruise on your side doesn't look too good." I bowed up and said, "No. It's too close to Christmas and I'm going home." And I did!

The next morning when I got up, I was sore in places I didn't know existed on my body. Soreness I could live with, but I was passing blood from places a person is not meant to pass blood. I knew that staying active—and a little time—would take care of the soreness; and I hoped the same would happen with the blood passage. I got dressed and went to the courthouse to file my complaints against the two DWI's.[26] But after finishing my reports, I was passing as much blood as ever. I knew it was time to get help. Doctor Tate and I were good friends. When he first got out of medical school he occasionally rode around with Webb and I. I will never forget this particular phone call to George.

I said, "George, I'm having problems. I need to see you."

He replied, "I'm not your doctor. Call someone else."

I was sore, bleeding in places that the human body is not meant to bleed from, and I was especially not in any mood for a load of you-know-what from a "supposed" friend.

I said, "Look, I didn't call you up for a bunch of bull. I've got problems and I need your help."

It didn't take George long to put old Glenn in his place. "Are you going to let me treat you, or are you going to treat yourself? If you want me to treat you, get on down to the emergency room. If you are going to treat yourself, call another doctor."

I went to the emergency room and spent Christmas, 1959, in Good Shepherd Hospital.

George did a good job. He was afraid that I had injured my spleen, but after a few days in the hospital, the blood cleared up and I went home. To this

---

[26] Co-author's note: From this time in 1959 until his retirement in 1987, Glenn missed only one day from sickness.

day I have had no problems from what could have easily been a fatal encounter. George has passed on, but until the day he died, as far as I am concerned, he was a great friend and a great doctor.

I want to talk about two of the most important and powerful men in Texas' history: the Director of the Department of Public Safety, Homer Garrison, and the publisher of the *Longview News-Journal*, Carl Estes.

Colonel Homer Garrison served as the Director of the Department of Public Safety for thirty years. In Texas he was Mr. Law Enforcement. Carl Estes, owner and publisher of the *Longview News-Journal,* could have been a powerful force either for or against the DPS. He was, thankfully, a great friend of law enforcement. I have nothing but extreme admiration for both men. I proudly counted both as friends, even if Colonel Garrison was my boss.

My first dealing with the two together could have been quite uncomfortable, to say the least. From this meeting, I learned how a true leader operated.

Texas Eastman had just starting moving people into Longview in the early '50s. Carl decided to throw a big wing-ding on his ranch south of Longview on Highway 149 for the Eastman people. He had invited Senators, Representatives, and anyone else he thought was important. If you were a politician in East Texas and Carl Estes sent you an invitation to his party, you went.

A day or two before the party I received a call from Colonel Garrison's office requesting that Webb and I pick him up at the Gregg County Airport the day of the party. Our Captain, Guy Smith, knew the Colonel was coming to Longview, so we called him and told him of the Colonel's request. "Fine," he said. He would meet us at the airport.

At the appointed time, Captain Smith, Webb, and I met the Colonel's plane. After the traditional handshakes, the Colonel told the Captain to ride in the back seat with him—he had several things he wanted to discuss with him. This would be his only available time, since the Colonel had to get back to Austin that night.

Before we ever got into our car, Captain Smith looked at the Colonel and said, "I'm not invited to this event, and Carl very well may ask me to leave."

The Colonel wanted to know why.

Captain Smith related that a few weeks before he had given a speech to one of the civic clubs in Tyler. Then, as now, all of Smith County was dry, and

65

most of Gregg County was wet.[27]   Captain Smith remarked during the speech that Highway 31, which ran between Gregg and Smith Counties, had earned its nickname, "Bloody 31." He remarked that one side of Highway 31 ran with whiskey, while the other ran with blood.

In an editorial, the *Tyler Courier-Times* had sided with Captain Smith. This was too much for Carl. He already had a major burr under his saddle. He called Captain Smith and tore into him, then blasted the highway patrol in his paper. Not only did he consider the remarks by Captain Smith an insult to the good people of Gregg County, but the highway patrol was obviously—at least to him—not doing its job. He really raked us up one side, then down the other.

As is the case with most things, there was more than what met the eye to this story—much more. Carl had formerly owned the *Tyler Courier-Times*, but in a very messy and even more public divorce, Carl's wife ended up with the paper. Not to be outdone, Carl bought the *Longview News-Journal* and moved to Longview. Everything was a major battle with Carl, and most certainly anything that concerned his former paper.

Be that as it may, I now learned from Colonel Homer Garrison the meaning of leadership.

The Colonel looked Captain Smith straight in the eye and said the words I will never forget: "We came here together; we leave together."

We all went to Carl's big bash, together—stayed until we got ready to leave—then we all left, together. That is leadership. Even a person as powerful as Carl Estes knew he could not push Homer Garrison.

I learned a great deal about Colonel Garrison and leadership in the just-described incident. I learned as much about Carl Estes, and what it meant to stake your position and stay with it only as long as you are in the right, when I had another incident with him a short time later.

Carl would jump on something and stay with it until the end, unless you confronted him and explained your position to him in detail. Having done this, I always found Carl Estes to be an extremely fair man. He might not change to your way of thinking, but you would know why he didn't. And then again, if your facts were straight and he knew you were right, he would change.

---

[27] Gregg County is wet or dry by precinct. It is not unusual for one side of a street to be wet while the other side is dry. Where Highway 31 crosses between the two counties, it is wet.

I was a personal witness to this once. One Saturday evening there was a traffic accident at the intersection of Airline Road and Hollybrook Road in Longview. One of the vehicles, a truck, was driven by a young student from Longview's LeTourneau College. He was working his way through school, supporting himself and a wife by cutting and hauling pulp wood. With him were two boys he had brought to help him in the woods. In the other vehicle, a car, was an attorney who had spent too much time at happy hour.

The student was going south on Airline and was just about through the intersection. The attorney, coming west on Hollybrook, ran a stop sign, entered the intersection and slammed into the truck's left rear dual wheels. The force of the impact turned the truck over and it caught fire. The two boys were not hurt badly but the student received some minor burns and other injuries. The attorney was not hurt at all.

Sunday morning, just as I was getting ready to leave for church, my phone rang. It was Carl. He called the attorney's name, and said, "I understand he's been involved in an accident.

I said, "Yes, he has."

"Glenn, I want you to come out here. I need to talk to you."

"Okay, I'll come out there in a little while."

When I arrived at Carl's house, he asked me if his friend had been drinking.

"Yes, but I don't think I could make a drunk driving case on him, because he wouldn't give a blood test, and he was injured. I'm going to file on him for aggravated assault with a motor vehicle because he violated the law when he ran a stop sign and hit the truck. He caused the truck to turn over and caused bodily injury. I can prove that case without any problem. I can also prove he was drinking, because I could smell it."

This seemed to satisfy Carl, so I went on about my business.

Tommy Carlisle Wrecker Service had picked up both the car and truck and taken them to his yard in Longview. The next morning, I went to Tommy's garage to take some pictures of the vehicles. Carl and the attorney were also there.

Carl had a voice you could hear a mile away in a thunderstorm. I distinctly remember him saying to the attorney, "Well, you convinced me that Glenn Elliott doesn't know what he's talking about. He's as wrong as he can be."

There was no doubt about it, Carl Estes was a powerful man in Gregg County. I knew that if I expected to have any credibility with Carl in the future I had to straighten this out—and right then. I walked over to Carl and the attorney, and said, "Mr. Estes, I heard my named called out. I thought I better come over and defend myself."

He pointed to the attorney and said, "You know he's an attorney. He's got an altogether different story from what you say. He's convinced me you're wrong."

I told him ". . . to hold on for a minute." I went to my patrol car and got out my highway patrol law book. I had them follow me over to a patch of sand beside the driveway. Picking up a stick, I drew an intersection in the sand. I showed Carl the position of both vehicles at the time of the wreck.

Then I said, "Now here's the car right here," and I drew a figure in the sand representing the car. I then drew another figure in the sand representing the truck. Then pointing to the truck sitting in the yard, I said, "You can see the damage to the truck is to the left rear tandem. You can see the imprint of those tires here in the grill and on the hood of this car," this time pointing to the attorney's car.

"The truck is going south on Airline Road and there's no stop sign on Airline, it's through traffic. Mr. Attorney is going west on Hollybrook, and there is a stop sign there."

Then I said, "Let me read you a little law."

I proceeded to read from the law book that if two vehicles approach an intersection about the same time, you must yield to the vehicle on the right if there's no traffic control. If there is traffic control you must come to a complete stop, and yield the right-of-way to any vehicle in the intersection, or so close thereto that it might become a hazard.

Finishing, I again pointed to the point of impact on the left rear dual, and said, "Now is there any question in either one of y'alls minds that this truck was in the intersection before the car was? There are no skid marks. The truck didn't even hit his brakes."

"When Mr. Attorney hit the truck, the front of the truck was already past him. If he had been a split second later, he would have missed the truck completely."

With that I looked at Carl and asked, "Who do you think was in the intersection first?"

Carl turned to the attorney and said, "You better go hire you a lawyer. You're not smart enough to represent yourself."

Turning to me, he asked, "Mr. Elliott, will you carry me back to my office?" He would not even ride back to town with Mr. Attorney.

Once in the car, Carl asked, "Could we go to that intersection? You didn't find any whisky in his car, did you?"

I said, "No."

"Well, he threw it out in the woods," Carl replied. "I can tell you right now what he drinks."

It did not take us long to find the bottle. I did not bother getting it checked for fingerprints. I did not need to. I had enough on him already to more than make a case.

Obviously, Carl Estes was an extremely important person to the attorney. Just as obviously, he had lost a lot of face with Carl. I don't know if he ever got it back. But knowing Carl, I doubt it.

I am glad that I took the time to explain the truth to Carl. I am just as gratified that he allowed me the time to explain my side. If I had failed, Carl would have gone to his grave thinking I had tried to wrong an innocent man.

Give Carl Estes the facts, and he would listen, and make a fair judgment. That's the type of man he was.

In September, 1957, Lone Star Steel in Lone Star, Texas, employed 4,300 workers, making it easily one of the biggest employers in the area. Of the 4,300 workers, 3,300 were union members represented by Local 4134. The previous September, Lone Star Steel and The United Steel Workers of America had signed a two-year contract. During the ensuing year, twenty-nine grievances had been submitted for arbitration. The company won nineteen cases; the union won seven; three cases were compromised. Declaring that they did not like the arbitration methods used to settle grievances with its members, at midnight, September 21, 1957, union workers called an unauthorized wildcat strike. Of the 3,300 union workers, 2,700 walked out.

To help keep the lid on the situation, on Sunday, September 22, the first full night of the strike, Webb and I were ordered to the plant to assist two Texas Rangers, Jim Ray and Red Arnold,[28] who were already there.

Arriving at the plant, we were assigned to the south gate with Jim Ray. Red Arnold was at the north gate. I do not remember the highway patrolmen who were assisting Red. I do remember that there must have been at least a thousand strikers around the south gate. And only Jim, Lloyd, and I stood between them and the gate.

Webb and I were left alone for a few minutes because Jim had to leave to pick up papers from District Judge Morris Rolston, of the 76th District Court. He returned about midnight carrying a restraining order from the Judge ordering the strikers to disburse. The restraining order said that pending the outcome of a hearing set for Wednesday, September 25, the strikers could leave only two people on each gate, and they could not prevent entrance or exit from the plant.

Those strikers were a pretty rowdy bunch, but I was sure they would

---

[28] Jim Ray was stationed in Tyler, Red Arnold in Mount Pleasant. Jim and Red were shortly joined by R. L. Badgett, Ernest Daniel, and E. J. Wimberly—all stationed in Dallas.

listen and obey the order. Jim asked for the leader of the strikers to step forward. When he did, Jim read the court order to him. Finishing the order, he said, "This is a court order from Judge Rolston and properly issued. We have no problem with you having pickets, but you can not have but two people."

Turning to his followers the strike leader said, "Well, this is what we thought was going to happen." Much to our relief, they disbursed and we went home.

It looked like this was going to settle easy. Looks can be deceiving.

The next morning at least six hundred people were on the picket line preventing anyone from entering the grounds. Needless to say, this did not sit well with Judge Rolston. He did not wait for Wednesday. He ordered the Morris County Sheriff's Office and the Texas Rangers to keep Lone Star Steel's property, state highways and roads leading to the plant's main gate clear of all pickets, loiterers and automobiles.

As earlier stated, this was a "wildcat strike." This made the situation even more difficult. The president and vice-president of Local 4134, W. T. Follis and Pete King, and the representative of the International Steelworkers, L. H. Brantley, disclaimed any connection with the strike.

The president of Lone Star Steel, E. B. Germany, buckled down and told members of his supervisory staff that there would be no compromise with the leaders of the strike. Leaving no doubt as to his determination, he ordered the six hundred or so strikers who had been identified at the plant gates on Monday morning permanently terminated. Then he ran "help wanted" ads in the local papers advertising for replacement workers. "These men," speaking of the six hundred pickets and strike leaders, "are being replaced, and right now," said Germany.

Within twenty-four hours, twelve secretaries were working full time processing the nearly two thousand applications that were received—three hundred from union members wanting to come back as new hirees. Germany showed his resolve to hold out for as long as it took. The plant sat up sleeping accommodations for over 1,250 people. Nearly 1,800 stayed in the plant's facilities twenty-four hours a day. Besides beds, Germany provided laundry service, meals, cigars and cigarettes—all free.

With this many people living in the plant around the clock, supplying them presented a problem. Twice trucks containing supplies for the plant had been fired on. Thereafter, President Germany ordered supplies flown to the company's private airport located on the plant grounds.

The situation continued to worsen. Threats were made. Shots were fired. It was so bad that on October 3 the company announced it would pay a $5,000 reward for information leading to the arrest and conviction of anyone threatening or intimidating an employee or any member of an employee's family. Additionally, Lone Star Steel said it would pay a $10,000 reward for information leading to the arrest and conviction of anyone who caused injury to any employee, any member of their family, or damage or destruction of that employee's, or family member's, property which was a direct result of the strike.

While most of this was going on I was back in Longview—but not for long. Jay Mayes, a Trooper from Mount Pleasant, and I were made Special Texas Rangers ordered back to Lone Star Steel. For the next few weeks we shared a room in a motel in nearby Hughes Springs. Our duty was mainly to patrol the area and try to prevent as much trouble as possible.

At one time the authorities considered putting me into the plant for undercover work, but it was decided that I was too well known in the area to be effective. That was all right with me. I have always found that type of work distasteful.

On October 31, 1957, near the end of the strike, the commander of Ranger Company B, Captain Jay Banks, arrived to personally take charge of the situation. He had not been on the scene long before the strike came to a dramatic conclusion.

A few strikers made a terrible mistake for their cause. Thinking they were blowing up the main gas line that fed the plant, in order to force a complete plant shutdown, they instead blew up the main feeder line to the city of Pittsburg.

It was cold when they blew up the line. Everyone in Pittsburg was out of gas: homes, churches, businesses, schools, hospitals, everything. This really turned public opinion against the strikers, and it was only a short time later that the strikers gave up and went back to work.

Unfortunately my work was not done. Ranger Jim Ray and I continued working, building a case against the bombers. We worked hard following up leads, and it paid off. All the people we thought were involved were arrested. One, we felt sure, was one of the bombers. While questioning him, Jim and I did not play the "good cop, bad cop" routine. We simply, and truthfully, told him how bad his situation was, and how things would go a lot better for him if he confessed. He agreed, and confessed—orally. Jim had just sat down at a typewriter to prepare the bomber's confession, when another officer came strutting in. He proceeded to read our suspect the proverbial "riot act," with the predictable results. The bomber clammed up and never said another word. I don't know that I have ever been more aggravated. We had the bomber, and he had confessed. All we had to do was write it up and he would have signed it. Instead, we walked out with nothing, and the bomber walked free.

That pretty well ended my involvement in the '57 Lone Star Steel Wildcat Strike. I was glad to get out of there. I hate working strikes. It's a no-win situation. Little did I know that my days working a strike at Lone Star Steel were just beginning.

HOMER GARRISON, JR.
Director
JOE S. FLETCHER
Deputy Director

Commission
W. E. DYCHE, JR.
Chairman
TOM HICKMAN
HOXIE H. THOMPSON
Commissioners

TEXAS DEPARTMENT OF PUBLIC SAFETY

5805 N. LAMAR BLVD.
BOX 4087, NORTH AUSTIN STATION
AUSTIN

December 12, 1957

Mr. Glenn Elliott
Texas Highway Patrolman
Box 373
Longview, Texas

My dear Friend:

Major Guy Smith, your Regional Commander, and Texas Ranger
Captain Jay Banks have highly commended you for the long hours
you worked under trying conditions during the Lone Star Steel
strike. I wish to join with them in expressing my sincere appreciation to you for the excellent manner in which you carried out
your responsibilities beyond the call of duty. Governor Price
Daniel has also requested that I express his appreciation to you
for your outstanding accomplishments in this situation. Your actions have brought credit upon our Department and you, and it is
service like this that has made the Texas Department of Public
Safety the greatest organization of its kind in the world.

I am placing a copy of this letter in your personnel record.

Thanking you again for your outstanding service during the strike,
and for the service you have rendered to the Department over the
years, I am

Sincerely your friend,

Homer Garrison, Jr.
Director

HGJr:ec

When you worked with Jim Ray, it was not hard to stand out.

During the Lone Star Steel strike I mentioned that Captain Jay Banks, the commander of Ranger Company B, came to Lone Star to take personal control of the situation. This was not the first time that I had met Jay.

All through my career I was (and still am) extremely active in law enforcement organizations and functions. So was Jay. I saw him often at functions like the East Texas Peace Officers Association, (Of which, I am proud to say, I am a charter member and Past-President.) and other affairs.

Jay was a very high profile type person. He was always on the cover of a magazine or newspaper. In 1955 he went to New York where he appeared as a mystery guest on the old television show, *What's My Line?* I don't think the panelists guessed his occupation. While on the same trip he appeared on the *Today* show with Dave Garroway, June Pritchard—Miss Texas of 1955—and J. Fred Muggs.[29] He was one of American Airlines special guests when they made their inaugural flight from Dallas to Los Angeles. He loved having his picture taken with movie stars. I remember a picture he had made with actor Robert Culp.

Of course, Jay had some distinguished Ranger company when it came to the camera. The legendary Lone Wolf Gonzaullas was never known to have shied away from the lens. In fact, when Gonzaullas retired in 1951, he went to Los Angeles to be the technical advisor to Joel McCrea's radio show, *Tales of the Texas Rangers.*

Undoubtedly, the thing that Jay is best remembered for is the eight-foot bronze statue of a Texas Ranger entitled "One Riot, One Ranger." Clint Grant sculptured that statue in 1958. Jay was the model that Grant used. Today the statue stands proudly in the main lobby of Love Field Airport in Dallas.

Jay had more than just the love of a camera lens in common with Lone Wolf Gonzaullas. Both were truly great Rangers. And that is what is most important.

By the time of the strike at Lone Star, I already knew I wanted to be a Ranger. As a matter of fact, I first applied to the Rangers in 1956, the year before the strike. I am often asked why I wanted to be a Ranger. That's easy: (alphabetically) Red Arnold, Jim Ray, my old teacher-coach Jim Riddle, and Lewis Rigler. Four finer men I have never known. If this was the type of men that were Texas Rangers, I wanted to be one of them.

I talked to Jay quite a bit about becoming a Ranger. He always encour-

---

[29] J. Fred Muggs was a chimpanzee that appeared on the *Today* show. For a while J. Fred was as well known and popular as any of the stars on the show.

aged me to work hard, and one day in the near future I would be a Texas Ranger. I had at least one thing in common with Jay; neither one of us was afraid of work.

In 1956, the way you became a Ranger was totally different than today. You did not test and go before a review board to become a Ranger. Officially, you wrote a letter to the Colonel and told him that you wanted to apply for the Rangers. If you were considered worthy, and if an opening developed, you might get the slot—that was the official line. In actuality, when a Ranger Captain wanted you in his Company, and when there was an opening, you became a Ranger.

One day in 1956 I was in Austin to pick up a new squad car. I decided that rather than mail my letter of request to Colonel Garrison, I would hand carry it to him. Homer Garrison's door was never closed to one of his men. Any person, from the lowly State Trooper like me on up, had the freedom of seeing the Colonel, without an appointment.

I went into the Colonel's office and handed him my letter. I told him I was interested in the Rangers. I knew not to expect the next appointment, because I knew how popular a Ranger appointment was. But I would like to be considered for a future appointment.

Colonel Garrison never ceased to amaze me. He said, "You know, Glenn, most folks hear of a vacancy and they come down here and want it right now. Then they're upset because they don't get it. You're the first person to ever come in here with the attitude that you've got, knowing that you are not going to get the next appointment, and not even expecting it. I am going to promise you that you'll be considered as a Ranger in the future."

In 1958, the East Texas Peace Officers Association was meeting in Houston. I remember that both Jay and Clint Peoples showed up. The Ranger force was being increased from fifty to fifty-one men. Everyone thought that the opening would go to Clint People's Company F, based in Waco. I don't mind telling you, I wanted that appointment in the worst possible way.

Jay had already told me that with all the trouble in Lone Star, Dallas, Sherman, Longview, and all over his area, he had asked Clint if Company B could have the opening if it went to Clint's Company F. Company B was badly in need of an extra man and Clint realized it, so he had agreed.

I had caught the eye of both Jay and Clint during the trouble at Lone Star. While we were in Houston, Jay came to me and said that if he was given the extra opening, it was mine. Later, Clint visited me and told me that if he could not transfer his opening to Jay, he would like for me to join Company F.

Unfortunately, neither Clint nor Jay knew the whole story behind the fifty-first opening. It was a political move. The opening was filled by a former Sheriff from Southeast Texas who was subsequently assigned to an area near the home of Governor Price Daniel. Political move or not, he turned into an excellent Ranger.

I did not have any hard feelings about not making Ranger. In those days that is how almost anyone became a Ranger. To this day, I don't necessarily disagree with the method that was once used to pick Rangers. Some of the greatest Rangers of all time were picked like this.

In 1960 the State Legislature passed appropriations to increase the Ranger force by ten, effective September, 1961. Every year I had renewed my request to join the Rangers. Word had it that Company B would get two of the new men. Unfortunately for me, Jay Banks had resigned from the Rangers and had been succeeded by Captain Bob Crowder.

Crowder was raised just south of Henderson in the community of Minden, so he was an East Texan himself. I barely knew Captain Crowder, but every time I went to Dallas I made sure I stopped by the Ranger office to visit and remind Captain Crowder that I wanted to be a Ranger.

My boyhood friend, Charlie Moore, from nearby Honey Grove, also wanted to be a Ranger. I knew Charlie had the inside track on me. He was stationed in Dallas and saw Captain Crowder often. But things have a way of working out; both Charlie and I made Ranger.[30]

I am getting a little ahead of myself. I knew that Charlie and I were going to be made Rangers a couple of days before Charlie. Early one morning just as I was getting ready to leave, my phone rang, it was Colonel Garrison. "This is Garrison. Can you keep a secret?"

"I'm the best hand you've got," I replied.

The Colonel then said the words that were music to my ears. "Well, you're going to be made a Ranger, but I want to make the announcement from here in Austin. I can't do it right now. I've got to wait until Hurricane Carla blows herself out. She's really causing havoc along the coast. It may be a few days before I am able to make the announcement, but I want to be the one to make the announcement, not someone else. So keep it to yourself."

I asked, "Is it a fair question to ask where I'm going to be stationed."

"Somewhere in Company B."

The reason Colonel Garrison wanted to make the announcement was that a total of ten Ranger positions were being created. This was the largest expansion since the reorganization in 1935. The Ranger force would be going from fifty-two to sixty-two men. This was big news.

---

[30] On October 8, 1961, six other highway patrolmen, two intelligence agents, and one sheriff made Ranger. Their ages and duty stations were as follows. From the highway patrol: Butch Albers, 38, Canyon; C. W. Bedner, 37, Liberty; Frank Horger, 34, Corpus Christi; H. A. White, 31, Houston; A. Y. Allee, Jr., 27 (Son of the legendary Captain Allee) Del Rio; and Ott Luther, 45, Waco. From the Intelligence Agency: Charlie Moore, 37, Dallas; William W. Wilson, 32, Waco. And Knox County Sheriff Homer Melton, 51, Lubbock.

Charlie Moore was in the Intelligence Division at the time. He and a fellow Intelligence Officer from Tyler came to Longview on business and asked if I could meet with them. When I met them, the first thing out of Charlie's mouth was, "Have you heard anything?"

I hate a liar worse than anything in the world, but I had given my word to Colonel Garrison.

"Not a thing," I reluctantly answered untruthfully.

Even now, almost four decades later, I hate that I had to lie to Charlie. But if I had told him the truth, then I would have lied to Colonel Garrison. I promised him I would tell no one. And I didn't. Not even my wife or children.

Ironically, Charlie and I rode to Austin to be sworn into the Rangers together. Charlie was in the Intelligence Division and he had to turn in his car and get a car assigned to the Rangers. My patrol car would stay in Longview, so Charlie came over from Dallas and picked me up. On the way to Austin I told Charlie the truth, explaining that I had no choice. He understood.

My home station would be in Marshall, a little over twenty miles east of Longview. Harrison County District Attorney Charlie Allen and Sheriff Earl Franklin had been requesting a Ranger. Colonel Garrison granted their request by stationing me in Marshall. Harrison County, along with the counties of Gregg, Panola, Marion, Cass, and part of Bowie, would be my territory.

The only downside was that we would have to move to Marshall. Regrettably, as far as Catherine and I were concerned, Longview and Marshall might as well have been two hundred miles apart, instead of twenty miles. Diane was a senior at Judson High School and she desperately wanted to finish there. I asked Captain Crowder if I could continue living in Longview until she finished school. I told him that if he wanted me to, I would rent an apartment in Marshall. He told me that would not be necessary, but when school was out we would have to move to Marshall.

I know I am jumping way ahead in my story, but one day I was in Marshall during this transition period when I ran into District Judge Sam B. Hall. During our conversation, I told him that I was looking for a house in the Marshall area.

Judge Hall said, "Don't worry about it. I'll get you a house. How much are you paying in rent now?"

I said, "Judge, I own my house."

"Well, what's your house payment?" he asked.

"Fifty-five dollars per month."

Judge Hall lived on Highway 80 between Marshall and Hallsville. His son, Sam, Jr.,[31] had lived in a house a short distance west of his father. How-

---

[31] Sam Hall, Jr., later became a United States Representative.

ever, he had just built a new home in Marshall and was vacating this house. "Well, that's what we'll rent you Sam, Jr.'s house for."

The Halls were the finest people in the world.

When Diane graduated from Judson High and our move could be put off no longer. Unhappily, Catherine gave a wonderful job she had with Doctor Bud Colquitt, a Longview bone specialist. We rented out our house on Ruthlyn, and made the move to Marshall.

We came to really enjoy our new home. Sam, Jr.'s children stayed with their grandparents a lot. Whenever they visited their Grandpa and Grandma, they always made a beeline to our house, which was only about two hundred feet from their grandparents. Catherine and I may have lived out our lives right there, except for one thing. Catherine was a typist who could spell all the big words that doctors use, but she could not find a good-paying job in Marshall. We had been living in Marshall about a year when she got a call from Doctor Colquitt asking her to come back to work.

I went to the Harrison County District Attorney and Sheriff and asked if they had any problem with me requesting that the duty station be changed from Marshall to Longview. I explained why we needed to move back to Longview, but at the same time assured them they would not see a drop-off in my work. They said it would be fine. I then went to Captain Crowder and made the same request. He said he had no problem if Colonel Garrison, and the District Attorney and Sheriff had no problem with it. I assured him that they did not. Things worked out, and we moved back to our home on Ruthlyn. We still live there.

Enough jumping ahead. Back to the story. In 1961, there was no testing or review boards; you became a Ranger because the Captain wanted you to be one of his men. I had proven my worth to Colonel Garrison and Captain Crowder. On October 8, 1961, yours truly became a Texas Ranger.

Before entering into my Ranger career, there is one thing I want to say about my days as a State Trooper. I say this from the very bottom of my heart. You will never meet anyone who was prouder being a Texas Ranger than I was, but I am every bit as proud to have been a Texas Highway Patrolman. No state has two greater organizations than the Texas Highway Patrol and the Texas Rangers.

From the co-author. Before leaving the highway patrol segment of this book, there is one other incident I asked Glenn to relate.

I am often asked: "Of all the Glenn Elliott stories you know, what is your favorite?" Almost always I get a look of shock and disbelief when I relate that it was not a Ranger story, but one that happened while Glenn was a State Trooper. The story has no John Wayne-type heroics, no wild shoot-out, no desperate fight to the death. No, it's story of a Texas Highway Patrolman simply doing his sworn duty. It is a story that, I suppose, is as plain as ... well, as plain as Glenn. What you see is what you get.

It happened late one night in the early '50s. Glenn and Webb were patrolling between Longview and Kilgore on Highway 26.[32] At that time Highway 26 was a two lane road, and I-20 was still in someone's imagination.

They had just crossed the Sabine River bottom, when they observed a car weaving all over the road in front of them, heading toward Kilgore. They turned on the patrol car's emergency lights, but instead of pulling over, the drunk took off. As they were approaching the first small hill,[33] leaving the river bottoms, the drunk crossed into the oncoming lane and hit a car head-on.

Glenn continues. There were two teenagers in the car. The drunk hit them with such force that it not only threw the teens out of the car, but it actually tore the front seat out of their car.

Stopping, we jumped out of our car. Lloyd headed for the boy and I went to the girl. I remember the girl was screaming at the top of her voice—one long continuous scream.

Then, as now, we carried long-handled flashlights. The handles were long enough so that we could stick them under our arms when we checked driver's licenses, wrote tickets, or whatever. When I reached the girl, I stuck the flashlight under my arm and leaned over her to check her for injuries and to help in any way that I could.

I remember it as if it was last night, her eyes did not look me in the face. They went to my cap.[34] When I bent over, the light from my flashlight shined on the shield on the front of my cap with the Department of Public Safety written on it. As soon as she saw the shield, she quit screaming and said, "Thank God."

I told her, "We've got an ambulance on the way out here now. I don't think you're hurt all that bad. You're not bleeding, but you may have a few broken bones—I'm not sure. Don't worry. We're going to be right here

[32] Now Highway 31.

[33] About where Oakwood Mobile Homes is located today (1998). This area is locally known as Romeo Hill.

[34] In 1957 the highway patrol changed from caps to hats.

where we can take care of you."

She held my hand until they loaded her into the ambulance. I am happy to say that everyone involved survived. After insuring the well-being of the teenagers, we checked on the drunk. As is often the case with a drunk, he would survive with few, in any, serious injuries.

That's it. In our entire forty-one hours of taped interviews, Glenn mentioned this once and then only in passing. To Glenn it was no big deal, like countless other police officers in similar situations; he was simply doing his duty. Other situations similar to this happened to him many times, but to me it spoke volumes about the way law enforcement personnel should be.

The girl was hysterical until she saw Glenn's shield; then she became calm and uttered, "Thank God." She knew that the police were there and everything was going to be all right. That's the way it should be. And when Glenn said to her, "Don't worry. We're going to be right here where we can take care of you." It was just as it should be.

THE RANGER'S PRAYER

O God, whose end is justice,
Whose strength is all our stay,
Be near and bless my mission
As I go forth today.
Let wisdom guide my actions,
Let courage fill my heart,
And help me, Lord, in every hour
to do a Ranger's part.
Protect when danger threatens,
Sustain when trails are rough;
Help me to keep my standard high
And smile at each rebuff.
When night comes down upon me,
I pray Thee, Lord, be nigh,
Whether on lonely scout, or camped
Under the Texas sky.
Keep me, O God, in life,
And when my days shall end,
Forgive my sins and take me in,
For Jesus' sake, Amen.

Pierre Bernard Hill
Chaplain, Texas Rangers

SECTION 3

Texas Ranger

DEPARTMENT OF PUBLIC SAFETY

IN THE NAME AND BY THE AUTHORITY OF

The State of Texas

To All to Whom These Presents May Come -- GREETINGS:

BE IT KNOWN, that the Public Safety Commission, and the Director of the Department of Public Safety of the State of Texas, reposing special trust and full

confidence in the integrity and ability of_____GLENN ELLIOTT_____

of the city of_____AUSTIN, TRAVIS_____County, Texas,

do by virtue of the authority vested in us by law, constitute and appoint him a

TEXAS RANGER

and do hereby commission him as a law enforcement officer of the Department of Public Safety of the State of Texas as authorized by Chapter 181, page 444, General Laws, Acts of Regular Session of the Forty-fourth Legislature in said State of Texas, giving and hereby granting to him all the rights, privileges, and emoluments appertaining to said appointment.

IN TESTIMONY WHEREOF, I have, with the approval of the Public Safety Commission, hereunto signed my name and caused the seal of the State of Texas, Department of Public Safety, to be affixed at the City of Austin, the___9th___

day of_____OCTOBER_____A. D., 19 61

Age 35___Height 5'11 1/2"Weight 180___Hair BROWN Eyes BLUE Complexion RUDDY

_____

(SEAL)

Director, Department of Public Safety

PUBLIC SAFETY COMMISSION

Tom R. Hickman, Sr., Chairman
C. T. McLaughlin, Member
W. E. Dyche, Jr., Member

CHAPTER VI
I WAS THERE

Before reporting for duty in Marshall, Captain Crowder wanted me to work in Dallas for a few weeks to gain needed experience. As an observer, I did not work any particular cases, but I watched closely and learned much.

I viewed men going about their jobs in completely different ways, but with the same efficient results. Ernest Daniel was there. Ernest was an easygoing man whom everyone liked. Jim Ray was in Tyler. The name Jim Ray says all that can or needs to be said about him. And there was Rig—Lewis Rigler. Earlier I said that Lewis was one of the main reasons I wanted to become a Ranger. Since the day I first met Rig, if I needed him, he was there—no questions asked. And I know he feels the same way towards me.

Bob Crowder was my first Ranger Captain. He had succeeded Captain Gonzaullas as Captain of Company B when Gonzaullas retired in 1951 and had remained at that post until the DPS reorganized in 1957. The powers in Austin decided that each of the six regions should have one commander over all DPS personnel. To accomplish this the rank of major was created. Colonel Garrison offered the Lubbock region to Captain Crowder and he accepted. At the same time my old Captain, J. Guy Smith, was promoted to major and transferred from Tyler to Dallas.

By 1959 it was plain that the experiment was not working with the Rangers, and it was abandoned, at least as far as it concerned the Rangers. The Rangers had never worked under this type of arrangement before, and frankly, except for Crowder, none of the new majors understood how the Rangers worked. Today majors still command each region, but not the Rangers.

When Captain Jay Banks retired in 1959, Captain Crowder jumped at the opportunity to return to Dallas as Captain of Company B. This sounds simply but it wasn't. In order to return to Dallas as Captain, not only did Captain Crowder take a cut in rank, but also the pay cut that went with the reduction in rank. Like all Rangers, Captain Crowder loved the Rangers more than anything except for his family. He never regretted putting the Ranger badge on again. And why would he. His actions and deeds while a Ranger were enough to get him elected to the Texas Ranger Hall of Fame.

Other than his time in the military, he spent his whole life in law enforcement. Early in his Ranger career he had almost single-handedly stopped a potential riot at the state hospital in Rusk, Cherokee County.[1] I am one of the luckiest men who ever lived. J. Guy Smith was my first Highway Patrol Captain. Lady Luck smiled at me when I was assigned to him. She smiled again when she gave me Bob Crowder as my first Ranger Captain.

By the time I became a Ranger in 1961 I already knew Captain Crowder fairly well. During his first tenure in Dallas, he had attended many of our East Texas Peace Officers Association meetings, and whenever I was in Dallas I always tried to stop by Ranger headquarters for a short visit. Remember, in those days if a Captain wanted you to be one of his Rangers, you became a Ranger. If he didn't, you didn't. Period.

I had been in enough courtrooms during my twelve years as a State Trooper to know that, however distasteful they are, reports are essential. Without good records, even a mediocre defense attorney can blow you out of the water. One of the first things I did as a new Ranger was ask around to find out who wrote the best reports. After all, who else would be better to pattern myself after than the best? In 1961, Bob Badgett and Jim Ray were the best in Company B. They were alike in the detailed way they wrote reports, they were as different as daylight and dark personality-wise. It was not easy to get next to Bob. He was pretty much a loner. He was always courteous, answered any questions I asked thoroughly and completely, and helped me in every way that he could. I never took offense to his stand-off nature; it was just his way. He, like many Rangers then and now, preferred working alone. Jim Ray was just the opposite. He enjoyed being around people. I will always be grateful to Bob Badgett and Jim Ray.

My two weeks went quickly and before I knew it, it was time to report to Marshall. My first day on the job, I visited every one of my Sheriffs. I let them know that I was available twenty-four hours a day, seven days a week. And I meant it. During the better part of the next three decades I worked with countless Sheriffs, District Attorneys, Police Chiefs, the Secret Service, the FBI, and agents from the ATF (Bureau of Alcohol, Tobacco, and Firearms), and the list could go on and on. You can not find anyone who will say I was not there when needed. I guess if there is any one thing in my career that I am proudest of, it's that I was always available. What would it do for my credibility if I went around telling one and all that all they had to do was call and I'd be there, then not be available. Their confidence and trust in me would have been out the window quick as a flash—and rightfully so.

---

[1] I love Texas more than anything in the world, but our practice of naming towns and counties sometimes defies logic. Henderson is in Rusk County. Rusk is in Cherokee County. Athens is in Henderson County. Houston is in Harris County. Crockett is in Houston County. The list could go on and on, but you get the point.

I am equally proud that I had the same relationship with Louisiana officials. Except for Gregg County, every one of my counties bordered Louisiana, and sometimes it seemed I worked as much in Louisiana as I did in Texas. Those old crooks did not pay the least bit of attention to state lines. In fact, most considered it a safe haven. I don't care what anybody says: Those north Louisiana boys are good peace officers—as good as any officers you will find anywhere.

I am not sure what my first case was, but looking back through my records I think it was the theft of some oil field sucker rods in Linden from the Pan American Oil Company. Sucker rods are used in the oil field. Being based in the heart of the East Texas Oil Field, I could have spent my entire career just working oil field theft if I had wanted to. And I did work it a lot. But it was never my first objective. During my career, I sometimes took a lot of heat from oil companies because I did not spend more time working their cases. My answer to them was always the same; "If someone robbed your folks of their life savings, or raped your women, or worse, murdered one of your loved ones, which would you rather I work? The theft of some of your oil field equipment, or catching the people who brutalized your family?" Needless to say, no one ever preferred that I work the theft of oil equipment.

Up until the last few years when the federal government, in all her infinite wisdom, said I couldn't do it, throughout my years as a Texas Ranger, it was normal for me to put in seventy to one hundred hours a week. I averaged putting eight hundred to a thousand miles a week on my car. Every single Captain I had, Trooper and Ranger without exception, told me that I did not have to put in the time I did. I figured the people of Texas hired me to do a job, and since I have never short-changed anyone in my life, I worked until I got the job done. I simply could not get the job done in forty hours.

One of the first things I learned was that, even putting in the time I did, there was only so much I could do. I could not work every case that came across my desk. In my first few weeks it seemed I had to be everywhere at once—Atlanta, Texas, to a bank robbery; Gilmer helping Red Arnold on a jewelry theft, burglaries in Longview, oil field equipment stolen in Linden; Hallsville to arrest a man wanted in Big Spring; over to Dallas to run a polygraph; plus still going to court finishing cases started while I was a State Trooper. I hit the ground running, and, in all honesty, I didn't quit for the next twenty-six years.

In November, 1961, though only on the very periphery, I worked my first high-profile case. During my career I was involved in several cases that gained a lot of statewide and national notoriety and publicity. Through my involvement in these cases I became acquainted with every Ranger in the state, plus ATF, FBI, and Secret Service agents. And, I am proud to say, I shook the hand of Presidents Harry Truman, Dwight Eisenhower, John F.

Kennedy, Lyndon Johnson, Richard Nixon, Gerald Ford, Jimmy Carter, Ronald Reagan, and George Bush.

Having said that, I guess this is as good a place as any to briefly mention a few of these high-profile cases and events.

SAM RAYBURN'S FUNERAL

On November 16, 1961, "Mr. Democrat," Sam Rayburn died. We had been briefed about a week beforehand that Mr. Sam's cancer was terminal, and that his death was imminent. He may have lived most of his adult life in Washington, DC, but in death he was coming home to Texas and Fannin County. Company B was assigned Presidential security for the funeral. Though we would be assisting the federal boys, this was going to be anything but a picnic.

In 1961 there was only eleven of us in Company B. Coming to Bonham were two past Presidents, Harry Truman and Dwight Eisenhower, and the current President, John F. Kennedy. But they were only the tip of the iceberg. Also attending the funeral would be Vice President Lyndon Johnson; members of the United States Supreme Court; members of the Joint Chiefs-of-Staff; Senators and Representatives; several members of Kennedy's Cabinet; the Governors of Texas and Oklahoma, Price Daniel and Howard Edmundson; my boss, Homer Garrison, countless other dignitaries; and relatives and friends like my wife Catherine and my Mother and Dad. Our work was definitely cut out for us.

I arrived in Bonham on Friday, November 17. After being briefed and given my assignment by Captain Crowder, I met with Secret Service and Fannin County officials. Everyone was extremely concerned. With all the high-ranking officials in Bonham, one madman could have done a lot of damage. It was our job to see that everything went smoothly and peacefully.

The funeral was held at Bonham's First Baptist Church.[2] I was stationed at the north door, right where the dignitaries entered and left the church. It was also where Mr. Sam's body was brought into the church. To see up close and personal the high and powerful, I could not have drawn a better station.

Most of the dignitaries arrived at Perrin Air Force Base in Sherman,

---

[2] Mr. Sam was a member of the Primitive Baptist Church in nearby Tioga, Texas. But the largest church in the area was Bonham's First Baptist Church. With the mass of people attending the funeral, that was where it was held.

about twenty-five miles from Bonham. From there they were driven to Bonham. Presidents Eisenhower and Kennedy, Vice President Johnson, and several dignitaries arrived in Bonham by helicopter, landing at different times and different locations. Some arrived at Bonham's Municipal Golf Course, while others landed at Bonham's high school football field. President Truman did not fly in. He hated flying and had taken a train from his home in Independence, Missouri, to Denison, Texas. There he had been picked up by a friend and driven to Bonham. I remember it as if it were yesterday, seeing President Truman getting out of a 1955 Buick Roadmaster, and walking, alone, toward the church. When he left the presidency, he refused Secret Service protection. Whoever his friend was who brought him from Denison remained in the car.

It may have been the largest church in Bonham, but the First Baptist Church could not begin to hold everyone who had shown up for the funeral. The people of Fannin County adored Mr. Sam, and they all wanted to pay their last respects. In an attempt to cope with the crowd, loud speakers had been installed for the crowd outside. As speaker after speaker spoke, all praising Mr. Sam, I happened to look up and saw sitting high above on the top of the church steeple a white turtledove. Staring at the dove I had a chance to reflect on my personal relationship with Mr. Sam.

Never in my life had I not known Mr. Sam. As I said earlier in this narrative, I was born right across the road from his birthplace. My dad and he had been good friends most of their lives. I remembered going several times with Dad to visit Mr. Sam at his home. I remembered the time he offered my Dad a real considerable housing contract during World War II. This man had given me an appointment to West Point. But the main thing I remembered was what a terrible loss Texas and the country had just sustained. Regardless of what anyone thought of his politics, no one ever questioned his fierce patriotism to Texas and the United States. I knew standing outside the church, that Texas and the country, in fact the whole world, had lost a man not easily replaced.

As assigned, shortly before the service ended I left the church and rushed to the Rayburn family plot in Willow Wild Cemetery on the outskirts of Bonham. It was here Mr. Sam would find his final resting place. I was stationed right behind the open grave. It was my job to make sure that only authorized people were allowed at the graveside.

After everyone had entered, I noticed Colonel Garrison standing outside the roped area. I motioned for him to join the others at the graveside. He was the commander of the Texas Department of Public Safety, and I figured he had as much right as several lesser dignitaries to stand near Mr. Sam. Nobody ever said anything to me for allowing the Colonel to join the graveside assembly.

THE SLANT-HOLERS

Working in the heart of the largest oil field in the United States at that time, the East Texas Oil Field, I could not help but work oil field cases a lot. One of the biggest cases in my career and in the history of the Rangers happened in 1962. At the time there were only sixty-two Rangers to cover the whole state. By the time the "Kilgore Slant-Hole Case" was over, almost every single Ranger had been involved, in one way or another.

The Great Black Giant[3] had come roaring to life with Dad Joiner's discovery of the Daisy Bradford Number Three in 1930. During the next thirty years the field had produced an astronomical amount of oil, but by the 1950s the field was showing signs of age. Many wells were operating under pump, instead of free flow.

The major oil companies controlled most of the oil patch. When an oil well faded and did not produce enough to be profitable, they would either close the well, or sell the lease to a small independent oil company. Not having the gigantic overhead of the majors, the independent could often re-work—"work-over"—a well, and squeeze a few more barrels from the tired old well.

This was all fine and dandy, and legal. Where they went over the line was when a "whip-stock" was brought into the game. Let me try to explain what a whip-stock is. Let's say that a layer of oil lies under a heavily populated residential area. Obviously it would not be practical to buy out and relocate all the homes in the area. To solve the problem, a well is drilled away from the homes. After the well is drilled vertically, a whip-stock is positioned in the well and the drilling continues in a horizontal direction toward the oil. Thus the valuable oil is retrieved, and the homesites are undisturbed. This is called "slant-holing."

Like I said, this is all fine and dandy, and legal. What's not legal is when a work-over well suddenly finds new life and starts producing forty, fifty, or more barrels a day instead of three or four barrels a day. You have to admit this is mighty suspicious—doubly so when a good-producing well is sitting only a couple of hundred yards away. What really gets your attention is when— and this really happened—a slant-holer taps into the casing of a big-producing well a quarter of a mile away. As a comedian once said, "Oops."

When a well is drilled or worked-over, a member of the Railroad Commission[4] has to make an on-site inspection. During drilling or work-over a

---

[3] Locals often refer to the East Texas Oil Field as the Great Black Giant.

[4] The Railroad Commission controls all Texas oil production.

well can deviate only a few degrees in its designed angle into the earth. This is to make sure that the drillers do not let a well wander onto someone else's lease. It is the Railroad Commission's responsibility to make sure everyone plays by the same set of rules.

The trial of J. D. Matthews really put the slant-hole business into the public's eye. Matthews was an investigator working undercover for the Exxon Oil Company. Suspecting what was going on, Exxon had sent Matthews into the oil field to gather proof. One night in a Henderson motel room, Matthews and a whip-stock man got drunk and got into a fight. During the fight a gun appeared and, according to Matthews, was accidentally discharged. The whip-stocker could not deny Matthews' allegation. He was dead.

Feelings were running hot and heavy in Henderson by the time of the trial in February of 1962. I was sent to Henderson to provide extra security. To the surprise of some, and the relief of others, Matthews was found not guilty. But during the trial he had ripped the lid off the slant-hole business exposing the gigantic degree of the fraud.

By the time Matthews came to trial in 1962, slant-holing had become epidemic. Naturally, the legitimate owners were screaming like a pig stuck under a gate. It was estimated that at a minimum three hundred illegal slant-holes were operating. Clearly, the slant-holers could not be getting away with their thieving without someone at the Railroad Commission being on the take.

There was only one way to prove a well was slanted—on-site tests had to be run. This was potentially a rough game we were playing. The men who were to run the tests refused to go on site without protection. With at least three hundred slant-holes it was going to take a lot of protection. The East Texas Oil Field lies mainly in Gregg and Rusk Counties. Rusk County was Jim Ray's domain. I was still a wet-behind-the-ears Ranger with only a few months' experience, so this was mainly Jim's show, with me trying to help. Plainly Jim and I could not hope to protect such a vast area, "One Ranger, One Riot" not-withstanding. So we got some help—sixty Texas Rangers. Not all were here at the same time. Obviously they all had their own territories and cases to work, but they rotated in and out protecting those who tested the wells in question.

I do not want to leave the impression that this all happened in a few days or weeks; it drug on for almost a year. Nobody ever accused the slanters of being stupid. When they realized we were going to start testing wells, they also sprang into action. They started dumping anything and everything down the holes to prevent investigators from checking the bottoms. Concrete, scrap iron—you name it; it went down the hole. There were plenty of Rangers in the oil field, and we checked any and every well the investigators wanted to check, all without any serious trouble.

The final result: We pretty well stopped slant-holing, but, as far as I know, not one person served one day in prison. Knowing and proving are two very different things.

I am often asked if it did not aggravate me to put the time and effort into a case—any case—with no tangible results. Law enforcement is no different than any other business; it's a team effort. When I know that I have upheld my end of the job, I never let it aggravate me if someone walks. Slant-holing is a lot like arson. If you don't catch them red-handed, it is almost impossible to prove. We may not have sent any slant-holers to prison, but we broke the back of their operation.

As far as getting no tangible results, I got a lifetime's worth. I met and worked with every field Ranger and most of the officers then on active duty. Imagine me, a country boy from Windom, Texas, working with the likes of my old coach, Hall of Famer Jim Riddle, Hall of Famer Charlie Miller, Jim Ray, Red Arnold, Lewis Rigler, Benny Krueger, Walter Russell, and the list goes on and on. No tangible results. You must be joking.

BILLY SOL ESTES

The extreme publicity of the O. J. Simpson trial reminded me of the time I was assigned duty at the first trial in which cameras were allowed—the Billy Sol Estes trial in Tyler.

Too much has been written about Billy Sol Estes and his scams for me to go into any detail about them here. Besides, he did not commit any crimes in my area; he operated out in West Texas. Through his association with Lyndon Johnson and other bigwigs his scam had drawn a huge amount of publicity. Feeling he could not get a fair trial in West Texas, his lawyers asked for, and obtained, a change of venue to Tyler, Texas.

I was assigned to provide additional security at the trial. Other than the cameras, I really can not remember anything special about the court proceeding, and if it had not been the first trial with cameras in it, I would not even mention it. But it was, and I was there.

90

JOHN F. KENNEDY'S ASSASSINATION

Friday, November 23, 1963. Like everyone who is old enough to re-member, I know exactly where I was and what I was doing that terrible day.

Red Arnold[5] and I were working a common case. We had apprehended a couple of suspected burglars who had been operating in our areas. Early that Friday we took them to Dallas to be polygraphed. About lunchtime, the first man being polygraphed confessed, so there would be no need to poly-graph the second. Red and I decided to grab a quick lunch before heading home. In 1963, Company B was headquartered on the Northwest Highway in Garland. We drove down the street about a mile to a small restaurant. We had just finished eating when word spread through the restaurant from a radio announcement that the President had been shot.

We paid our bill and hooked 'em back to headquarters, double-quick. We were able to gather a few bits of scant information over the police radio on our way to the office. The phones were ringing off the wall as we entered the door. I grabbed the closest phone. It was Colonel Garrison. He did not mince any words "I want to know what's going on in Dallas. Keep this line open until I find out."

I told the Colonel what little I knew. Captain Crowder was not at the office, but was on his way back. Our sergeant, Lester Robertson, and Charlie Moore were headed downtown to the Dallas Police headquarters. A couple of the boys, Bob Badgett and Ernest Daniels, had left for Parkland Hospital[6] to provide additional security for Governor John Connally. That was all I could tell him.

Until relieved I kept the phone line open between Company B head-quarters and DPS headquarters in Austin. I do not want you to think that I sat there like a dummy doing nothing but holding a phone. While making sure the line stayed open, I was passing messages, forwarding orders, and doing whatever else needed doing. It may not sound like it, but I had an extremely busy three hours.

Meanwhile Red and I still had two prisoners we had to do something with. We had locked them in a small room adjoining the polygraph room while all this was going on. If we stayed any longer, we were going to have to put them in a jail. I told Captain Crowder our problem. He told Red and me to go on home; he had all the help he needed. And that is the extent of my involvement in the John F. Kennedy assassination. But I was there.

---

[5] Red was the Ranger stationed in Mount Pleasant.

[6] Parkland Hospital was where President Kennedy and Governor Connally were taken after the shooting.

CHAPTER VII
MURDER IN UNCERTAIN

Deep in the Big Thicket of East Texas, sitting on the banks of Caddo Lake,[1] is a community called Uncertain. On a busy day it has maybe one hundred or so people. With the exception of an auto parts distributor, its economy is based almost entirely on fishing, hunting, and other vacation and resort activities. It is a place where people from all over come to kick back, rest, have a little fun, and enjoy themselves.

In 1966 I worked a murder case that had the most bizarre ending of any case I ever worked. Take my word for it, in almost forty years of law enforcement I worked more bizarre cases than I care to remember. On Wednesday, March 2, 1966, Judge Andrew J. Roe, called Judge or A. J. by his friends, was shot to death as he walked from his car to the front door of his home in Uncertain.

As far as I know, Judge Roe was not, nor had he ever been, a judge. Somewhere along the way someone had hung the title of Judge on Mr. Roe, and it stuck. At the time of his murder the Judge was sixty-six years old and had lived in the Uncertain area most of his life.

For more than twenty years he had been the caretaker of the Dallas Caddo Club. The club is made up of people who want a place to come and do a little hunting and fishing. They had a large cabin that could sleep several people. It was the Judge's responsibility to keep the property maintained, arrange for guides for hunting or fishing trips, and generally take care of the club and members' needs when they were at the cabin.

After retiring from the Dallas Caddo Club, Judge Roe and his wife, Martha, bought a house next door to the club. Regretfully, retirement would not be kind to the Judge and Martha. After a lengthy illness, Martha died in November of 1965.

Uncertain was and is a place where everyone knows everybody. They know one another's habits, who is running around with whom, who is sick

---

[1] Caddo Lake is part of the border separating Northeast Texas and Northwest Louisiana.

and what's ailing them. Everyone knew that the Judge was financially secure. It was common knowledge that twice a month he wrote checks to pay his bills; then he would withdraw thirty to fifty dollars in cash for walking-around money. Records would reveal that his last withdrawal was on February 26 in the amount of thirty dollars.

It was almost a ritual; every morning at seven o'clock the Judge would meet with friends at Haddad's Cafe to drink coffee and talk. On Thursday morning, March 3, the Judge did not show up, but even that did not raise undue alarm. All his friends knew he had a slight heart problem, and would take a little nip occasionally—you know, to thin the blood a little so his heart would not have to work so hard. Though not a common practice, occasionally the Judge drank a little too much blood thinner. When he did, he usually did not get up and around for the morning coffee session.

That afternoon at about 1:30, the Judge's next-door neighbor and the current caretaker of the Caddo Club, Wendell Gene Fuller, was standing in his yard talking to a friend, Ray Fasen. Looking over at the Judge's house, he saw the Judge laying face down in the yard. Rushing to the scene, Fuller and Fasen could tell that the Judge was dead. It was not difficult to tell. He had been dead for more than sixteen hours and rigor mortis had clearly sit in.

Their first thought was that the Judge had suffered a heart attack. After a quick consultation, it was decided that Fuller would stay with the body while Fasen went to call the Harrison County Sheriff's office. Deputy Fletcher Shivers came by, looked at the body, and agreed that the Judge must have had a heart attack. In a situation such as this, under Texas law the only person who can declare a person legally dead is a Justice of the Peace. Fletcher called the Justice of the Peace, J. G. Stauts, in Waskom and asked him to come over. Arriving at the Judge's home, the JP looked at the still unmoved body, and agreed. "Yeah, Judge Roe's had a heart attack. Call Sullivan's Funeral Home in Marshall and tell them to come get him."

Attendants from Sullivan's Funeral Home in Marshall arrived and started to load the body onto a gurney. When they rolled the body over they discovered that the Judge had died of a heart attack all right—a heart attack caused by a shotgun blast in the chest. Before criticizing all these folks for failing to realize that a shotgun blast, not a heart attack, had killed the Judge, let's examine the situation more. First, they had no reason to suspect foul play. It was common knowledge that Judge Roe had heart problems and he was still grieving the recent death of his wife Martha. Second, there was no blood around the body.

The community was stunned; nothing like this had ever happened before. Who in the world would have killed the Judge, and why? Everyone liked the Judge, and he was friendly and kind to everyone. He was a religious man who attended church regularly. In fact, he had attended Prayer Meeting the night before at the Karnack[2] Methodist Church. Surely it was not robbery. Everyone knew that the most cash the Judge ever carried was the thirty-to-fifty dollar allowance he withdrew twice a month.

On March 6, I received a call from Harrison County Deputy Sheriff Fletcher Shivers[3] requesting my assistance. The day after the murder, March 3, Dr. Mildred Cariker, a pathologist in Marshall, had performed an autopsy. He determined that the time of death had been at about 9:00 p.m., March 2. During the autopsy he determined that a sixteen-gauge shotgun was the murder weapon. The examination further showed that one hundred twenty-eight, number six pellets had ripped into his chest, fifteen in the heart. The blast was centered near the Judge's right nipple, and measured approximately twelve inches in diameter. Obviously, whoever killed the Judge had been close in proximity. We removed two other things from his body: a one-dollar bill from his wallet, and some small change from his pocket.

Investigation showed that on the day of his murder, Judge Roe arrived at Haddad's Cafe at seven o'clock for his normal morning coffee. Later in the morning he went to the office of his attorney, Joe Bibb, in Marshall. Coincidentally, and investigation would prove it was purely coincidental, Judge Roe had signed his will the very day of his death. He had divided his estate equally among his and Martha's four children.

He left Bibb's office at approximately 11:30. Between 2:30 and 3:00 that afternoon, Zephyr Dee Charles, who lived across the street from the Judge, saw him enter his driveway. At about 6:50 p.m., Alton Charles, Mrs. Charles's son, was walking home after having gone fishing when the Judge passed him heading toward Karnack. Witnesses confirmed that the Judge had attended Prayer Meeting from 7:00 p.m. until 7:50 p.m. at the Karnack Methodist Church. It is about a twelve-minute drive from the Karnack Methodist Church to the Judge's house. The pathologist, Dr. Cariker, had confirmed that his time of death was at nine o'clock. We were never able to determine the Judge's whereabouts during the missing hour.

It was clear that when Judge Roe got home, he had parked his car in the garage and was walking down a narrow walkway toward his front door when he was shot from ambush.

After finishing our review of the reports, Deputy Shivers, Constable Buck Little, and I went to the crime scene. We found shotgun wadding thirty-one feet from where the Judge's body was discovered. We also discovered numerous footprints at the southwest corner of the Judge's house. Apparently, someone had waited patiently for the Judge.

We began questioning people in the area. As stated earlier, Judge Roe's

---

[2] Karnack, Texas, is the hometown of former First Lady, Lady Bird Johnson.
[3] Shivers would later become Sheriff of Harrison County.

next-door neighbors were Wendell and Mildred Fuller. On the night of the murder, Mrs. Fuller had gone to Tatum to visit with Mr. Fuller's father. Wendell had called his wife's sister, Betty Ward, and invited her and her husband, Tom, over for coffee. Living only a short distance from the Fullers, she and her husband arrived at the Fullers house at 7:45. Around 8:30 they were sitting at the kitchen table drinking coffee when they heard a shotgun blast.

After Mrs. Ward turned on the back porch light, Fuller and his brother-in-law went outside to investigate. Fuller and Ward went to Fuller's pickup, hooked up a spotlight, and shined it around the area. They neither saw anything, nor did they hear a car or motorboat crank up. They shined the light at the Judge's house, but it was dark. They assumed the Judge had already turned in for the night.

After discovering the body the following afternoon, Fuller had walked around the Judge's house while Fasen was calling the Sheriff. He checked all the doors and windows and found them to be locked.

As with any investigation, we asked Fuller if he owned a shotgun. Yes, he did. Could we test fire it? Yes. It was a twelve-gauge loaded at the time with number nine shot. Had he fired it recently? Of course, shortly before and shortly after the discovery of the Judge's body. Since this was (and is) hunting country, there was nothing unusual about that. Would he consent to a polygraph test? Yes.

At the time, the closest polygraph-testing site was in Dallas. We took Mr. Fuller to Dallas and administered the test to him. Test results showed that he had no knowledge of or association with the murder.

We interviewed Ray Haddad, Glen Turner, and Charles Glover. The three had been frog-gigging the evening of the murder. Haddad and Turner stated that they heard a shot at 8:35 that night. Haddad was certain of the time. He happened to be looking at his watch just as the shot was fired. Glover had been operating the boat motor and had not heard the shot. But even if he had, like his partners, he would have thought nothing about it. They stayed in the area another fifteen minutes, but did not see or hear a vehicle or boat after the shot.

In the ensuing days we interviewed nearly everyone in Uncertain. Almost everyone in town had heard the gunshot blast but, like the frog-giggers had thought nothing about it. Gunshots, day or night, were not unusual in this rural area located deep in the woods on the banks of Caddo Lake. If someone wanted deer meat, they seldom worried about whether it was deer season or not. They simply went out and shot a deer, cut it up, and put it in the freezer. No big deal.

At the time of the murder it seemed almost everyone in town was either drinking coffee, frog-gigging, playing dominoes, or watching *The Big Valley* on television. We took countless people to Dallas to take the polygraph test.

They all returned negative. Everyone seemed to have an airtight alibi.

We continued to dig, and finally one alibi sprung a leak. Alton Charles was a senior at Karnack High School. He and his parents, James "Boadlum" and Zephyr Dee Charles, lived across the street from Judge Roe. In his statement he claimed he went to school that day. After school he went fishing and had seen the Judge driving toward Karnack as he was returning home. After arriving home he had watched *The Rifleman* and *Batman* on television. After *Batman* went off he walked down the road to Jessie Hanson's Liquor Store. He had played the pinball machine awhile, bought a package of Winston cigarettes and left. He then went to Henry Lewis' house, arriving there at about 8:30. He remembered that there were eight or nine people in the house at the time, but the only ones he was sure about were Henry and his wife, Mary, Eura Black, Robert Rivers, Mann Perry, Jr., and Fred Hood. Some were playing dominoes while others watched television. After hanging around for an hour or so he left. He had heard a shot, but like everyone else he thought nothing about it.

That was his story. I confirmed that he had gone to school, and had gone fishing. His mother and father confirmed that he had watched *The Rifleman* and *Batman* before leaving the house. Witnesses remembered seeing him at Jessie Hanson's Liquor Store, but they were not sure of the time.

During our interviews with the people who had been at the Lewis house, none mentioned Alton Charles hanging around. I questioned them again, and yes, they remembered Alton being there, but they could not be sure when. People were going in and out all night. It could have been 8:30, or 9:00, or anywhere in between. Most remembered that he had left at about ten o'clock, and they remembered he had not stayed long.

Questioning Alton again, he simply could not remember exactly when he got there; however, he was sure that he had left at ten o'clock. His family did not have running water. He remembered picking up his water bucket and going to an outside faucet at Hanson's Liquor Store, filling the bucket and going home. I told him I did believe him, but would he consider taking a polygraph. I told him that a whole host of people in Uncertain had taken the test. He said, "Sure, I'll take the test."

Harrison County District Attorney Charles Allen advised Alton that he did not have to take the polygraph, nor did he even have to talk to us without an attorney present. Yes, he understood, but he did not need an attorney. We took him before Judge T. G. Stauts who again advised Alton of his right to an attorney, and assured him yet again that he did not have to take the polygraph. Again, he assured us he had nothing to hide; thus he needed no attorney, and he was more than willing to take the lie detector test.

Meeting my sergeant, Lester Robertson, at the DPS office in Dallas at four o'clock on the afternoon of March 17, we escorted Alton directly to the polygraph room. Awaiting us was Burl Reed, the polygraph operator.

Whenever anyone is taking a polygraph, the operator always asks simple yes or no questions before starting the actual test. The person being questioned answers these to establish a pattern. The questions are always very basic: "Is your name Alton Charles?" "Are you a senior at Karnack High School?" "Have you ever drunk a Coca-Cola, or played baseball?" Real simple questions. Also, the operator asks the person being questioned to deliberately lie. This too shows a definite pattern. Alton could see the marks the lie detector made when he told the truth, and when he lied.

Completing the briefing, Burl started asking Alton the basic questions like those already mentioned. Finally he asked Alton, "Did you kill Judge Roe?"

I have had countless polygraphs run but never have I received the answer that Alton Charles gave.

"Yes."

I know my mouth had to have dropped open a foot. I couldn't believe it. This had never happened before, and never would it happen again. Surely this must have happened to someone, someplace, but in all my years I have never heard of it happening any other time.

I knew immediately that we were at a critical stage. If we did not handle this just right, we could lose the whole case, confession or not.

Even when a person makes a confession, you cannot assume anything, or lead the person in any way. For instance, it would have been easy to rush into the room and say things like: "Did you shoot Judge Roe with a sixteen-gauge shotgun?" Or, "Did you wait for him beside the southwest corner of his house?" A sharp defense attorney would have been on that like a bird dog. He would have rightfully pointed out that we were leading the witness and would have gotten the confession thrown out of court in an instant.

I did not want Alton to know I had been watching from the other side of a two-way mirror, so I walked into the room and said as casually as possible, "I understand Alton's getting his business straightened out. I hate to interrupt y'all, but why don't we all just sit down here and let him tell us all about it."

Alton and his father, Boadlum, had been fighting for over a year. The Tuesday before the murder, Alton and Boadlum had a terrible fight over money. If Alton had any uncertainty about leaving home, it disappeared after this latest fight. He knew for sure that he wanted more than anything in the world to get away from his father, and dreary little Uncertain. Dallas was where he belonged.

Regrettably, he needed money and a car to get to Dallas. He had neither, but he knew that Judge Roe had a car, and he just knew he had lots of money, much more than the puny fifty dollars a week he got out of the bank. In Alton's mind, no one could possibly spend that kind of money every week in a one-horse town like Uncertain, Texas.

After the latest fight with his father, Alton decided he would kill Judge Roe, take his money and his Chevrolet, go to Dallas and live the good life that he felt he so richly deserved.

He planned well. On the day of the argument with his father, he slipped his father's shotgun[4] out of the house and hid it in a pile of brush in the woods behind his house. Searching his house, he was able to find one Remington-Peters Express, number six shot, sixteen-gauge shotgun shell. He considered himself a good shot and one was all he would need.

The next day he went to school, smugly self-assured that he would soon put this hick country school and two-bit, boring little town behind him for-ever, and head for the city lights of Dallas. When school dismissed he still had several hours of daylight before he could commit his "deed of freedom," so he decided to go fishing. Along the way, he hid an empty water jug in a ditch near the home of a family named Blackmon. Later he would retrieve the jug, get it filled as usual, making sure that as many people as possible saw him. After he hid the jug, he continued to the lake where he spent several enjoyable hours fishing. As he walked home he met Judge Roe headed for Karnack and Wednesday Prayer Meeting. The Judge might be driving while Alton walked right now, but he wouldn't be walking much longer. It was time to put his carefully laid murder/robbery plan into action.

He went straight to the woods, and exchanged his fishing pole for the hidden shotgun. Loading the weapon, he walked to the Judge's house. Know-ing where the Judge had gone, he knew he had awhile to wait. He sat down on the front steps of the Judge's house, and waited. Finally, he saw the head-lights that meant freedom and the good life. He ran around to the corner of the house and sat up his ambush.

Just as Alton knew he would, Judge Roe pulled into the driveway and parked in the garage, got out of the car and started walking toward the house. About halfway between the garage and the house, the Judge saw a figure standing in the shadows. Evidently he did not recognize his assassin, for he called out, "Who is that standing there?"

Alton had the shotgun resting on the edge of the house to steady his aim and, in answer to the Judge's question, pulled the trigger. The Judge did not fall immediately; he stood in disbelief. Dying, he cried out, "Oh, my God!" Standing yet another second or two, he finally collapsed forward on his face.

Alton rushed forward to his victim and started looting his pockets. In-stead of enough money to live the good life, he found a one-dollar bill in his wallet and some loose change in his pocket. Disgusted with the Judge for

---

[4] This was a J. C. Higgins, sixteen-gauge, bolt-action, full-choke shotgun with a twenty-eight inch barrel. On the stock the name "Alton" had been carved.

carrying so little cash, he did not even bother to take the tiny amount of money he found.

Just as he was about turn the body over, a neighbor's[5] yard light came on. Alton jumped up and ran between the garage and Judge Roe's house. He continued running until he reached the lake. As he ran in front of the Caddo Club's boathouse, he bolted the empty shell case out of the shotgun and threw it into the water. Continuing in his mad rush, he went to where he had hidden the water jug. Grasping it, he ran to the woods, where he once again hid the shotgun.

Still running, he ran to Hanson's Liquor Store. Then, showing the calmness of a true sociopath, he entered Hanson's and bought a pack of Winston cigarettes. Now walking slow and easy, making sure that everyone saw him, he entered the adjoining cafe where he partook in a game of Skill Ball on a pinball machine.

Still as calm as a hardened killer, he completed the game and walked to Henry Lewis' house. He stayed there, making himself visible, until about ten o'clock. Leaving the house, he saw Raymond Broadnax, a man from Dallas that he knew slightly, walking down the road. Running to catch up with him, he walked with him until they reached the home of a neighbor with whom Broadnax was going to try to catch a ride into Marshall. Parting with Broadnax, he ran back to where he had left his water jug, went back to Hanson's Store where he filled it with water. Then, he went home.

Alton knew his father would have to leave the house the next day before anyone got up. Hearing him leave, Alton ran into the woods, retrieved the shotgun and put it back in the house. No one had missed it. He then dressed and went to school. As he got on the school bus, he looked over at Judge Roe's house and saw his victim still lying on the sidewalk, exactly as he had left him the night before.

On Monday, March 21, 1966, Deputy Shivers and I returned to the crime scene. We needed the shotgun and the shell casing. Going to Alton's home, we secured the sixteen-gauge shotgun. His father assured us that the gun had not been out of the house. I did not think then, nor do I think now, that Boadlum was trying to cover for his son. This is not to say that he would have hesitated to lie for his boy; he honestly did not think the gun had been out of the house.

Next came the hard part—finding the shell casing. Fletcher and I donned hip-high wading boots, took a garden rake and waded into Caddo Lake in front of the boathouse. After two hours of hot, muggy, stinking work in moss-covered water, we found a sixteen-gauge Remington shotgun shell about seventeen feet from the shore. From the condition of the shell it was obvious it had not been in the water long. Tests would prove that the shell had been fired

[5] The Fullers.

from the murder weapon.

Alton Charles pled guilty and was sentenced to death. As is the case with most killers, justice was never served. In the late 1960s the United States Supreme Court, in all its supposed wisdom, found the death penalty to be cruel and unusual punishment. His sentence was changed to life imprisonment.

At the time of this writing, I do not know if Alton is alive or dead. If he is still alive, he is probably out on parole, or soon will be.

I have been asked, "Why did he say yes during the polygraph test?" I don't know. I only have an opinion. When Burl Reed ran the sample questions on him, and it clearly showed every time that he lied, he must have convinced himself that lying was useless.

There is one thing of which I am sure. Alton Charles may have been only a high school teenager, but he was as hardened a killer as I have ever met. He didn't blink an eye when he gunned down Judge Roe.

CHAPTER VIII
A STRIKE GONE MAD

I had all of the strikes I wanted during the wildcat strike at Lone Star Steel in 1957. I hoped I would never again have to work a strike, but such was not to be the case. At midnight, October 16, 1968, 2,500 members of the United Steelworkers of America Union struck the Lone Star Steel plant in Lone Star, Texas.

I did not think then, or now, that a Ranger has any business working a strike. No matter what we do, we lose. Regrettably, this strike would be no exception to the rule.

As bad as the '57 strike was, the '68 strike was worse. The '57 strike lasted only forty-three days, of which I worked only a few weeks. The '68 strike lasted 210 days and my direct involvement lasted for more than seven months. As violent as the '57 strike was, it was a walk in the park compared to '68. Shootings, bombings, Molotov Cocktails, threats, intimidation, beatings, killing of children's pets, families breaking up, murder—you name it, and we had it in the '68 strike.

Mention the '68 strike to any Ranger on duty in 1968, and he will not ask what you are talking about—he will know. With the possible exception of a handful of officers, I think every Ranger in the state worked the '68 strike at one time or another. Each and every one has his own horror story, but only two, Bob Mitchell and yours truly, were there from beginning to end. Either of us could write a book of horror stories about that ungodly mess.

In 1957 Jim Ray had been Tyler's Ranger, but by 1968 Jim had become a Ranger sergeant in Midland and was well on his way to becoming the head of the Criminal Law Enforcement Division in Austin. His replacement in Tyler was Bob Mitchell. When the strike started, Bob and I had already become close friends; by the time the strike ended we were more like brothers.

According to the strikers, money was not the main issue. Lone Star Steel offered the union insurance and pension benefits, plus a twenty-five cent an hour wage increase. This was a nickel more than was being granted by other steel companies around the country. The way I understood it, the union was demanding numerous changes in working conditions.

Negotiations went nowhere with each side apparently ready for a fight. In 1957 E. B. Germany had been the president of Lone Star Steel. By 1968 he had retired and been replaced by George Wilson. Just as Germany had dug in against the union in 1957, Wilson dug in just as strongly, maybe even more extensively, in 1968.

Like his predecessor, Wilson vowed to keep the plant running. Unlike Germany, Wilson's position was strengthened by the Vietnam War. Because of its production of shell casings, he claimed that the plant's continued operation was vital to national security. And he left no room for doubt that whatever it took, Lone Star Steel would meet its obligation to our troops in the field. Naturally the strikers claimed this to be hogwash. Any number of plants around the country could fulfill the contract. Wilson vowed to keep the plant open and the strikers vowed just as emphatically to close it down.

Again like E. B. Germany, but even more elaborately, Wilson started preparing the plant for the impending strike. He imported and prepared tents, cots, additional kitchen equipment, portable bathrooms, foodstuffs, movie rooms, housekeeping facilities, recreation areas, and additional security. Anything and everything management could think of to withstand a long siege was brought inside the fences of the plant. Then Wilson issued a statement that salaried personnel would keep the plant running, and if a settlement was not quickly reached, replacement workers would be hired. You can imagine how this went over with the union.

In Mount Pleasant, District Court Judge Morris Rolston issued an order that restrained gate blockading by pickets. Like '57, the strikers defied the court order and blocked the gates, daring anyone to remove them.

We setup headquarters just north of the Lone Star Steel Plant at the Hilltop Motel in Daingerfield. Other Rangers rotated in and out of Lone Star during the following months, but Bob and I did not check out of this room for the next seven months and three days.[1] This room was un-

---

[1] At the time Bob and I would have given odds that we would never forget this room number, but we have.

doubtedly one of the smallest rooms in Texas. And with every passing day it got smaller. Bob is a big man and he needed more than this room offered, just for himself. Fortunately or unfortunately—it's all in how you look at it—we had precious little time to spend in our room.

There were so many acts of violence that I will not even attempt to recount but a few that for one reason or another still stick out in my mind.

The strike had been going on for only a few days when the guns were brought out. After the guns came out, it was not long before we were involved up to our ears. Some of the strikers were determined to stop production at the plant—preferably by violence. Like most "wanna-be" tough guys, they were only tough from ambush. Several trucks and a few drivers were shot up from ambush or from unknown person(s) firing from speeding vehicles. We desperately wanted to nip this in the bud before it could take hold. Tragically, we were not successful.

On Tuesday, October 22, three drive-by shooters came as close to dying, and yet living to tell about it, as any three men who ever lived.

Our Captain, Bob Crowder, and Bob Mitchell decided to try and drawout some of these would-be tough guys who liked to shoot at un-armed men from speeding vehicles. One morning at about five o'clock, Bob and the Captain borrowed a Lone Star Steel pickup and headed south down Highway 259 in the direction of Ore City. They had barely cleared the main plant gate when a red and white pickup carrying three men swung in behind them. No doubt they believed they had found easy pickings. If they had known Rangers were in the pickup, there is no doubt they would have given them a wide berth. But they didn't. Bob and the Captain had gone only a short distance when the men in the pickup opened fire. They put bullets into the left rear tire of the Rangers pickup. Unfortunately for them, they had taken on the wrong boys.

Captain Crowder was driving, while Bob literally rode shotgun. I have already told you what I think of Bob. Captain Crowder's picture hangs on the Hall of Fame Wall at the Ranger Museum in Waco. Nothing else can or needs to be said about him.

Fortunately the hole shot into the tire did not cause an immediate deflation, but rather a slow seepage of air. Captain Crowder was able to control the pickup, and the chase was on. (I have always thought that even if the tire had been flat, it would not have mattered. Captain Crowder would not have let a flat tire stop him.) Going south on Highway 259, the two vehicles sped towards Ore City, another ten miles down the road. All the while Bob was either firing at the fleeing pickup or using a handheld bullhorn yelling at them to stop. They ignored Bob's warning and continued trying to evade the Rangers. Bad for them.

The Captain finally boxed in the pickup on a dead-end street in Ore City. Bob came out of the pickup with fire in his eyes. Captain Crowder was older and undoubtedly wiser—at least that morning. He stopped Bob in his tracks with four words. "Robert, don't shoot 'em."

Bob Mitchell: I knew Captain Crowder for years, and that was the only time he ever called me Robert.

Inside the shooters' pickup Bob and the Captain found two jars of illegal moonshine whiskey, a .22 caliber rifle, a 7.65 millimeter German automatic pistol, a short piece of chain, and several rocks.

The three men—William E. Montgomery, 43, of Gilmer; Leo White, 51, of Mount Pleasant; and Archie W. Connor, Jr., 41, of Omaha, Texas— were charged with assault with intent to murder and destruction of property valued over $50, both felonies, and possession of a handgun and possession of untaxed alcohol, both misdemeanors. All three were mechanics at Lone Star Steel's maintenance department. Upshur County Precinct 1 Justice of the Peace, Shine Simpson, set bonds at $7,000 each. To the best of my knowledge none of the men ever served a day in jail. But I guarantee you one thing; if at any time thereafter, Montgomery, White, or Connor ever suspected that Bob Mitchell was anywhere near, no power on earth could have gotten them in the same area.

We all hoped that this was as bad as it would get. Were we ever wrong. The situation went from bad to worse.

In 1968, Preston Smith was running for Governor in the Democratic primary. One day after making a speech in Marshall, he had planned to fly into Lone Star Steel's airport, then take a car to Gilmer to speak at the annual Yamboree celebration. While in the air, Smith's pilot, James Griswold, a World War II fighter pilot, was informed that he could expect possible ground fire if he attempted to land at Lone Star Steel. Griswold, who had survived the Battle of Midway, was no fool. He landed at an alternate site.

On Saturday, October 26, another steel company employee, Lonnie Helms of Pittsburg, was arrested for threatening the wife of a steel mill employee who had chosen to continue working. After pounding his chest and making his he-man threats against the woman, he got his gun and started shooting at random around her house. Fortunately, he neither hit anyone nor inflicted any property damage. When arrested, Helms had a .38 caliber pistol, a .22 rifle and a shotgun in his possession. He was charged with threatening to take a life and aggravated assault, both misdemeanors. Justice of the Peace T. H. Miller placed him under a peace bond. As far as I know, he never served a day.

On November 5, the lid really blew off. George Wilson carried out his threat to hire replacement workers. No one was surprised when shortly someone ended up dead.

It seemed that every day brought further acts of violence. C. V. Moore, head of Lone Star's employment office in Mount Pleasant,[2] had three 30-30 high-velocity rounds fired into his house and automobile in the early morning hours as he and his wife and two children slept. Luckily an oak china cabinet stopped one 30-30 bullet that was headed directly into the babybed of one of his children.

Another employee, Joe Stacks, who lived directly across the street from the Moore's, also had his house shot into six times. Luckily for the Stacks and their two children, this shooter was using a .22 which did not have the penetrating power of the 30-30. One of the shots did shatter a bedroom window near where the Stacks slept.

Trucks were particular targets of the strikers. I could not begin to guess how many trucks were shotup or blownup during the strike. It is miraculous that none of the drivers were killed. It wasn't like the shooters and bombers didn't try. I remember one Lesco[3] truck that was loaded with bomb material that had just left the plant headed for the LeTourneau Company in Longview. The truck[4] had just crossed the Cypress Creek bottom and started to climb the long hill directly south of the bottom when it was hit by gunfire. Eleven shots entered the cab, one barely missing the driver's head. Another shot inflicted a superficial wound in the driver's right leg. Six shots blew out the left front dual tires of the truck, and other slugs ripped open the left side fuel tank.

All of these cases had one thing in common. The shooters were usually operating in the dead of night, and they were always either lying in ambush or in a speeding vehicle. We worked until I thought I would

---

[2] Moore lived in Naples, Texas.
[3] Lesco was the name of Lone Star Steel's private trucking company.
[4] The driver asked not to be identified.

drop, but to no avail. Several things have to be remembered. Lone Star Steel was not only the big fish in the pond in the Lone Star-Daingerfield area—it was the only fish in the pond. Thousands worked at the plant. When we were able to make an arrest and get an indictment, the odds were slim to none that we could get a conviction by the neighbors and fellow workers of the accused. Your fault, my fault, nobody's fault; that's just the way it was.

Be that as it may, we could not, and did not, stop working and trying. Hundred hour weeks were the norm for Bob and me as we did our best to keep a lid on a boiling situation. Shootings, beatings, ambushes, and bombs—yes, bombs—were common. Every time a striker looked up and saw smoke belching from the smokestacks at the plant and realized his efforts and sacrifices were going for naught, the madder he got. And the madder they became, the more violent the situation became. Likewise, with every act of violence, the more determined plant management became. It was like the two toughest kids in school fighting it out.

We could not win; we were caught in a catch-22. As far as I was concerned, "Doom on both your houses." The strikers claimed we favored the company. In their eyes, it was unforgivable that we sometimes ate in the plant's cafeteria. Of course, the plant management was equally outraged that the Rangers were showing too much partiality to the strikers. After all, did we not sometimes drink coffee with the strikers at their union hall? As I said, the Rangers have no business working strikes. We can not win.[5] Our job should have been working murders, bank robberies, and other major criminal cases, not trying to keep two sides apart—especially when both sides down deep wanted to fight. Catch-22 it may have been, but quitting never entered our minds.

During the night (as usual) of November 26, two plant security officers, Norris Tigert and W. E. Gossett, were shot from ambush (again, as usual). Both were hit in the legs, Gossett so severely that it was feared that amputation would be required, but fortunately this was avoided. Lone Star Steel offered a $5,000 reward for the arrest and conviction of anyone performing any kind of act of violence. The United Plant Guard Workers of America—both guards were members of the Local 258—put up a $1,000 reward for the arrest and conviction of the person or persons responsible for the shooting. Neither reward was ever claimed.

---

[5] I guess someone was listening. Today Rangers no longer work strikes.

On the 21st of December I worked a case that really made my blood boil, and still does today. A seventeen year old high school boy, Tommy Visage, was trying to make a few dollars on the side by delivering portable toilets for Ray Carter's Longview-based, Port-a-Can. The C. A. Hackett Construction Company was one of Lone Star Steel's independent contractors and a customer of Port-a-Can. At 10:10 a.m. Visage had delivered a portable toilet to the Hackett Company, and was returning to Longview. At 10:45 a.m., three miles south of Ore City, he was flagged down and told that he had a low tire on his trailer. He looked, and indeed the right rear trailer tire was low. The man who stopped him was forty-one year old Tommy Mathis. Visage recognized Mathis as one of the pickets at the gate from which he had entered and departed.

I always found it amazing that Mathis would know that Visage was going to have tire trouble—ESP, I guess. Before he could reach the rear of the trailer, Mathis sneered at Visage that because he had crossed the picket line, he had more trouble than just a flat tire. While talking, Mathis had kept his hands behind his back. Visage, suspecting trouble, started walking back to his pickup. At this point, Mathis attacked Visage with a chain. Visage fled across the highway and into a patch of woods trying to evade the deadly chain. He was in better shape than his attacker and finally escaped with only minor injuries. I guess "I-Want-To-Be-Known-As-A-Tough-Guy" Mathis thought he could prove to his friends that he was "bad" by beating up an unarmed seventeen-year-old boy with a chain.

Mathis showed a typical coward's brand of bravery. He was quite willing to attack a defenseless boy with a chain, but he and his type had no stomach to go one-on-one with anyone near their equal. I would bet that if Visage had noticed anything suspicious about Mathis when he stopped, and shown the least bit of resistance when approached, Mathis would have tucked his tail and run. Mathis was arrested in Upshur County and charged with aggravated assault. He was released on a $1,000 bond.

The situation continued to get hotter and hotter until the unavoidable happened. At about 6:30 p.m. on Thursday, January 17, 1969, near Daingerfield, Aubrey "Smithy" Blackburn, 27, of Pittsburg, Texas, was shot to death as he drove to work. He was survived by his wife, Joan, and two small children, Aubrey Robert, 5, and Rhona Lorrane, 4. Not surprisingly, he was shot in the back.

Blackburn was no stranger to strike violence. The year before, on October 25, his car had been shot up while parked at his home. On January 2, the same thing had happened again.

On the fatal night, Blackburn and a fellow employee, T. A. McFarlin, also of Pittsburg, were traveling southeast on Highway FM-557, in Blackburn's 1955 Chevrolet pickup. They were working the 7:00 p.m. shift. About seven miles from Pittsburg a car dropped in behind them. At least four shots rang out, one hit Blackburn in the middle of his back. Before dying, Blackburn was able to stop his pickup in the intersection of highways FM-557 and FM-1975, open the door and collapse onto the highway's pavement. McFarlin was uninjured, but extremely rattled. He was unable to give us any information until he received a sedative. Then all he could add to the story was that persons in a car had fired at them and that he thought Blackburn was hit by the first shot.

He did tell us one very interesting story. When Blackburn was hit he managed to stop the pickup, pull out his .38 special, get one foot on the ground and return fire. McFarlin was of the opinion that Blackburn emptied the pistol at their attackers.

During questioning, Alton Morton of Pittsburg related to Rangers Frank Kemp and Sergeant John Wood that he came upon the murder scene shortly after the shooting. He looked into the pickup and saw a pistol and a package of L & M cigarettes lying on the seat. Later the pistol was nowhere to be found. As much as we looked, we were never able to find the pistol during the investigation.

Other leads were slim, but we did have a few. Three men met Blackburn and a pursuing car, and had to dodge Blackburn's car. They also heard shots being fired. Like everyone in the area, they knew of the trouble going on at the plant, so they sped down the road about three miles to a farmhouse and called the Sheriff's office in Pittsburg.

The men could make no identification of the car or its occupants. They felt, but could not be sure, that the pursuing car had been a Mustang. Unfortunately, this led nowhere.

Sergeant Wood[6] found three 30-30 rifle bullets close together in the center of the road. It was obvious from their placement that the men in the car had stopped, gotten out of car, and taken careful aim at Blackburn's pickup. The rifleman's aim was good—to good. Regrettably, we were never able to tie the shell casing to a rifle.

Sadly, that is about as far as the case ever went. I wanted to solve

---

[6] John would later become Captain of Company D in San Antonio.

this case as badly as any I had ever worked. And we worked long and hard trying to solve it, but got nowhere. Lone Star Steel put up a reward of $10,000, which they quickly doubled to $20,000. *Citizens, Friends and Fellow Pipe Mill Employees* posted another $1,000 reward. Neither reward was ever paid.

The plant ordered its flag flown at half-mast until the end of the strike. Later they placed a marker honoring Blackburn on the plant's grounds. Following the funeral services at the plant's Chapel of the Pines, Blackburn's father, A. C., was heard to say to no one in particular, "I wonder what the feeling is today in the heart of the man who did this thing." I would bet that the assassins have not had a completely restful day since the murder—the statute of limitations never runs out for murder.

The blowing of the gas main in Pittsburg pretty well took the wind out of the sails of the '57 strike, but Blackburn's murder did nothing to cool either side. If anything, both sides dug in deeper.

Workers continued to be shot at, have their houses and cars shot up, be run off the road and beaten up, and bombs were exploded on and off the grounds of the plant. There was potentially deadly bomb in particular that came close to killing and maiming dozens. Two hundred employees were eating in the plant cafeteria when a bomb was discovered. It was set to go off at noon—only ten minutes away—when the cafeteria would have been filled to capacity. Thank God it was discovered. With only ten minutes I didn't have time to wait for a bomb squad to disarm the bomb. It was not an elaborate bomb and I was able to easily and quickly disarm it. There is no telling how many would have died if it had gone off.

Everywhere we looked it seemed there was a bomb. One was on the motor of a supervisor's car. Fortunately it too was discovered. Unfortunately we did not discover all the bombs. Where the strikers had been shooting up people's homes, some now turned to dynamiting them. Miraculously no one was killed.

Some—and only a very few—of the strikers and their fellow-travelers claimed the bombs were planted just to scare people, not to hurt them. That's the biggest load of garbage I have ever heard. They were meant to kill and maim as many people as possible. You don't plant a bomb and say, "Gee, I didn't mean to hurt anybody. I just wanted to scare 'em." You bet, and I've got a terrific deal on a bridge in Brooklyn I want to make you if you believe that.

The violence never seemed to end. Like the rabbit in the Energizer

Battery TV commercial, it just kept going, and going, and going. It was so bad that whenever negotiations broke down, newspapers would run headlines such as: "War Resumes As Talks Fail In Long Strike," or "A New Declaration Of War In the Strike," and "Tension And Terror Grip Northeast Texas Region—Citizens Fear To Talk As Striker Violence Spreads." The one I found most appropriate was in the Sunday, April 20, 1969, *Dallas Morning News*: "A Strike Gone Mad." It was war, and it was mad.

Each side naturally blamed the other. The union felt that Lone Star Steel was trying to break the union. The company felt that the union was behind the violence, a charge the union officials hotly denied. They credited the violence to an extremely small minority of their members. I have no doubt that only a few people were committing the violence. I do not believe that high-ranking union officials orchestrated or planned such action. I am not sure I can say the same about some of the lower echelon union management. There is one thing I do know, Lone Star Steel, the United Plant Guard Workers of America, and some private groups offered cash rewards for the arrest and conviction of persons responsible for acts of violence. To the best of my knowledge, the United Steelworkers of America never offered any reward, of any kind, for anything. Sometimes what a person does not say tells you as much as what he does say.

Another thing I know for a fact: regardless of who knew how, what, where, when, who, or why, on many a day Mitchell and I worked around the clock.

An ancient wise man once wrote, "This too shall pass;" and finally on May 11, 1969, it ended. The union voted to go back to work. No one was happier than Bob and me that it was over, but I do have one regret. To the best of my knowledge, for all the shootings, bombings, beatings, destruction of property, woundings, and killing, no one ever served any serious time for their crimes. Who won? I have no idea, and I could not care less. That was not my job, nor should it have been. I do know two losers. One was the people of Texas. Even today bitterness and hatred lingers in the Lone Star area. The other was a young widow who had to raise two small children without their father. Perhaps they are the biggest losers of all.

Violence was so common I could not begin to relate it in one chapter of this book. I said earlier that Bob or I could write an entire book on the

'68 strike. Maybe someday someone will write that book. I know I won't, and I don't think Bob will, but someone should. These are but a few of the incidents that I was involved with during the strike.

That's me in front of Mother, and D.L. in front of Dad on our homeplace in Windom.

That's me and brother D.L. in the early 1930s.

I was 15 years old in 1941 when this picture was taken at Windom High School. A few years later, while in the Army, boxing would earn me a leave to New York City.

Yours truly and Woodrow Crossland in Lacrosse, Washington, in 1942. Though similar, this was not the Caterpillar I described in this book.

Lacrosse, Washington, had more to offer than just work. Unfortunately I did not realize a beautiful lady was nearby when this picture was taken.

That's my brother, D.L. on Dad's right and me on his left, in front of the old homeplace in Windom. This picture was taken while I was on my way from Fort Hood, Texas, to Fort Mead, Maryland. D.L. was on his way to an airbase in Maine.

Kobe, Japan. That's Sergeant Alley, Louie Tillman, Domini Tallerico, and yours truly. Louie Tillman was someone very special to me. In 1995 a major earthquake leveled Kobe, so naturally I watched the news with a special interest. Everywhere the camera panned showed only devastation, but right in the middle was this great big old concrete building we are in front of.

Catherine and I while I was home on leave.

The Elliotts — yours truly, daughter Diane, Catherine, and son Dennis.

Five genera-
tions: Grand-
mother
Winchester,
Mother, yours
truly holding
granddaughter
Paige, and
daughter
Diane.

The graduating Texas Highway Patrol Training School, Number 15, from April 1 through May 21, 1949. *Left to right, front row*: D.K. McDaniel, L.M. Hancock, W.A. Brandon, C.R. Hoffman, B.N. Carroll, J.B. Montgomery, H.L. Robuck, W.R. Thompson, W.A. Cowan, W.M. Cawyer, Jr., H.M. Henderson, S.J. Locklier, R.E.L. Scholl. *Second row*: R.R. Jones, L.F. Poore, A.J. Clinton, Patrolman W.B. Hawkins, Sergeant R.M. Hammett, Sergeant Sam B. Guynes, Chief W.J. Elliott, Colonel Homer Garrison, Assistant-Director Joe Fletcher, Captain J.O. Musick, Sergeant A.E. Jones, E. Upham, M.D. Stout, C.C. Matlock, D.C. Miller. *Third row*: W.S. Grandberry, P.S. Lacey, L.G. Buslett, Leo Gossett, yours truly, M.N. Davis, Johnny Krumnow, R.Q. Quintana, B.T. King, L.C. Christensen. *Fourth row*: J.L. Bergstrom, W.V. Edwards, G.W. Burks, R.E. Grimmett, C.P. Richardson, D.J. Saunders, E.G. "Butch" Albers, H.L. "Lefty" Block, H.E. Hale, J.W. Parks.

125

My first Highway Patrol picture, taken in 1949.

In Longview, shortly after becoming a Highway Patrolman. You might take the boy out of the country, but you will never take the country out of the boy. Nothing has changed — I still wear my overalls.

My first partner and one of the greatest friends I ever had, Lloyd Webb.

I never thought I could have a partner equal to Lloyd Webb, but I did —
Howard "Slick" Alfred.

Between Lloyd Webb and Slick Alfred, I had another fine man for a partner — Kenneth Walker.

This picture, taken on the grounds of the Gregg County Courthouse in Longview, has always been one of my favorites. Those old bloodhounds very seldom failed. You can just see my face between two of the dog handlers behind the first dog. To the far left is my partner, Lloyd Webb. Beside Lloyd is Sheriff Noble Crawford.

This is the shield that calmed the hysterical young lady described in the chapter dealing with my Highway Patrol years.

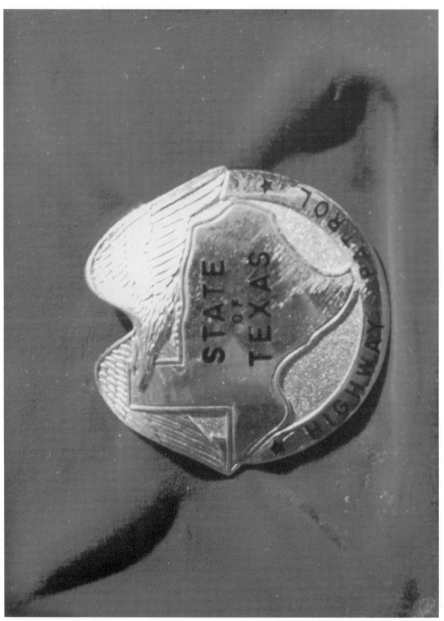

My proudest day as a Texas Ranger, October 8, 1961. That's Colonel Homer Garrison pinning my Ranger badge on me.

This is a group of men I attended a Ranger school with in October, 1961 — *Front row, left to right*: Captain Bob Crowder, Assistant Director of the DPS Joe Fletcher, Director of the DPS Colonel Homer Garrison, Captain A.Y. Allee, Inspector J.L. Rogers, Captain Frank Probst, Sergeant Jim Riddles. *Middle row*: Frank Kemp, Frank Horger, Homer Melton, Butch Albers, Charlie Moore, yours truly. *Back row*: H.A. White, Hollis Sillivan, Ott Luther, G.W. Burks, A.Y. Allee, Jr., Clay Bednar, Bill Wilson, Johnny Krumnow.

This was my first picture as a Ranger.

My first picture
as a member
of Company B.
Front row:
Bob Badgett,
Red Arnold,
Jim Ray,
G.W. Burks.
Standing:
Lewis Rigler,
Ernest Daniel,
yours truly,
Captain Bob
Crowder,
Sergeant Lester
Robertson,
Frank Kemp,
Charlie Moore.

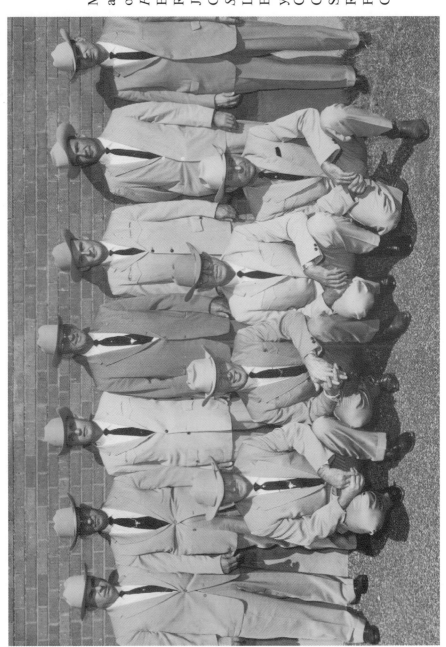

Some dear friends, including Howard "Slick" Alfred, Roy Scott, yours truly, Red Arnold, Bob Mitchell, and Max Womack, during the construction of the Company B cabin on Lake O' The Pines.

137

A company meeting in 1961 at Lake O' The Pines: Pet Green (a great friend of the Rangers), Lewis Rigler, Ernest Daniels, Jim Ray, Charlie Moore, Bob Badgett, Captain Bob Crowder, G.W. Burks, yours truly, Sergeant Lester Robertson, Red Arnold, and Assistant Director Joe Fletcher.

138

My first Company B Christmas party in 1961. It was held at Captain Bob Crowder's home in Dallas. *Seated, left to right:* Legendary Captain M.T. "Lone Wolf" Gonzaullas, Lewis Rigler, Frank Kemp, Red Arnold, G.W. Burks, Captain Bob Crowder. *Standing:* Lester Robertson, Bob Badgett, Charlie Moore, Jim Ray, yours truly, and Ernest Daniels.

Company B in
June, 1968 —
*Front row, left
to right:*
Ernest Daniel,
Lewis Rigler,
Captain Bob
Crowder,
Sergeant Lester
Robertson, Bob
Badgett.
Back row:
Charlie Moore,
G.W. Burks,
yours truly,
Bob Mitchell,
Red Arnold,
Frank Kemp.

With the rain
cover on my hat, it
was obviously
raining the day
this picture was
made with Bob
Mitchell and the
Director of the
Department of
Public Safety,
Colonel Pat Spier.

141

Taken near Lone Star, Texas, during the Lone Star Steel strike in 1969. That's Bob Mitchell, Red Arnold, Sergeant Lester Robertson, and yours truly.

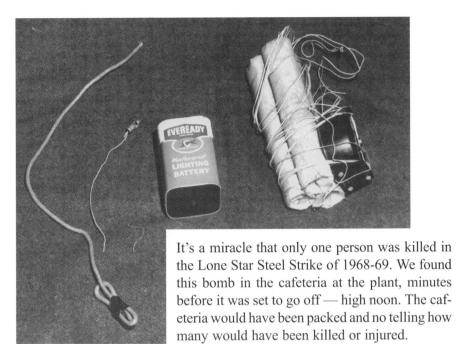

It's a miracle that only one person was killed in the Lone Star Steel Strike of 1968-69. We found this bomb in the cafeteria at the plant, minutes before it was set to go off — high noon. The cafeteria would have been packed and no telling how many would have been killed or injured.

The violence was not confined to the plant. This house was sprayed with rifle fire. God must protect the children. Only He could have protected the infant sleeping in this baby bed as bullets slammed all around it.

Wiley College in Marshall was the scene of racial problems in 1969. We shut the college down so that cooler minds could prevail. *Left to right:* G.W. Burks, Charlie Moore, yours truly, Highway Patrolman George Reese (face not visible), Sergeant Lester Robertson, Bob Mitchell.

144

I have always liked this picture. We found this wig after a bank robbery in Elysian Fields (near Marshall).

Company B. *Seated, left to right:* Lewis Rigler, yours truly, Sergeant Lester Robettson, Captain G.W. Burks, Tom Arnold, Frank Kemp, Charlie Moore. *Standing:* Roy Scott, Max Womack, Howard Alfred, Bob Mitchell, Red Arnold, Stuart Dowell.

Panola County Sheriff Johnnie Spradlin and I in Las Vegas, Nevada, in 1976.
We were on our way to Reno on the Michael Koon murder case described in
these pages. We had a long layover in Vegas, so a local FBI agent who was a
friend of ours, picked us up and took us to the Horseshoe Casino.

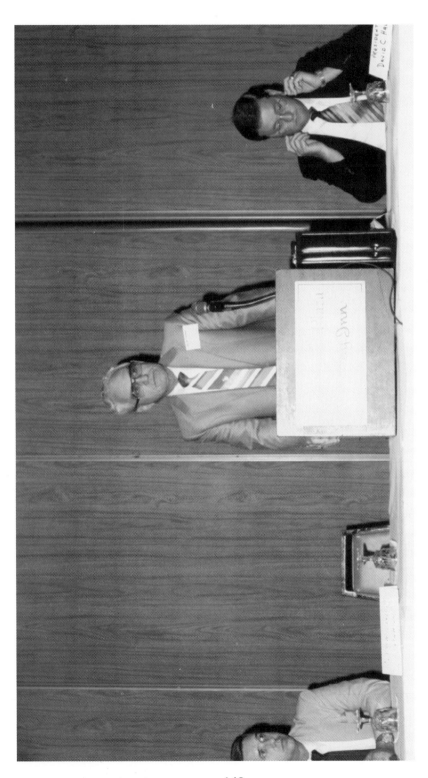

I proudly served as president of the East Texas Peace Officers Association.

I am flying to
Midland, Texas, in
my friend Richard
Harvey's plane to
testify in court.

Accepting an award for the East Texas Peace Officers Association from Bruce Brookshire. With me are fellow Rangers Captain James Wright, Max Womack, and to my left, Stuart Dowell.

I am proud to say I have known some of the greatest Rangers who have ever lived. Here are two: Jay Banks and Red Arnold.

"Pet" Green of Longview was a close friend of Lone Wolf Gonzaullas and had collected many of the legendary Ranger's guns. Shortly after Pet died, his widow thought the appropriate place for the guns was in the Texas Ranger Hall of Fame and Museum in Waco. I had the privilege of delivering these guns to the Museum.

This picture was done on a lark. I never wore two guns. This picture was taken during the Lone Star Steel strike in 1969.

Howard "Slick" Alfred

Lewis Rigler

154

Red Arnold

Jim Ray

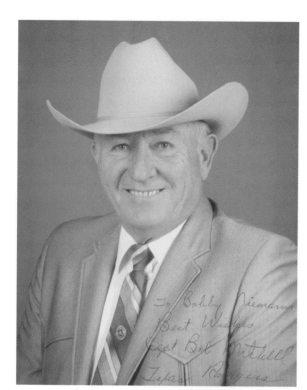

Bob Mitchell

Max Womack

156

Politics aside, I met a lot of governors in my years as a Ranger, but none ever showed me more respect than Governor Mark White.

That's me with my good friend, Paul Harvey. Paul is almost as good a fisherman as a storyteller. I have spent many a night over a campfire in a fishing camp in Canada listening to Paul tell many "Rest of the Stories." Over 400 people showed up to wish me well at my retirement party. Paul Harvey mentioned it on his daily broadcast.

The day I retired friends and colleagues said many flattering things, but the most important was my son Dennis' remarks.

Photo used by permission of Dan Winters

I am very proud that this picture was voted one of the all-time
favorites in *Texas Monthly.*

Yours truly with Mother and Dad.

For many years this picture hung above my desk. Felons just hated it. I had a caption under it that read, "The picture that convicts liked least."

CHAPTER IX
HE'D STEAL ANYTHING THAT WASN'T TIED DOWN

Some people believe things are preordained, so I guess it was inevitable that Charles Robert Mathis and I would eventually cross swords. It was a battle that started in Kilgore, Texas, in 1963 and would continue until its tragic end in 1970 on Harry Hines Boulevard in Dallas.

There have been better-known thieves than Mathis, but in all my years in law enforcement, never have I known one who stole more. Mathis' theory was simple: "If it's not tied down, steal it." Of course, he considered anything he could pry loose, not tied down.

You would think being in the Army would be a full-time job, but I think he looked upon the Army only as a source of backup income for his chosen field—being a thief. In fact, only a very short time after our first encounter, Mathis left the Army. While in the Army, more often than not, he was suspected of one thing or another. I guess the Army didn't want any part of him; they just got rid of him. In 1963, even though Mathis was under a cloud of suspicion for robbing an Officers' Club at Fort Rucker, Alabama, they ridded themselves of him via an honorable discharge. At the time he was a seventeen-year veteran with only three years to go before he would have been eligible for retirement.

Even while in the Service, Mathis had headquartered his illicit operation in the Texarkana area. By the time he became a full-time civilian in late 1963, I had developed a large file on him and knew his M.O.[1] well. I don't know if he considered the Longview-Marshall-Texarkana area his home turf or not, but he was not hitting my duty area very hard at the time. But in other places in Texas, Arkansas, Louisiana, and Oklahoma, he and his associates were stealing everything in sight. Mathis was very broadminded in his criminal activities, but his specialty was safe-cracking, and let me tell you, he was as good a safe-cracker as ever came down the pike. I knew it was only a matter of time until we met

---

[1] M. O. Modus operandi. Method of operation. Crooks are no different than honest people; they develop set patterns in the crimes and in the way they commit them.

163

up. That time came at 10:10 p.m., Sunday, November 17, 1963.

That night Gregg County Deputy J. W. Pruitt called me at home and said the Kilgore Police Department had Mathis in custody. A local night watchman, E. F. Mayo, had spotted Mathis behind some stores in an alley in the downtown area.[2] Seeing a pistol in Mathis' belt, Mayo ordered him to halt. He surrendered meekly, and Mayo ordered him to start walking to jail, which was only a few blocks away. There was one problem; Mayo was extremely nearsighted and unwittingly allowed Mathis to get too close to him. Mathis suddenly turned and knocked Mayo to the ground, and made a run for freedom. When he struck Mayo he knocked his glasses off, and without his glasses Mayo was as blind as the proverbial bat. Regardless of his impaired eyesight, Mayo fired two shots in the general direction of the fleeing Mathis. Luck just wasn't with old Charlie that night. The second shot struck him in the right leg, and sent him scrawling onto the pavement. From the way he was screaming you would have thought Mayo had blown his leg off instead of just nicking him. That little superficial wound wouldn't keep him from stealing for long. But Charlie's tolerance for pain was obviously extremely low. He flopped around on the ground screaming, "You killed me. You killed me."

Meanwhile, Mayo got to his feet. As he cautiously approached the screaming Mathis, he saw another fuzzy figure run from the same alley, but was unable to make an identification. For once we were in luck. Jerry Davis, from Odessa, Texas, was working in Kilgore for an Odessa construction company and he was living in the old Kilgore Hotel. As anyone who travels on business a great deal knows, hotel rooms become very lonely and boring. And Davis had become bored. About ten o'clock, in an attempt to relieve some of the boredom, he decided to take a walk. The old Kilgore Hotel[3] was located in the downtown area. As Davis was about to cross an alley intersection, he heard a gunshot, then a man screaming, "You killed me. You killed me." Just as he stepped into the alley, a man ran past him with a pistol in his hand. Fortunately for Davis, the gun-toter was not concerned about witnesses; his full attention was centered on getting away. The man ran down the street to a car parked in front of the Kilgore Hotel, jumped into the automobile and sped away.

When we questioned him, Davis identified the car as a late-model, white Plymouth, with a dark colored license plate. Regrettably, he had not gotten the license number.

I was home in bed when I received a phone call ten minutes later from the Sheriff's office. Getting dressed, I immediately went to the Sheriff's of-

---

[2] The night watchman's duty was to make sure the doors were locked, not to see if anyone had broken into a building through the roof.

[3] Currently the Citizens Bank in downtown Kilgore is located where the Kilgore Hotel stood.

fice in Longview. While it is true that Mathis had not been working my area heavily, I was very familiar with him and his known associates. As I said, I already had a thick folder on him. Remember, at that time the southern part of Bowie County[4] was part of my assigned territory. A few days before the Kilgore burglary I received a memo from the Kansas Bureau of Investigation concerning a burglary in Jamestown, Kansas. On the night of October 15-16 the safe in the Jamestown Co-Op Elevator had been burglarized. Jamestown's City Marshal had seen a 1962 or 1963 Chevrolet earlier in the day bearing the Texas license number LW-2284. They forwarded this information to Texas requesting any information we could provide. The owner of the car was identified as a known burglar, Henry Clift of Texarkana. Two of Clift's neighbors were also known burglaries: Lyman Birtcher, Jr., and, you got it, Charles Robert Mathis.

We had Mathis in custody and an unknown associate on the loose. Where there's smoke, there's fire. We figured the fugitive would be either Birtcher or Clift, possibly both. Just because Mayo and Davis had seen only one person, that did not mean the second was not around. Deputy Tex Pruitt and I broadcast a pickup on Lyman Birtcher and Henry Clift. Meanwhile, Kilgore Judge King Russell, after receiving evidence presented by Deputy Walter Jernigan, issued warrants for the arrests of Mathis, Birtcher, and Clift for attempted burglary.

When I heard Jerry Davis describe the man he saw fleeing the scene, and the Plymouth he drove, I had no doubt that we were looking for Lyman Birtcher. I contacted Bill Dowd, the Sheriff of Cass County,[5] and asked Bill, ". . . to get out there and set up a road block. Lyman Birtcher will be coming through there pretty quick on his way back to Texarkana." Birtcher managed to evade Sheriff Dowd, but not for long. Birtcher's car was found abandoned south of Texarkana. At 1:30 a.m. I got a call from the Texarkana, Texas, Police Department. Two of their officers, Patrolmen Dave Wilson and B. W. Fant, had arrested Birtcher.

Birtcher was no fool. He knew a man, Jerry Davis, had gotten a good look at him and his car. He had been in the stealing business a long time, and knew we would throw up a roadblock. So he had to move, and move fast. But like Mathis, this just wasn't his night. All the way from Longview, his car's battery had gotten weaker and weaker. By the time he reached Linden, the battery was finished. He was able to limp the car into a small country store that was still open. Fortunately for Birtcher, the store had a battery charger. Once recharged, the battery carried him to just outside Texarkana before it again played out. This time there was no store with a battery charger any-

---

[4] Texarkana, Texas, Mathis' home base, is located in northern Bowie County. It sits astride the Texas-Arkansas line, adjoining it's twin sister, Texarkana, Arkansas.

[5] Linden is the county seat.

where around; he had to dump the car. He managed to find a pay phone, and called his wife to come down from Texarkana to pick him up.

She picked him up, but then his luck gave out. Officers Wilson and Fant had been notified of the pickup request on Birtcher, and when they saw Mrs. Birtcher as she entered Texarkana, they stopped her. They found her husband laying in the backseat trying to avoid detection. They ordered him out of the car and arrested him. Texarkana Chief of Police, Jack O'Brien, took him back to Linden, where he deposited him in Bill Dowd's jail. The next morning Bill brought him to Longview.

Meanwhile, about midnight the Longview Police Department reported that one of the vehicles we had issued a pickup request on was parked in front of Jackson's Cafe in downtown Longview. Arriving at the cafe, I immediately spotted Clift's pickup. Accompanied by Longview Police Officers Sergeant O. R. Lockett and Patrolman Jim Thomas, we entered the cafe and arrested Clift and his companion, Johnnie Hopkins, Jr.

At 7:55 the following morning I received information from the Kilgore Police Department that the Lahaie Finance Company in Kilgore[6] had been burglarized. Lahaie Finance was one of several stores and businesses located along Main Street that shared a common roof. The burglars had climbed onto the roof, via an oil derrick,[7] and entered an office that adjoined Lahaie through a skylight. Inside the building the burglars had crawled through the attic until they were over Lahaie's offices. They removed a panel from the ceiling over a back office, and dropped to the floor of the finance company.

Lahaie's had a freestanding safe located in the front of the office. Once in the office, the burglars pushed it to the bathroom in the rear of the office suite. Safely away from the windows in the front of the office, they turned the safe onto its back, and peeled it.

Safes are constructed differently, but most are not a single sheet of steel. They are several layers of steel welded and riveted together. Every burglar had his own method of opening a safe. After you work enough safe peelers, their methods almost become a set of fingerprints. You could look at a peeled safe and most of the time you had a good idea who opened it, but regretfully, unlike fingerprints, the peeler's method could not be presented as conclusive proof in a court of law.

Two things you have to remember about peeling a safe—it's not quick, and it's hard work. In the movies when thieves burglarize a place, they have it down pat—in for so many seconds, and then out. Believe me, it doesn't work that way. It can sometimes take hours to peel a safe. And it is hard, hot,

---

[6] The Lahaie Finance Company was located at 205 East Main Street in downtown Kilgore.

[7] Remember that Kilgore was the heart of the East Texas Oil Field. Oil derricks in downtown Kilgore were as common as fence posts around a farmer's field.

sweaty work. It's also noisy. Take a sledge hammer and beat on a solid sheet of steel in a small, enclosed, area and see how quiet you are. That and any inquisitive eyes from anyone walking down the street was why Mathis moved the safe into the bathroom.

You would not believe some of things I have found at crime scenes: in addition to burglar's tools, it was not uncommon to find drinks and food. Some were so brazen as to leave their calling cards. One old burglar drank only Old Milwaukee Beer. I remember going to a crime scene and right there on top of the safe was a bottle of Old Milwaukee. Of course there were no prints, but I knew that he had left me a message—he wanted me to know who had peeled the safe. Well, I thought to myself, "OK, Partner, you won this hand, but we'll get you. Time is on our side."

Peeling a safe is pretty much a thing of the past now, but in the early '60s it was still a booming business. Peeling a safe is an art. I know that sounds foolish, but it is. At the risk of sounding redundant, each peeler has his own method, but they usually followed the same pattern. The first thing they do is lay the safe on its back. Most freestanding safes are on wheels, and if you don't lay it down, when you start beating on it, it will "walk" with you. So they lay it on its back, and knock the combination dial off. All safes have a main locking pin directly behind the dial that regulates all the locking pins. Every safe also has locking bars that go all the way around the door into the walls of the safe. With the door closed and the locking pins in place, the safe is locked. After knocking out the dial, most peelers try to punch the main pin. Using a hammer and punch they try to drive the main pin out. If they're successful, the pin will drop down and the rest of the pins will fall in place. When this happens, the safe is unlocked, and they simply open the door.

To stop someone from punching the main pin, safe makers started putting a canister of tear gas directly behind the pin. Their theory was simple: when the peeler punched the pin, it would rupture the canister; the tear gas would spill out, and, presto, the peeler is stopped in his tears. I'll admit it looks good on paper, but a lot of things that look good on paper are not worth a flip in reality. Old Charlie Mathis knew how to handle the tear gas problem. He always carried a handkerchief. If he ruptured a tear gas canister, he would urinate on the handkerchief, put it over his nose and eyes, and go right on working. You think I'm kidding; I'm not.

If Plan A, punching out the main pin didn't work, Plan B was fairly simple.[8] Take a heavy hammer, usually a sledgehammer, and hit it pretty close to one of the corners of the safe until it crimped. As soon as it crimped, the peeler would work a bar into the opening and force the metal back until it

---

[8] I have heard some old timers talk about a safe cracker using nitroglycerin, but in all my years I never saw nitro used.

167

started popping the rivets around the door, or, in extremely rare occasions, in the safe's back section. Like I said, it's hard work peeling a safe, but I guess in a thief's mind, it beats picking cotton.

In this case two tire irons had been used on the back of the safe.[9] Hello, Charlie. Apparently, old Charlie got heated up working so hard. He had moved a fan from the front office into the bathroom. It may have been November outside, but swinging a hammer in Lahaie's bathroom made it feel like it was August in Texas—and you haven't experienced hot until you've spent August in Texas. Like I said, thievin' can be, and usually is, hard work.

One thing you had to give old Charlie, he always tried to complete what he started. He opened the safe and gathered up the $359.69 that had been left in the safe over the weekend. Putting the money in a bank zipper bag, he knocked another hole in the ceiling of the bathroom, threw his tools through the opening, and pulled himself into the attic. On his way out, he dropped in on the office of Lahaie's neighbor, Dr. J. W. Fleming. This time he was not so successful in finding something to steal; Dr. Fleming reported nothing missing.

Charlie also believed in "equal opportunity thievin'." While he was in the attic he tried to gain entry into another office located beside Dr. Fleming. This time he was unsuccessful in gaining entry. I think he realized he had pushed his luck at not being discovered as far as he could. It was time to get out.

But he had already stayed too long. Climbing back down the oil derrick, he realized he had been spotted by the night watchman, E. F. Mayo. He dumped the moneybag behind an air conditioning unit. Obviously, he meant to evade Mayo, then come back and get the money. But this just wasn't Charlie's night—not only did he get himself shot, he got caught. The following morning, while searching the area, the Kilgore Police recovered the bank bag with the cash still in it.

Since it was only a superficial wound, it didn't take the doctor long to patch up Mathis and get him out of the hospital. Then he was taken to the Gregg County Jail. Once he was booked, Gregg County Deputy W. H. Owen and I questioned Mathis and Birtcher at length. Mathis would not give up, but Birtcher did.

In a sworn statement, Birtcher revealed that the previous Saturday, November 18, he had met Mathis in Texarkana. Mathis told him that he was AWOL[10] from the Army and he had to go back. But before he went back, he was going to Kilgore to burglarize a finance company that he believed had a

---

[9] In addition to the two tire tools, we also found a large ball pen hammer, a new large Craftsman screwdriver, one small screwdriver; one new pair of vice grips; and one pair of battery pliers.

[10] Absent Without Leave.

lot of money in its safe. It was a two-man job, and he wanted Birtcher to help. Birtcher wasn't sure, but he told Mathis he would let him know.

The next afternoon, Sunday, Birtcher decided that he could use some easy money, so he drove to Kilgore and found Mathis walking down Main Street casing the offices of his intended victims. Mathis got into the car and together they planned the robberies.

Returning after dark, they climbed onto the roof via the oil derrick and entered the building. Birtcher stood watch, while Mathis peeled the safe. As they climbed across the roofs of the buildings making their escape, Birtcher followed Mathis. While Mayo was busy nabbing Mathis, Birtcher was lying out of sight on top of the building. With Mayo occupied with Mathis, Birtcher made his break for freedom.

Still not totally satisfied that Mathis and Birtcher acted alone, Deputy Owen and I took Johnnie Hopkins, Jr. and Henry Clift to Dallas for a polygraph test. Both were cleared of any knowledge of the Lahaie robbery, but showed knowledge of other burglaries in East Texas. But those are other cases not in the scope of this book.

Mathis and Birtcher were both convicted, but for whatever reason, neither served any time. And for being AWOL Mathis received an honorable discharge from the Army.

As the years rolled by, Mathis was a constant thorn in my side. With the advent of all-night deposit slots at banks, no longer did businesses leave their next day bank deposits in their safes. Burglarizing safes suddenly became extremely unprofitable, and Charlie clearly had to find a new way to make a living. He did not consider honest work an option. Besides safes, throughout his career his area of operation was mainly rural area farms, ranches, and oil fields. Many thieves were already working the oil field, obviously too much competition, but farm and ranch equipment was another matter. The field was wide open to a smart, hardworking thief like Charlie Mathis.

Farm and yard equipment cost a great deal of money on the retail market, and the pluses in this field were many. Farm equipment was normally used in densely populated rural areas, far away from the general population. Even on the rare occasion when the equipment was run on the highway, licensing was not required, thus preventing a busybody lawman from running a plate. Another plus was that most brands of tractors, lawnmowers, bulldozers, backhoes, etc., looked pretty much the same. You almost always have to have the serial number to make a positive identification, which brought up maybe the most important point. To make a positive identification of the serial number, you had to get real close. Most people stored their equipment in barns and sheds when not in use, away from the prying eyes of a watchful lawman.

As for getting rid of the equipment, that would be the easiest part of the whole racket. All he had to do was line up his buyers before making the hit. Since the equipment was usually in a dealer's yard, most of the time he could make his hit during the night, or better yet, over the weekend, move it to another state, and have it sold before the victim even knew he had been burglarized.

I believe that most people are not stupid. If word starts getting around that an old boy has got several pieces of new, or almost new, equipment worth, say, $10,000, but he will let it go for $1,500, it doesn't take a rocket scientist to figure out that there is a fairly good chance that the equipment is hot. Regretfully, there are a lot of dishonest people in this old world who would swear on a head-high stack of Bibles that they consider themselves to be honest people. When we recovered stolen equipment, we almost always heard the same excuse, "Well, I had no idea that tractor (or whatever) was stolen." Of course not. They were just trying to help a poor old boy out who was so far down on his luck that he was having to sell truckloads of equipment for ten cents on the dollar.

From Mathis' point of view, it wasn't going to take a lot of money to get into business. He took a three-axle mobile home frame—which he also probably stole—cut it down to legal size, and built an enclosed van on it that was big enough to haul two or three tractors. He didn't bother to register it. He simply stole an old farm plate that no one would bother to report—after all the farmer would naturally think he had lost it in a field somewhere. As for a truck, that was easy. He could steal it. After finishing with it, he could sell it to a chop shop, or abandon it altogether.

Mathis was a wide-ranging entrepreneur. Yes, I said he changed his M. O. from safes to farm, industrial, and yard equipment. This is not to say he quit safes altogether. If he found one he thought had something of valuable in it, he still remembered quite well how to peel with the best of them. And, heavy competition or not, if he saw an easy heist of oil field equipment, he hit it. He even stole mobile homes.

To show you how brazen this guy could be, one time he stole a mobile home with the owner in it! I kid you not. It happened in Jacksonville, Texas. The owner had disconnected the utilities, unblocked the mobile home, and hooked his truck to it. Since it was late in the day, he decided to get a good night's sleep before pulling out. Quite naturally, he decided to sleep in his mobile home. Why rent a motel room when he had a perfectly good bed with him? I don't know who was in for the bigger shock, the victim or the thief. When his bed literally started moving, the owner jumped out of the mobile home and went one way. Mathis, equally bewildered seeing a man jump out of the mobile home, went the other way—but with the mobile home. (It was eventually recovered.) Mathis was a real piece of work.

Mathis was good, or he would not have lasted as long as he did; but even the best foul up, and it's usually something pretty small they foul up on. Mathis was no exception.

At 1:00 a.m., on June 3, 1967, Mathis and an accomplice, his juvenile stepbrother, were seen driving a stolen 1967 Chevrolet pickup near Avinger, Texas, by Highway Patrolman Ralph Allen and Linden Constable O. R. McMillon. The chase was on. Roaring up Highway 155 between Avinger and Linden at a very high rate of speed, Trooper Allen was able to get his patrol car beside Mathis, but Mathis turned into Allen, forcing him off the road and wrecking his patrol car. Fortunately, Allen was not seriously injured.

Meanwhile, Constable McMillon continued the chase and opened fire on Mathis, hitting one of the pickup tires. Losing control of his vehicle, Mathis left the road and smashed into a ditch. He and his stepbrother jumped out of the pickup and fled into the woods. They managed to evade capture until about eleven o'clock the next morning when Highway Patrolman Paul Boone[11] located them hiding in the woods near Pruitt's Lake. Spending the night in the woods without any food or shelter has a way of taking the starch out of a would-be tough guy's spine. Both meekly surrendered to Boone.

The pickup had been stolen in Mineola on May 24. The same day, a 1965 Chevrolet pickup that had been stolen in Texarkana (Mathis' home at the time) was found abandoned in Mineola. As for the '67 pickup, Mathis had made a few modifications to it. He had equipped it with a special rear bumper made of heavy steel, mounted on pieces of stout two-inch pipe. He designed the pipe so that it would slide in and out at the rear of the pickup. He had also added sideboards, a rear door made of three-quarter-inch plywood, a gas can, and two-by-six-inch boards in the bed of the pickup. It was apparent he had designed the truck to haul small garden and yard tractors.

Also, the license plate on the pickup was stolen, as was the mobile home license plate we found in the truck. We also found a stolen Enco credit card on Mathis. The card had been issued to the Atlas Tile Company of Longview. J. C. Steel, the owner of the card, had used it at Monty Hill's Humble Service Station in Longview and left it by mistake. Mathis was in Hill's shortly thereafter, saw the card, and grabbed it along with Hill's personal card, which was also lying on the counter. (As I have said repeatedly, this guy would steal anything.) Mathis' stepbrother advised me that Mathis had used the card in Atlanta, Texas, forging Steel's signature to buy five dollars worth of gasoline.

Mathis' stepbrother and accomplice, also from Texarkana, was a sixteen-year-old juvenile. (I guess Mathis figured that the family that stole together, stayed together.) He said his stepbrother had picked him up in Texarkana, and they had both been drinking heavily. At the time Allen started

---

[11] At the time of this writing Paul Boone is the Sheriff of Cass (Linden) County, Texas.

chasing them, they were on their way to Longview.

We charged Mathis with grand theft auto, contributing to the delinquency of a minor, and forgery (the credit card purchase). This happened on a Saturday. By Sunday, Mathis had made his $5,000 bail, and never served another minute. Even then, you sometimes had to wonder about our justice system.

The years rolled by and Mathis continued stealing everything in sight. He was hitting mainly in Texas, Arkansas, Louisiana, and Oklahoma. In 1967, he slipped up in Oklahoma and they sent him to jail on a two-year sentence, of which he served only a few months. When he got out, it was back to business as usual. Everything ends, and by 1970 things were building to a climax.

During most of his career, Mathis had lived in Texarkana, Texas, but by 1970 he had moved to Longview and was living in a mobile home park on Gilmer Road. I do not to this day know why he moved to Longview. He claimed to be a mechanic, and was running a so-called auto repair shop out of a garage beside his home. He was a pretty good mechanic, but I can assure you, that was not how he was making his living.

On December 4, I arrested Mathis on a Fugitive Warrant from the state of Louisiana. I went out to his mobile home at about eight o'clock that morning and woke him and his wife. When he came to the door I told him to get dressed because I had a warrant for his arrest, and I was going to take him to the county jail.

He asked if it would be all right if he shaved and showered before going to the jail. I told him he could. There was no need to get into a knockdown, drag-out over something like this. Both of us had been down this road many, many times in the past, and knew there was nothing to get excited about. We both knew he would probably make bond and be home before I finished the paperwork booking him in. (We were right. I booked him at 9:05 a.m.; at 11:15 a.m. he had made $2,500 bail and left the courthouse—before I had finished the paperwork)

He invited me to come in and sit down while he cleaned up. He asked his wife to make coffee and fix me something to eat. I told her I would appreciate the coffee, but not to fix anything for me.

I sat at the kitchen table talking to Mathis as he shaved. I told him he better knock off the stealing. If he didn't, sooner or later I was going to get him. He assured me that I had nothing to worry about. He and his sons were going to purchase a convenience store in north Longview and straighten up and act right. I couldn't help thinking to myself, "Yeah, I'll bet."

You may wonder why I let him shower and shave before going to jail, or how in the world I could sit in a thief's home and drink coffee. Take my word for it, we both knew this was no game we were playing. I knew, and never forgot for an instant, what his business was. Likewise, I have absolutely no doubt he knew the same about me. An adage says, God gave each one of us

172

one mouth and two ears for a reason. I have sat around and listened to many a thief talk himself into prison. You would be amazed at how much information they will inadvertently give you. A Ranger Captain once said, and it's probably true, that ninety percent of the people in prison today are there because they can't keep their mouth shut.

A few days later, I finally got the big break I had been waiting for. In western Harrison County, Bob Mitchell and I arrested one of Mathis' running buddies, Larry Fyffe, with some televisions, radios, and other items; he had stolen them from an appliance store in Tyler, which was Bob's territory. Fyffe was not made of real strong material. He was much more concerned with saving his own butt, than Mathis'. You've heard of "the twinkling of an eye"; that's about how long it took Fyffe to roll over on Mathis.

To save his own hide he agreed to become an informant on Mathis. I knew now was the time to take Mathis down with major prison time. "One riot, one Ranger" notwithstanding, I needed help. I have never been too proud to ask for help when I needed it, and I needed it now.

The Department of Public Safety had formed a major crime task force for operations against major criminals like Mathis. Mitchell and I went to our Captain, Bill Wilson, and told him the situation and why we felt we needed the assistance of the task force. With an inside informer, Larry Fyffe, if we put Mathis under twenty-four hour a day surveillance, we thought it would not take long to bring Mathis down. Captain Wilson agreed. He took our case on up the ladder until it reached the Chief of Criminal Law Enforcement, Jim Ray—the same Jim Ray that I had worked with in the past. Jim had worked his way all the way up to the second highest law enforcement officer in the State of Texas.[12] Chief Ray studied our request and agreed that the task force was needed.

We rented a mobile home across the street from Mathis' movile home and started twenty-four-hour surveillance. Mathis was in the process of building another trailer, like the one discussed earlier. Our snitch, Larry Fyffe, didn't know for sure where it would take place, but a hit was definitely on. They were going to steal a John Deere 450C bulldozer on Sunday, December 20. Mathis had already collected a $2,500 payment in advance.[13] They had surveyed three different John Deere dealers in Decatur, Huntsville, and Dallas. It was going to be one of the three, but Mathis had not yet decided which one. Fyffe thought Mathis was leaning toward the dealership in Dallas.

Huntsville is in Company A's area, headquartered in Houston; Decatur

---

[12] Since the reorganization of the DPS in 1935, Jim Ray has achieved higher rank in the Department of Public Safety than anyone who has ever been a Texas Ranger. I know I am biased, but it could not have happened to a finer person.

[13] In 1970, a new John Deere 450C bulldozer was worth about $20,000.

is in Company C's, headquartered in Lubbock. We informed each as to what information we had. Each, in turn, sat up surveillance at the John Deere tractor dealers in their respective cities.

On Saturday night, December 19, Red Arnold, Bob Mitchell, Max Womack,[14] and I sat in the shop building of Riverview Equipment Company in Dallas,[15] and waited. In the unlikely event that Mathis got away from us, Stuart Dowell, a new Ranger stationed in Dallas and a member of the organized crime task force, along with members of the Dallas Police Department, waited in the surrounding area.

Even though we thought Dallas was where they were going to hit, we still did not know for sure. That is, we didn't know for sure until about noon that Sunday morning. To make sure no one happened to be at his intended target, one of Mathis' favorite tricks was to call the intended victim before breaking in. If anyone answered, he simply hung up and walked away. Shortly after noon the phone started ringing. And it rang, and rang, and rang.

Bob Mitchell: "I know it rang for only a minute or so, but it seemed like it rang forever."

It wasn't enough to simply catch Mathis on Riverview's property, which would have been only trespassing. He would have laughed himself to death if we had arrested him for that. We had to catch him in the act of stealing. We didn't have long to wait.

Both Mathis and Fyffe shortly appeared in the dealership's back lot. The first thing Mathis did was hot-wire a three-ton Chevrolet truck that was designed to haul heavy equipment. After positioning the truck and dropping the bed to its loading position, he jumped out of the cab and disappeared out of sight. Almost immediately we heard an engine start and saw Mathis come into sight driving a new bulldozer. While this was going on, Fyffe was lying low. He thought we were on the grounds, but he didn't know our exact location.

Meanwhile, the four of us were still in the shop building. When Mathis came into sight sitting on the dozer, that was what we had been waiting for. Now there could not be the slightest doubt he was stealing. I came out of the shop door first, followed closely by Bob Mitchell, Max Womack, and Red Arnold.

Mathis was looking over his shoulder so intently as he backed the dozer onto the truck that he did not see us until we were directly in front of the dozer and yelled, "Police. Stop." Hearing our warning yell, he snapped around, stood

---

[14] Mathis had been working all of our areas: Red Arnold in Mount Pleasant, Bob Mitchell in Tyler, and Max Womack in Atlanta.

[15] In 1970, Riverview Equipment was located at 7919 Harry Hines Boulevard, Dallas, Texas.

up, and reached for a pistol he carried in his belt. He shouldn't have done that. All of us were armed for the occasion.

When he grabbed his pistol, we fired. Our shots lifted him up and over the side of the dozer and onto the ground. As he was falling, he became entangled in the dozer's steering clutches and the dozer also went over the side of the truck, landing directly on top of Mathis. Being hit the way he was from our fire, I do not believe Mathis ever felt a thing.

Seeing his body entangled in the churning tracks of the still-running dozer, all of us ran to the dozer, but by the time we managed to kill the engine, the rotating tracks had done terrible damage to Mathis' body.

We had promised Fyffe that we would not arrest him in return for his help. So while we were busy shutting down the dozer, he left the area. I have been asked how we could let a known thief like Fyffe walk away. Given this situation, you have to ask yourself, "Is it better to recover countless thousands of dollars of people's hard-earned money, or take down a two-bit little thief like Larry Fyffe." If we had not given up something—freedom to Fyffe—he would have had no reason to help us catch Mathis, which also led us to over a million dollars of stolen equipment.

Another thing: a guy like Fyffe would believe that he beat the system, when actually he didn't. We knew it would be only a matter of time before he stole again, and one of us would be waiting for him. We were right. He would shortly steal again; the law was waiting, and he did go to jail.

Since the shooting had taken place inside the city limits of Dallas, the Dallas Police Department did the crime scene investigation. On January 6, 1971, the case was presented to the Dallas Grand Jury. It reported the shooting as "Justifiable Homicide."

I have been asked what it felt like to have been involved in the taking of a human life. Let me tell you, if a man is pointing a gun at you, and you know he will use it,[16] you sleep with a clear and untroubled conscience.

In the ensuing weeks Rangers Red Arnold, Stuart Dowell, Bob Mitchell, Roy Scott, Max Womack, and I started gathering up stolen property in Arkansas, Louisiana, Oklahoma, and Texas. Besides the places that Fyffe told us about, we subpoenaed the telephone records of Mathis, Fyffe, and some of their other known associates. By the time we finished we had gathered up over one million dollars in stolen equipment. That's in 1970 dollars. What would a million dollars be worth today?

---

[16] A few years earlier, Mathis had pistol-whipped a man he thought was messing around with his wife. When he hit the man, the pistol went off, barely brushing his victim's scalp.

CHAPTER X
DEATH OF A MATRIARCH

On a rainy night in July, 1975, seventy-five year old Inez Phillips was murdered at her home in Gladewater. Mrs. Phillips, widow of oilman and former Gladewater mayor, Loyce Phillips, was a wealthy woman. We have all seen the typical Hollywood portrait of the wealthy person—arrogant, selfish, and self-centered. In no shape, form, or fashion did Inez Phillips fit that mold. I have known my share of wealthy people, but not one gave more freely of herself, her time, and her wealth to community and church work than did Mrs. Phillips. Without question, she was one of Gregg County's most beloved matriarchs.

Inez Scarborough was twenty-one years old when she stepped off the train in Gladewater in 1921. Raised in Cameron, Texas, Gladewater's newest schoolteacher had only recently earned her teaching certificate at San Marcos, Texas. She was the type of person who was easy to like, and in short order she conquered the hearts of the citizens of her new hometown.

When she received her first paycheck, she headed to the closest bank—the Everett Bank—to cash it. At the bank she met Loyce Phillips. It was a case of love at first sight. Loyce and Inez were made for each other, and only a few short months passed before they were married. Staying in Gladewater, they prospered and in 1927 they built a new home at 428 North Main Street—the last address either would ever have.

In 1930 Dad Joiner brought in the Daisy Bradford Number Three, thus starting the greatest oil field in history up until that time, the East Texas Oil Field. It also set off one of the wildest booms anyone had ever seen. Taking advantage of a smart business situation, wise lending and investing, during the boom years that followed, Loyce and Inez became a prosperous and affluent couple. In later years Loyce became mayor of Gladewater. But even with all their wealth and influence, they did not horde their money. Church and community activities ranked at the top, and they never missed an opportunity to help both.

As the years passed, Loyce and Inez enjoyed a very happy and fulfilling marriage that would only end with his death early in 1975. Mrs. Phillips continued living at their home until that fateful night on July 8, 1975.

The morning of July 9 started as most mornings for Frankie Howard, the Phillips' maid. As usual, Mrs. Howard entered the house through the sliding patio doors in the rear of the house. Though Mrs. Phillips normally kept all the other doors in the house locked, she usually left the patio doors unlocked for her maid. Mrs. Howard arrived for work at 8:30, her normal time. She proceeded with her regular house duties for about twenty minutes. By 8:50 Mrs. Phillips still had not joined her. This was most unusual.

Concerned, she started searching for Mrs. Phillips. Entering the master bedroom she found her lying on her bed in a pool of blood. A butcher knife, buried to the hilt, was protruding from the center of her chest.

Terrified, Mrs. Howard ran screaming from the bedroom to a phone in an adjoining room. She called the office of the Phillips Oil Company located beside and north of the Phillips home. A long-time Phillips employee, Bill Sorrells, took the call. Unable to make heads or tails of the frantic Mrs. Howard, he was finally able to calm her enough to determine that Mrs. Phillips was hurt badly. He placed an emergency call to the Phillips' family doctor, then rushed to Mrs. Phillips' home. As soon as he saw Mrs. Phillips, he called the Gladewater Police Department.

Gladewater Police Department log records show Sorrells' call came in at 9:15 a.m. Gladewater Chief of Police, Jay Banks,[1] called me immediately at my office in Longview. I immediately left and headed the fifteen miles to Gladewater, arriving at the Phillips home at 9:39. I had no idea that for the better part of the next two years this case would dominate much of my time and efforts.

Entering Mrs. Phillips' bedroom I was met with a grizzly sight. She was laying on her back near the edge of her bed. She was fully clothed, wearing white slacks and a blue blouse. Her hairpiece was found near her left knee. Her right leg was hanging off the side of the bed, with her foot on the floor. Likewise, her left leg was also hanging off the bed, almost reaching the floor. She did not have her shoes on. The shoes were on the opposite side of the bed, lying in a very irregular position, indicating they had either been removed by the attacker, or had come off while the body was being dragged across the floor. Adhesive tape had been used to bind her hands and to gag her. It was obvious that she had been struck on the head by at least two blows. As if this were not enough, protruding from the center of her chest was a butcher knife—buried to the hilt. Later investigation showed it to be an eight-inch knife, with a six-and-a-quarter-inch blade.

---

[1] This is the same Jay Banks who had been a Texas Ranger Captain. Jay retired from the Rangers in 1959. Subsequently he served as the Chief of Police in Big Spring, Texas; Palestine, Texas; then Gladewater.

Joining me at the crime scene investigation was Bill Roach and Frank Odom[2] of the Gregg County Sheriff's office, and Bill Brown of the Gladewater Police Department.

From the condition of the bedroom, there had apparently been little or no struggle. The only bloodstains were those on the bed. We saw a bullet hole in one of the windows, but could find no apparent bullet wounds or powder burns on her body. We suspected the killer had either fired the gun to scare Mrs. Phillips, or she had made a break for freedom and the gun had been fired to stop her. Whatever the reason, the bullet had gone through the drapes of the south window of the master bedroom, across a small yard, and entered through the top left pane of a window to a bedroom in an adjacent wing of the house. We found the spent bullet lying in the middle of a bed.

We correctly assumed the bullet to be a .38 caliber. Later our lab confirmed that not only was it a .38, but it had been fired from an Arminius .38 Special revolver. The land and grooves of the Arminius were unusual—a right twist, with ten lands and grooves.[3] In the upcoming months this unusually-marked bullet would lead me on many a wild-goose chase all over the Southwest. After we solved the case we learned that the pistol had gone off accidentally when the killer struck Mrs. Phillips on the head, but I'll say more about this later.

It was obvious that the killer, or killers, knew what they were looking for. The only part of the house that had been disturbed was the bedroom and closet where the murder took place. This part of the house had been turned upside down. The clothes from the closet were thrown about, the drawers in all the furniture had been emptied with the drawers thrown on the floor.[4] It did not appear as if Mrs. Phillips' body had been robbed of any jewelry.

Further examination of the body revealed one piece of broken adhesive tape around her wrist. We believed that sometime before being killed, she had possibly worked her hands loose. We felt that this was possibly when the gun had been fired. Closer examination showed several marks on her back, two of which were superficial. We theorized that these were inflicted as tor-

---

[2] Within a few months of Mrs. Phillips murder, Frank became a Special Investigator for the Gregg County District Attorney's office

[3] The accuracy of any modern pistol or rifle is the result of the bullet spinning as it travels down the bore of the weapon. This is accomplished by grooves in the barrel that force the bullet to spin as it travels down the barrel. Thus, how many times it "twists" in its journey down the barrel is different for different guns. Each gun leaves its own distinct marks (called "lands and grooves") on a fired bullet. Just as no two sets of fingerprints are exactly the same, no two guns leave the exact same "lands and grooves" on a bullet.

[4] Earlier I said that it was apparent there had been little or no struggle. There is a big difference in a room that has been ransacked and one where a struggle has taken place.

ture to obtain the combination to the safe, or the location of other valuables. It was my opinion then, and now, that if Mrs. Phillips had told the thieves what they wanted to know, they would not have killed her.

Laying on top of a closet dresser we found a labeled folder that had once contained, or had been intended to contain, the owner's manual to a floor safe like the one in Mrs. Phillips' kitchen. Continuing the investigation, we found the safe and the paper with the combination on it in a closet in the rear of the house. The safe was open—and empty. Not knowing what was in the safe and finding no inventory list anywhere in the house, we had no way of knowing if anything had been taken from the safe.

By the time we finished the on-site investigation late that evening, several things had become clear:

1. Obviously, there had been a killer-thief in the house. We thought there could have been two robbers, or more. But due to her age, one person could have easily overpowered her. Regrettably the crime scene gave us no clues as to how many persons had been in the house. It was not until the end of the case before we were positive that more than one person was involved.

2. The killer-thief had known the layout of the house, or at the very least had very good information about the house.

3. Robbery of the floor safe was the apparent reason for entry.

4. Resistance by Mrs. Phillips to the robbers had been minimal.

5. The night of the murder had been rainy and few people were on the street. The Phillips' house, like most of the houses in the area, was on a large lot with no neighbors close by. The house directly south of the house was also owned by the Phillips and was vacant. The building to the north was the Phillips Oil Company headquarters and it too was vacant at night. Also, sound does not carry well in the rain. A shot could very well have been fired without any of the neighbors hearing it.

Shortly before finishing our crime scene investigation, Mrs. Phillips' son, Jack, returned from Midland where he had been on business. He requested that his mother's body be sent to the Malcolm Stone Funeral Home in Gladewater.

Before preparation for burial, Justice of the Peace Ross DeLay ordered an autopsy. Until the autopsy report returned, we worked under the assumption that the knife wound was the cause of death. However, the autopsy showed that Mrs. Phillips had died instantly from one of the blows to the back of her head. She was already dead when the knife was plunged into her chest! Even though she had not been violated sexually, it was hard not to think we were up against some kind of sadist.

Things started moving quickly. Because of prior testing obligations, state polygraph operators could not be sent immediately, so Jack Phillips hired a private operator to fill the void. When two State operators finally arrived,

180

one from Austin and the other from Dallas, we set them up at the Gregg County Courthouse in Longview. Rangers Red Arnold from Mount Pleasant and Max Womack from Atlanta came to Gladewater to assist me. We had fingerprinted the whole Phillips house and several prints could not be identified. When we questioned any suspect they were fingerprinted and Red, a fingerprint expert, compared their prints with whose we had lifted at the Phillips home.

Meanwhile, Max was in charge of an 800 watts "Hot Line" we had installed in a local motel on Highway 80 between Gladewater and Longview. We hoped that someone would supply us a tip via the "Hot Line", and for the better part of the next three weeks we manned it around the clock. When time allowed, Red and I, with occasional help from Ranger Charlie Moore from Dallas, assisted Max. And we did need occasional help. Manning the Hot Line was in itself a full-time job.

Meanwhile, Jack Phillips, Mrs. Phillips' son and the president of Phillips Oil Company, offered a $50,000 reward for any information that would lead to the arrest and conviction of anyone related to the murder of his mother. The reward was offered for thirty days, then extended another thirty days. We knew that anyone who had information about the killing would more than likely come forth in that time frame. Usually people who come forth beyond that time frame are mainly cranks.

Jack Phillips was very active, as anyone would have been, in keeping abreast of his mother's case. I kept Jack as informed as best as I could. Jack was—and is—a real go-getter and a couple of times he became impatient. Feeling that I did not have sufficient manpower to solve the case, he called the Chief of the Criminal Investigation Division[5] of the Department of Public Safety, Jim Ray,[6] and suggested that I might need more help. He went so far as to offer to pay for any extra help out of his own pocket.

Jim called me and asked if I needed any further help. I told him I didn't. With Max Womack and Red Arnold's assistance, I had all the help I needed. Max mainly manned the Hot Line. I had worked with Max a lot in the past few years and I knew how good he was. Red handled the fingerprints. He had worked in the Identification Bureau before joining the highway patrol and there was nobody better at connecting fingerprints than Red. Charlie Moore, stationed in Dallas, was spending a lot of time helping. Besides the

---

[5] At that time the Rangers were under the immediate command of the CID. (Criminal Investigation Division)

[6] This is the same Jim Ray who as a Ranger had been stationed in Tyler. Later Jim was promoted and became Captain of Company C in Midland. Then Colonel Pat Spier asked Jim to go to Austin and assume command of the CID. Jim served, with great distinction, as the Chief of Criminal Law Enforcement (CLE) for ten years. The Chief of the CLE answers directly to the Colonel of the DPS. Since the reorganization of the DPS in 1935, no Ranger has risen to this high rank in the DPS.

Rangers, we had two polygraph operators, Sheriff Tom Welch's Gregg County Sheriff's Office, the Gregg County District Attorney's investigators, and Jay Banks and his Gladewater Police Department. We had more than enough help. I knew if I needed more assistance, all I had to do was pick up the phone and call the Captain in Dallas and help would be on the way. Chief Ray agreed that I obviously had a firm grip on the situation.

I knew this case was going to be tough and long. If I could not do all the work myself, and I knew that I could not, there was no one I had more confidence in or wanted more than Max Womack and Red Arnold. No better men have ever worn the badge of a Texas Ranger than these two men.

I visited Jack and told him I understood his frustration, and asked if he would please bear with me. I promised we would do everything in our power to catch his mother's killers. It was a promise I meant to keep.

Much to my regret, I have seen officers promise grieving families not to worry, one way or another they would solve their case. I never did; I never could. Neither I nor anyone else can make such a promise with the certainty that we can keep it. There are too many unsolved crimes on the books—some of them mine—to make such a rash statement. The most we can offer is to promise to do our best. And we can never, ever, do less.

Unfortunately we got some offers of help I could have done without. A psychic guaranteed she could solve the case. When you don't want to leave any stone unturned, sometimes you accept unwanted assistance, even when you know what the results will be. And the results were exactly what I thought they would be. Zero.

Almost immediately people started coming to us from all over, trying to be helpful. The overwhelming majority simply wanted to be helpful. A few wanted to collect the fifty thousand dollars. Most of the reports were well intended, but of little value. While passing Mrs. Phillips' home near the time of the murder, they had seen so-and-so with so-and-so near the house. We followed every lead. All turned out to be either false, or, as in most cases, the suspect had a legitimate reason for being there.

Every lead was a deadend until Darline Henderson came forward on July 10. She related a story that gave us our first positive glimmer of hope. Mrs. Henderson worked nights at the 7-11 Store on Highway 80 in Gladewater. About 12:30 or 1:00 on the morning of July 9 a regular customer had come into the store and made two small purchases. She said this was unusual because he usually came into the store every morning just before she got off duty at 7:00 o'clock.

Seeing him nearly every morning she had learned that his name was James and that he was from West Texas. She described him as being about 5'10" and weighing about 150 pounds—large enough to have overpowered a frail seventy-five-year-old lady.

On the day of the murder, not only had James come into the store at a different time than usual, but he was also bleeding slightly from the corner of his mouth. He also had blood on his hands and on his shirt. Darline thought he had been in a fight, but she did not question him. Of course this was before she had any knowledge of the murder only a short distance from the 7-11.

Darline described his vehicle as an older model, dark blue El Camino pickup. She had never had a reason to learn the pickup's license number, but if he came back she would write it down. Unfortunately, he never came back, at least not while he was a suspect.

A few days later, on July 14, we eliminated James as a suspect. We tracked James down and found out that he had arrived in Gladewater three months earlier to work in the oil patch. At the time of the murder he was working for Ranger Well Service in Kilgore.

When he got off work at 5:30 on the afternoon of July 8, he had a message from his girlfriend. She wanted to see him. Would he come by for short visit? She had been living with him for several weeks, but they had a falling out and she had taken up with another man.

They met, but after talking for about thirty minutes, he begrudgingly admitted to himself that reconciliation was not possible. He asked her if she wanted him to bring the rest of her clothes to her. She did. He left and went to his house in Gladewater and picked up the remainder of her clothing. When he arrived back at Kilgore he found, much to his injured pride, his former girlfriend outside talking to her new boyfriend. He asked her where she wanted him to put the clothes. She pointed to her mother's home. He bit his tongue and kept his mouth shut. Taking the remainder of her clothes out of his pickup, he sat them on the porch and left.

He was hungry so he went to the local Pizza Hut for supper.[7] He finished eating at about 10:00 and went to the Capri Club in Kilgore for a few beers.

Drinking more "Who Hit John" than was good for him, James left the Capri Club at about 11:30. Emboldened by the liquor, he decided to give reconciliation one more try. Arriving at her house he was met at the door, not by his former girlfriend, but by her new boyfriend. Heated words quickly followed and soon fists were flying. James broke the new boyfriend's nose. Retaliating, the boyfriend grasped a pair of scissors lying on a nearby table and slashed James in his left side. Fortunately, the wound was just a scratch, but it was enough to end the fight.

James left and headed back to the Capri Club. By the time he arrived it

---

[7] It was easy to collaborate James' meal at the Pizza Hut. Employees of the Pizza Hut remembered him well. For whatever reason, the sandwich he ordered took such a long time in being served that he was not charged for his meal. This was about the only piece of luck James had all night.

had already closed. Realizing the possible serious implications of the fight, he went back to the girlfriend's house to try to smooth things over. The new boyfriend had also had all the fight he wanted. He told James he was going to the doctor to get his nose worked on. In the spirit of reconciliation James gave him twenty dollars to pay the doctor.

About this time, the girlfriend's mother arrived at home and demanded to know what was going on. After explaining to her mother what had happened, her mother ordered James to leave. He left and returned to Gladewater. Arriving in Gladewater about 12:30 or 1:00 in the morning, he went to the 7-11 Store were Darline Henderson worked. It turned out he had only stopped to pick up food for his lunch the next day.

So much for a quick end to the case.

Shortly before her murder, Mrs. Phillips had an additional room and closet built onto her home. She dearly loved to can fresh garden produce and had built the new room near the kitchen to use as a canning room. In the new closet she had a floor safe installed.

About two years before the new room was added, her home had been burglarized and her safe stolen. It contained a substantial amount of her jewelry and other valuables. When the addition was built on she insisted on a floor safe. She did not want anyone to be able to steal the whole safe again.

I had not worked the 1973 burglary, but I was familiar with it. I requested and received the case file from the local authorities. Reviewing the pictures of the crime scene from two years earlier, I was immediately struck by the similarities of the two incidents. If you added a body to the first crime scene, the two crime scenes looked almost identical. The thieves had even parked their cars at almost the exact location. The earlier crime had never been solved, so it was no giant leap of imagination to suspect that the criminals could very well have returned to strike again.

As in the first burglary, the culprits knew exactly what they were looking for—the floor safe. One of the first questions I had to answer was, how many people knew about the safe?

Obviously the first people to question were the people who had installed the safe and the contractors who had built the add-ons. We questioned and polygraphed many, but not all, of the contractors and their employers—all with negative results.

Looking at evidence from the previous burglary, we found a piece of a key with the letter "H" stenciled into it. It was attached to a pull-apart key ring. From the half key I could make out the letters *B* and *Mc*. One of the largest automobile dealerships in Texas is Bill McDavid Pontiac in Fort Worth, so it was not illogical to assume the key came from there.

In the first burglary the thieves had rolled the safe out of the house and across the yard to the driveway of the house next door where they had left their car. It was in the driveway of the neighboring house that the partial key and key ring had been found. I asked the local authorities if they had done anything with this evidence. They had not.

I took the key and key ring to Fort Worth and looked up Tom Arnold, the local Ranger. I asked Tom if he would go to McDavid's Pontiac and try to match the partial key with an automobile. If he could do that, it would be no problem to find out who owned it, their address, and any lien information concerning the automobile.

Tom and McDavid's General Manager, Ken Yates, determined that this particular key blank was a trunk and glove box key of a 1969 or 1973 model General Motors vehicle. By placing the key in a key cutting machine they were able identify that the key was from cut number 533434. The key code book revealed that this number was prefaced by either 2J14 on 1969 model vehicles, or 20L2 on the 1973 model.

Tom went through 1,800 sales records for 1969 models with negative results. Undaunted, he turned to the 1973 models and searched another 2,400 records. And then, there it was. 20L2-533434, a 1973 red Pontiac Bonneville hardtop coup; serial number 2N57R3X161283. The man who had originally bought the car financed it with the First National Bank in Fort Worth on April 9, 1973. The buyer lived at 6433 Rosemont, Fort Worth, Texas. But what really lit up my eyes was the name of the purchaser, Henry Bowen.

Henry was well known to the Rangers. He was a known thief who ran with Jerry Ray James.[8] Jerry Ray was an all-around bad guy. In addition to bossing a gang of thieves, he ran a prostitution ring, and anything else that would turn a quick buck—legal or illegal. The gang's M. O. was to break into the homes and businesses of wealthy people, tie them up, terrorize them, and rob them. The list of their suspected crimes was very lengthy.

Following up on the lead, Tom went to the First National Bank in Fort Worth. He visited with Tom Turner, a loan officer of the bank. Examining the records, Tom learned that another well-known gambler, Curtis Garrett, had co-signed the note with Bowen. Furthermore, Mr. Turner revealed that the loan was continuously delinquent and he had finally insisted that the note be paid off in full. On January 21, 1974, it was.

Through vehicle registrations Tom learned that Bowen, on April 3, 1975, had traded the Pontiac for a new Oldsmobile at Worden McDavid Oldsmobile in Weatherford, Texas. The current owner of the vehicle was Harley Bradley

---

[8] Later, while in prison, Jerry Ray James's cell mate, Charles Harrelson, confided to James that he had killed, for hire, Federal Judge John Wood on the Bexar County Courthouse steps in San Antonio. To get out of prison, James rolled over on Harrelson. Harrelson is the father of Woody Harrelson, star of the popular television series "Cheers." Charles Harrelson received a life sentence. Jerry Ray James is today living in the Federal Witness Protective Program.

of Fort Worth. Tom contacted Mr. Bradley at his job at the Oak Grove Airport in the Fort Worth area. Mr. Bradley was totally cooperative. Inspection of the vehicle showed that the key would not fit the trunk, but it did fit the glove compartment. Sometime in the past the trunk lid and lock had been so severely damaged that the lock had to be replaced. As for the lid, repairs had been attempted, but without success. Bradley said that the trunk leaked and nothing he did seemed to stop it.

Coincidentally, "street talk" in the Fort Worth Police Department's files had it that Bowen once had a safe in the trunk of his car, but he had lost the key, and the only way he could get into it was to bust the lock. "Street talk" also revealed that Bowen had in the past owned a .38 pistol. Could it be an Arminius with ten right turn twists? As it turned out, no, it was not.

None of the local officials knew the present whereabouts of Bowen, so surveillances of his known associates were started. Weeks passed, and still no Bowen. But as the old saying goes, "There's more than one way to skin a cat." You can not be a Texas Ranger as long as I was and not know a few tricks.

It's common knowledge in law enforcement circles as to who makes bonds for certain thugs, crooks, and other lowlifes. Jerry Ray James' and Henry Bowen's favorite bondsman was none other than one Curtis Garrett—the same Curtis Garrett who had co-signed Bowen's note at Fort Worth's First National Bank for the '73 Pontiac. If anyone knew where Bowen was, it would be Garrett.

On August 20, 1975, I called Garrett and told him I was in Fort Worth and needed to see him. At first he was reluctant to meet, but when I assured him I was alone, he agreed. Even I gave a double take when he told me where he wanted to meet—an ice cream parlor on Fort Worth Avenue. The last thing in the world Garrett wanted was to be seen with a Texas Ranger. I presume he reasoned that none of his associates would ever be caught dead in an ice cream parlor, so he must have felt safe meeting me there. I couldn't have cared less why he wanted to meet there. I wanted to talk to him, so we met at the ice cream parlor. I didn't waste words with small talk. I told him I needed to talk to Bowen about an important case. "All I want you to do is get in touch with him. Leave it up to Henry whether he wants to talk to me or not." I knew Bowen would have no problem talking to me, unless he was the killer.

Trying to put the old con on me, Garrett said, "Well now, Mr. Elliott, I just don't have any idea where I can reach Henry."

"Get him the message, Garrett. That's all I'm asking you to do."

Leaving no doubt as to where I stood, I said, "Garrett, you and I both know you can't stand a whole lot of scrutiny from the Rangers. Get him the message."

Then I told Garrett, "I'm tired and I am going to Dallas to get a motel

186

room. You can get reach of me through the DPS headquarters in Dallas."

I left and headed for Dallas. Before going to the motel I went to our headquarters on Beltline and I-30[9] to fill my car with gas. I always filled up at night. You might not have time to get gas the following morning. You never knew when something would come up during the night and you would have to hit the ground running.

Anyway, I pulled up to the pump and called inside for someone to turn on the electricity to the gas pump. The person on the other end of the intercom says, "Mr. Elliott, you have a long distance call from Fort Worth."

I said, "Get a number and after I finish gassing my car I will call them back."

When I finished I went inside and called the number. Guess who? Garrett. He had contacted Bowen.

"Mr. Bowen said he wanted to talk to you tonight. But it will take him about five hours to get here. Would that be all right?"

I told Garrett to stay put. I needed to call to see if I could get a motel room in the Fort Worth area.

I called Garrett back and told him, "I'll be at the Western Hills Motel in Euless.[10] When he gets there tell him to come into the lobby and get on the house phone and call my room. I'll be asleep."

I went to Euless and checked into the motel and went to bed, like a tired man's supposed to. And I mean to tell you I was tired. Looking back and reflecting on the hours I put in, it is a small wonder I was bone tired all the time.

I do not remember what time it was when the phone rang, but I do remember I was sound asleep. It was Bowen. I gave him my room number and told him to come to my room. I got up and dressed. I expected him to be by himself and was mildly surprised when I opened the door to find both Bowen and Garrett. It really didn't matter, nor did it change anything. Looking back, I should not have been surprised. It stood to reason that he would have his bondsman with him. If I arrested him, he wanted his bondsman to immediately know where he was.

We spent the next two hours talking about the Inez Phillips murder. Not only did he claim to know nothing about it, he claimed he had not even been in the area the night of the murder. And, naturally, he had an airtight alibi. He claimed to have been with his girlfriend, Denise Morris Bailey, celebrating her birthday the night of the murder.[11] He clearly remembered going to a drive-in theater to see *Bonnie and Clyde*. After the movie they had gone to Curtis Garrett's house.

---

[9] The DPS office is actually located in Garland, a suburb of Dallas.

[10] Euless is a small community laying about halfway between Dallas and Fort Worth.

[11] Denise Bailey's birthday was July 7, 1946. Mrs. Phillips was murdered on July 8.

187

Any halfway intelligent person would make sure that he and his accomplice had the same story, but you would be amazed at how seldom they do. Garrett got real fidgety. He had already told reporting officers that Bowen had left the Fort Worth area the first of July. Garrett started mumbling something about this happening a long time ago and that his memory was a bit hazy. Even I shook my head at how full of holes Bowen's story turned out to be. Later when we checked the July 8 edition of the *Fort Worth Star Telegram*, it failed to show any listing for *Bonnie and Clyde* in the Fort Worth area.

When I turned to the 1973 burglary, Bowen claimed, unconditionally, to know nothing about it. After deep thought he seemed to remember that a friend of his, Charles Oden, had borrowed his car that night. Predictably and conveniently, Oden had since died. As for the busted trunk lock, that was easy. Thieves had broken into his car's trunk, and ripped off a bunch of his clothes. I would have expected nothing less. Only a very sorry professional criminal does not have a built-in alibi ready whenever he needs it.

Pressing a little harder I said, "Henry, I can get a warrant on you for the burglary two years ago. You know the statute of limitations is not out on it. I don't think I could send you to the pen on it, but I can cost you a lot of money. And you know it."

"Henry, for your sake, you'd better not be lying to me."

Then I hit him up to take a polygraph test.

He refused. "Mr. Elliott, years ago you offered me a polygraph and I refused. I had to spend my money to make the bond. If I have to, I'll do the same again. You know how us old thieves are, I just don't want to get the rap for taking a polygraph test, you know."[12]

With that he left and drove back to wherever he had come from. There was no doubt in my mind that he was responsible for the 1973 burglary. When he arrived at my room Henry was my leading suspect. When he left, he still was. I was confident that if he did not murder Mrs. Phillips, he knew who did. Unfortunately, knowing and proving are two very different things.

The days rolled by. They soon turned into weeks, then months. All the time I continued following leads. Hardly a day went by for nearly two years that I did not do some work on the case. I followed leads all over the United States—leads that went from Cheyenne, Wyoming, to Tulsa, Oklahoma, to Jackson, Tennessee, to Atlanta, Georgia, all the way to Fort Lauderdale, Florida, and it seemed everywhere in between. All showed promise at one time or another, but each turned into another deadend, at least as far as Inez Phillips was concerned.

---

[12] Years later Bowen was charged with a double murder in Oklahoma. He requested a polygraph. He told the arresting officer to ask me about his feelings about a polygraph.

A year after the murder it seemed that maybe I had finally caught a major break. Travis Roy Erwin and two other men were arrested in El Paso for aggravated robbery. A local check of M. O.'s showed this robbery to be similar to the Phillips case. The El Paso Police contacted me.

As soon as I saw Erwin's name I started getting excited. He was a known associate of Henry Bowen, Jerry Ray James, and Benjamin Thomas Tisdale. At the time, Jerry Ray James' Gang, of which Travis Erwin was a major player, was still my prime suspect in Mrs. Phillips' murder. I did a quick check of Erwin's records. They showed that he had been released from federal custody on June 7, 1975. Unquestionably he could have been in the Gladewater area.

For his latest crime he was in the federal lockup at the LaTuna Federal Institute just outside El Paso. When I told Jack Phillips I was going to LaTuna to question Erwin, and why, he insisted on flying me out there in his private plane. I accepted and on August 12, 1976, Jack and I flew to El Paso.

The local Ranger in El Paso, Pedro Montemayer, was working in McAllen with a drug task force, so a DPS Intelligence officer met me at the El Paso Airport. After a quick lunch, we drove straight to LaTuna Prison.

Before leaving Longview I had made an appointment with prison officials to see Erwin. I expected them to have Erwin ready for questioning. My expectations were quickly dissolved. Completing the normal procedures anyone, policeman or not, must complete before being allowed to see a prisoner, I was told to take a seat. A "counselor" would be with me shortly. About fifteen minutes later the "counselor" wandered in. After shaking hands I told him I needed see Erwin as quickly as possible. I wanted to get on with my business and get back to Longview. In more ways than one, federal prisons are different than our Texas prisons. The "counselor" informed me, "Mr. Elliott, you're going to have to wait awhile. Mr. Erwin is taking a nap."

It took all my will-power not to go completely ballistic. Showing as much calm as I could possibly muster under the circumstances, I explained to the "counselor" in as civil a tongue as my temper would allow, ". . . go back there and wake Mr. Erwin, and tell him he's got company. I didn't fly all the way from Longview, Texas, out here to interview a man that's in the penitentiary, just to sit around cooling my heels waiting for a prison thug to get through taking a nap before I can talk to him."

I must say, that rather startled the "counselor." But he went back and woke up Erwin, and brought him to the visitor area.

Erwin did not want to talk. He was a pretty tough old boy. Seeing that I was getting nowhere fast, I tried the oldest approach in the world. There are two things almost all crooks and thugs have in common—one is money, and two is their willingness to sell their own mother's soul, or anyone else's for that matter, to get it. I reminded him of fifty thousand reasons he should

189

talk—Jack Phillips' reward. Even though the reward had long since expired, I knew that if he wanted to talk, all I had to do was walk outside and Jack would reinstate the reward on the spot.

"Now look here, Partner," I said. "You're in the pen on a twenty-five year sentence. You will have to serve probably at least fifteen."

In the mid-70s interest rates were sky-high with every indication of going still higher. I said, "It doesn't take a genius to tell you what fifty thousand dollars would do for you for a month while you're in the penitentiary. When you get out it'll still be laying there in the bank waiting on you. You'll have quite a nest egg waiting for you when you get out."

Looking at me with a drop-dead look, he said, "I don't know who killed the old woman. Even if I did, I wouldn't tell you. It wasn't me. In fact, on the Fourth of July in '75 I was in jail somewhere in Kansas."

I later checked his story, and, sure enough, he was in a Kansas jail on July 4, 1975.

I said, "Now look here, you're not going to stay in the pen all your life; you're going to be out one of these days. I'm still a young man. I'm going to make sure that I know when you get out. You thieves are all alike; sooner or later you'll come back to East Texas and I'll be waiting."

He softened a little, but only enough to talk civil. "Look, the fifty thousand is not even tempting. I wouldn't snitch on anybody for all the money in the world."

Trying to anticipate what I would say next, he said, "Don't try religion on me. I was raised a Roman Catholic, but I converted to convict a long time ago. You know, and I know, I'll die in a penitentiary somewhere. There's no question about that."

If you admire such attitudes, he was a real tough guy.

I did not know it at the time, but back on March 8, 1976, I had gotten the break I needed that would eventually solve the case. I got a call from a local thief that I will call John,[13] who I knew fairly well. He was currently in the state lockup in the Sugar Land, Texas, facility. He said he had information on the Inez Phillips murder and he wanted to talk to me. Would I come to the Sugar Land Prison?

I was following every lead and this one was no exception. I called and made the customary arrangements with the prison officials at Sugar Land and flew down the following day. Unlike the federal "counselors" at LaTuna, the Texas guards and officials at Sugar Land did every thing they could to be helpful. They had my man waiting for me. We sat down and began to talk.

John was willing to help, but he wanted something in return. His mother

---

[13] In 1977 I promised this man anonymity. Through the years he has always shot straight with me, so I will not now break the pledge I gave him then.

was extremely ill and needed someone to watch over her. Currently his brother was helping their mother, but he had gotten into trouble and he too was going to the penitentiary. However, John would shortly be released and he wanted me to arrange it so that his brother would not have to start serving his term until he was released. I told him I would do what I could, but I could not make promises. He understood and said my word was plenty good enough for him.

John had overheard a fellow inmate telling about a burglary that he was familiar with. He had heard talk about a burglary in Gladewater. The target had been an extremely rich old woman who had recently installed a floor safe in her home. John was a crook, but he was no dummy. Being from the Longview area and familiar with the Phillips murder, he started listening closely.

John related to me what he had overheard. One prisoner was telling another that two men from the Longview area were both trying to date the same old barmaid who worked in one of the dives on Whiskey Bend in Longview.[14] As drunks tend to do, the more they drank, the more they bragged about their immense feats in the world of crime. He could tell from the conversation that the barmaid the men were competing for was, to say the least, no prize—but each to his own.

John did not know many details, but what he had overheard was enough to eventually break the case. He did not know either of the men's names. The only thing he knew for sure was that one of the men was a carpet layer for a local firm in Longview. The other was a Canadian national. The Canadian had been friends with a fireman in Longview who had been fired from the Fire Department for smoking marijuana.

As soon as I got back to Longview, the first thing I tried to do was delay John's brother's sentence, but it was too late. He had already been processed and was headed for prison. I requested from the proper authorities that John be released a few days early, if possible. He was.

I have always made it a point to keep my promise when I made one, even to a crook. Strange as it may seem, in the world that I operated in, it was extremely important to keep your word to a felon. Like any other business, the world of the crook is a small one. It takes no time for a crook to know whether or not your word can be trusted. You would not believe the cases I have solved because of things a crook told me. They knew that whatever I told them was the way it would be. And to the best of my ability, it was. But back to the story.

I visited the Longview Fire Department and asked if they had fired one of their men in 1973 for smoking pot. Yes, they had. They remembered the

---

[14] Whiskey Bend is located just south of Longview on Highway 149 where the road makes a slight bend before crossing the Sabine River.

man well. He had been a good fireman, but he had been caught red-handed smoking marijuana, so he had been dismissed.

I ran a check on the man[15] and discovered that he was presently living in Wood County[16] and working for a local oil drilling company that was currently drilling in Palestine, Texas. He was working twelve-hour shifts and driving back and forth between the well site and his home.

I made a couple of trips to Wood County, but missed him both times. Finally I went to his house at about the time I thought he would be getting home, and I waited for him. Sure enough, about dark, here he came.

I asked him if he had recently been friends with a Canadian. Having nothing to hide he was cooperative and answered fully. Yes, he had recently been casual friends with a man from Canada, but he had not seen him for several months. He knew his first name was Stan, but he had never known his last name.

"I don't know his last name, Mr. Elliott," he said. "I can tell you that he was arrested in Gregg County last year (1975) on July 4, for drunk driving."

"Mr. Elliott, if I knew any more I'd tell you."

I believed him.

The next morning I went through the Sheriff's traffic records for July 4, 1975, and there it was. Arrested for DWI, Stan Faulder.

I pulled his record and found out more about Stan Faulder—much more.

His full name was Joseph Stanley Faulder. He was born on October 19, 1937, at McLennan, Alberta, Canada. Standing 5'8", and weighing 175 pounds, he had brown hair and blue eyes. Reading on, Canadian authorities considered Faulder dangerous and advised that he be approached with caution.

Also in the file were Faulder's mug shots, rap sheet,[17] and fingerprints. During our crime scene investigation, Red Arnold had determined that the killer(s) had worn gloves, so his fingerprints were of no help.

Furthermore, he had been convicted of a felony in Canada for shooting some teenage kids and other acts of violence. As a convicted felon he was not supposed to even be in the United States.

There was one other vital piece of information in the folder. Immediately south and east of the railroad underpass, at 609 South Green Street in Longview, J. C. Bailey had owned a Fina Service Station. Being unable to operate the station himself because of his full-time job with a local oil pipe-

---

[15] Since the only crime this man committed was knowing the suspected felon, and as far as I know he may still live in the Longview area, there is no need to reveal his name.

[16] Mineola, Texas, is the county seat of Wood County.

[17] A list of a criminal's record.

line company, he had hired a Stan Cotter to operate the station on a daily basis. One day in the first week of July 1975, Cotter had failed to open the station. Fearing the worst when he was unable to contact Cotter, Bailey decided to perform an audit on the station's books. It did not take him long to find the truth—three hundred thirty-five dollars was missing. Unfortunately Faulder and his money were gone. Bailey was a working man and could not afford to spend the money or time to recover three hundred fifty dollars.

When I contacted Bailey he had closed the station and moved to Bartlesville, Oklahoma. I beat a path to Bartlesville and met with him. He informed me that he had never been able to locate Cotter, but he wanted to. He gladly agreed to cooperate in any way possible. We went before a local notary public and prepared, to the best of his knowledge, a sworn statement as to what Cotter had done.

With Bailey's sworn statement in hand, I headed back to Longview and the Gregg County Sheriff's Office. I immediately went before the Gregg County District Attorney, Odis Hill, presented my case, and on January 22, 1977, a felony warrant for Stan Cotter, a.k.a. Joseph Stanley Faulder, was issued and published in the National Law Enforcement Bulletin.[18]

After embezzling Bailey, Faulder had fled Texas and dropped completely out of sight. He stayed hidden until April 17, 1977.

It turned out that Faulder had gone to Las Vegas where he laid low until his itchy feet got the better of him. He bought an old Cadillac and headed for Miami, via the northern route through Denver. In Lincoln County, Colorado, a Deputy Sheriff stopped him for a routine traffic violation—a burned-out taillight.

The deputy became suspicious when Faulder presented the officer with his driver's license. The Cadillac had Nevada plates, but Faulder still had a Texas driver's license. He radioed for a NCIC computer check. The computer made a hit.

Lincoln County, Colorado, authorities notified Gregg County that they had arrested Faulder and wanted to know if we were going to extradite him. When the DA's office saw where I had written across the top of their file folder that this was the main suspect in the Phillips murder, I was immediately notified that Faulder was in jail in Colorado.

Faulder had no idea that he was a suspect in the Phillips murder and we were not ready to file a murder charge against him. He was being detained for embezzling from his former employer, J. C. Bailey. Before the Gregg County District Attorney would file the necessary extradition papers, he needed to know, ". . . if Bailey would still continue the case." I told the DA that I felt

---

[18] This is a network where all crime information is compiled in one center and can be dispensed quickly via radio and/or teletype.

sure he would, but I would have to contact Bailey to be positive.

There was only one problem; Bailey had left Bartlesville, and it seemed no one had a clue as to where he had gone. I like to have never found him. But I finally located him living on a lake near Hemphill, Texas. And, yes, he was more than willing to continue the prosecution of Faulder.

I pled my case to the DA explaining that this was the best suspect we had for the killing of Inez Phillips. To make sure that we would not lose him again, we had to get him back to Gregg County. My argument was convincing; the DA agreed. After preparing the necessary extradition papers, Sheriff Tom Welch dispatched Captain Jim Montgomery, one of his reserve officers, to Denver to bring Faulder back to Longview.

Faulder arrived in Longview on April 20 and I immediately visited him. I never mentioned the Phillips murder; all I talked to him about was the theft of Bailey's money.

He still had no idea that we suspected him for the murder of Inez Phillips. I guess he thought that it was not worth fighting over three hundred thirty-five dollars. He confessed to running off with the money and signed a voluntary confession statement.

We had him. Now we had plenty of time to build our murder case. With his confession for embezzlement, he was not going anywhere.

Once I had his signed confession for the theft, I starting questioning him about the killing. I caught him completely off guard, but he denied any knowledge. I asked if he would consent to a polygraph. "Yeah, sure. Why not."

At the time, the nearest place to have a polygraph test given was in Tyler, about thirty-five miles from Longview. Deputy Bill Roach and I made arrangements to have the testing done, and transported Faulder to Tyler.

As is the case anytime a person is going to take a polygraph test, the polygraph operator started briefing him on what would happen if he lied. The machine would know immediately. Obviously, Faulder had thought he could beat the polygraph, but when he realized that he could not, he had a change of heart. He decided he did not want to take the test—that he would ". . . like to think about it. I need a couple of days to get things straight in my mind."

You can not make a person take a polygraph. When he had the change of heart, I sat down and started talking to him, one-on-one. You never confront a person you are trying to get information from with definite statements, such as, "Joe said you did this, or Jean said that." If you do, and the person you are questioning catches you in a lie, you're dead meat. They will know immediately that you are on a fishing trip. Instead you say something along the lines of, "What if I said . . ." Leave yourself an out. You keep mentioning names of known associates of the person you are questioning. Usually their imagination takes over. "He must know about this, since he knows that I hang around with so-and-so." Faulder and I carried on a similar conversation for about forty-five minutes to an hour.

Finally he said, "Well, I can't tell you about it, but if you'll give me a pen and a piece of paper, I'll write it down."

He wrote about two paragraphs, and then he started talking about it. The more he talked, the more he confessed, until he had finally confessed to the whole thing.

The story he told was sordid.

One rainy night at a club south of Longview, he and James Millard Moulton were drinking heavily and competing for the attention of a barfly named Stormie Summers.[19] Trying to impress her, Faulder insinuated that he had underworld connections. And as for safes, according to his braggadocio, there was no safe in the world that he could not crack. Moulton responded saying that he had just laid some tile in this rich woman's house in Gladewater. Not only was he sure the safe was full of money and jewels, he bet Faulder he could not crack it.

Faulder accepted the challenge. After closing the bar, Faulder, Summers, Moulton, and Doyle Hughes, another ex-convict who was at the bar, headed for Gladewater. They cruised the area around the Phillips home several times. But it was raining, and an unattended strange vehicle in the area would arouse unwanted attention, so they decided to wait and come back later.

The next day Faulder and Summers decided that they did not need Moulton and Hughes. That Tuesday night, July 8, 1975, they went back to Gladewater, alone.

We had thought they gained entrance into the Phillips home via the unlocked patio doors, but they did not. They had parked in the driveway of the Phillips Oil Company, directly north of the elderly Mrs. Phillips' home. There was a gate in the backyard connecting the home with the office. Faulder and Summers had come through this gate to the kitchen door. They could see Mrs. Phillips making jelly, so Summers knocked on the door. The unsuspecting Mrs. Phillips answered. Summers told her that her car had broken down, and asked if she could please come in and call for help. Kind and trusting, Inez Phillips agreed. As Stormie came through the door, Faulder pushed his way through.

They demanded that Mrs. Phillips tell them the combination to the safe. She refused. Forced into the bedroom, Faulder tied her hands with tape and pushed her onto the bed. After ransacking the master bedroom and its closet, they finally found the safe's combination. Faulder handed Summers a pistol and told her to watch the "old woman" while he opened the safe.

Summers later testified that she was afraid Mrs. Phillips was so up-

---

[19] Her real name was Lynda Ziegler McCann, but she used the alias, Stormie Summers.

set by the sight of the gun that she was going to have a heart attack, so she laid the pistol down on a nearby table and backed off. But Mrs. Phillips worked her hands free, rolled across the bed, and grabbed the pistol. Just as she seized the pistol, Summers grabbed her. In the ensuing struggle, Summers wrenched the gun from Mrs. Phillips and struck her on the head with the gun, causing it to discharge. This was the bullet we found in another part of the house.

Meanwhile, Faulder angrily returned from the kitchen carrying a butcher knife. He gagged and tied Mrs. Phillips again. Once again forcing the frail, helpless lady onto the bed, he started trying to remove her wedding ring.[20] According to Summers, she objected, and Faulder ordered her to leave the room and go look for valuables in some other part of the house. Outside the room she claimed to have heard moans and groans, followed by a thumping sound as Faulder stabbed Mrs. Phillips in the chest.

Faulder almost made my stomach turn over when he told his version of the story. According to him, he could tell that Mrs. Phillips was in agony from the blow she had received. He claimed he could not stand seeing the poor woman in such agony. So as an act of kindness to stop her misery, he took Mrs. Phillips' butcher knife and buried it, to the hilt, in her heart.

Faulder related this story with no more emotion than you would use to tell about pulling a flea off your dog. It later turned out that it was not Summers who delivered the fatal blow to the old lady, but Faulder. Also, Mrs. Phillips was not in agony. The autopsy had shown that the blow to the head had killed her instantly.

With Mrs. Phillips stilled forever, he returned to the job at hand—opening the safe. To their total dismay, all they found was some cheap costume jewelry, and no money. She had insisted on a floor safe, but her confidence in it was minimal. She had hidden her real jewelry and money in a secret compartment behind a built-in corner linen cabinet. She had told only her granddaughter about the secret hiding place. Faulder and Summers did not find it.

Disgusted that such a rich old woman had so little money and jewels, they fled from the scene and enjoyed freedom almost two years. But their time had run out.

Before his murder confession, Gregg County Justice of the Peace, Charles Cashell, had placed Faulder under a $50,000 bond for theft of over two hundred dollars in the Bailey embezzlement. With the filing of the murder charge, Cashell denied Faulder bond.

We knew that Summers was living in neighboring Smith County. Armed with Faulder's confession and Summers' involvement in the murder, we contacted Smith County officers. They went directly to Stormie "Summers"

---

[20] Later when we found the body, Mrs. Phillips' wedding ring was still on her finger.

McCann's home in Tyler and arrested her.[21]   She was deposited in the Smith County jail, where she was put under a $100,000 bond. After filing the necessary papers, she was transported to Longview. Like Faulder, Cashell also denied her bond.

Three days later we arrested the carpetlayer, James Moulton. We had presented our evidence on him before a grand jury and they indicted him for conspiracy to commit burglary. Cashell put his bond at $50,000.

Ironically, the man who would take my place as Ranger in Gregg, Harrison, and Panola Counties, Ronny Griffith, had arrested Moulton shortly before the murders for DWI. At the time, Ronny was a State Trooper stationed in Kilgore. Also shortly before the murder, Moulton had laid carpet in the home of State Trooper Sergeant Elton Thane in White Oak.

You would think this was an open and shut case—but it was far from it. At the time of this writing, 1998, Faulder is still sitting on death row with no execution date set. The twenty plus year road from 1977 until today is both long and winding.

The court appointed Vernon Solomon, of Marshall, to defend Faulder. By a jury of his peers, Faulder was found guilty of murder in the first degree and sentenced to death. Solomon is a good criminal lawyer who knows his job. He filed an appeal on the grounds that the confession had been gained through undue duress.

Solomon maintained that Faulder had confessed only because of his intimidation and fear of a polygraph. That's bull. In all my years of law enforcement I have never had a suspect who was more cooperative than Faulder. During questioning we sent out for dinner, which we all, including Faulder, ate.

As a matter of fact, I did not have to do much questioning. The more he talked, the freer he became.

Be that as it may, the Court of Appeals agreed with Solomon. According to the Justices, when Faulder refused the polygraph, and said ". . . he wanted to think about it . . .," he was in a roundabout way invoking his Fifth Amendment right not to incriminate himself. According to the judges, we should have immediately removed him back to Longview. Any interrogation we did, according to them, we should have done somewhere else, and in the presence of his attorney. They overturned the conviction and ordered another trial.

A lot of things had happened since the first trial in Longview. For one, the case had received a ton of publicity in Longview and the defense wanted a change of venue. It was granted, and moved to Lufkin in Angelina County. For another, District Attorney Odis Hill had retired to private practice and had been replaced by Rob Foster. But that was only the start of the complications. The Criminal Court of Appeals had overturned the murder conviction and

---

[21] The actual arrest time was 3:30 a.m., April 26, 1977.

death sentence of Emmett Murray Holloway for the killing of Longview Police Officer Marshall Sowders. And to really stir up the pot, both cases were set for retrial in different courts at the same time.

This is where Inez Phillips' son, Jack, stepped up to the plate. He volunteered to hire Odis Hill and a well-known Dallas attorney, Phil Burleson, Sr., as special prosecutors to work with James McCoy, an Assistant District Attorney. Technically, Foster would remain in charge of the prosecution through his assistant, who in turn would be assisted by the man who had gotten the first conviction, Odis Hill, and Phil Burleson. Foster agreed to the plan.

Now that a prosecution team was set, they had a major problem to overcome. When Faulder's conviction was thrown out, that meant we could not use his original confession. There was only one way to get a conviction; we had to turn Stormie Summers. While Faulder had confessed everything, Summers would admit nothing. She had not even given us a statement. She had been convicted on conspiracy to burglarize Mrs. Phillips' home and had spent forty-two months in jail. But when Faulder's conviction was overturned, so was Stormie's.

But she was herself facing "the chair" this time. When offered a deal to save her own neck, it was bye-bye Faulder. In return for rolling over on Faulder, Summers was charged with conspiracy to commit burglary and sentenced to ten years probation. Also, she was terrified of Faulder and was afraid that if he beat the second trial he would come after her. Once again Jack Phillips stepped to the plate. He offered to pay any relocation expenses she needed, to move anywhere she wanted. Payment of this offer was never needed.

Since he did not participate in the actual robbery, Moulton, like Stormie Summers, was also charged with conspiracy to commit burglary. He was found guilty. Since he was still on probation for DWI, he was ordered to finish that term and was sentenced to the state penitentiary for a lengthy term.

Doyle Hughes, the fourth person involved, turned state's evidence and was a valuable witness against the other three. He received no prison time.

Assistant District Attorney Alvin Khoury[22] handled most of the work during the trial in Longview. Let me tell you, Alvin did a first-class job. James McCoy, Odis Hill, and Phil Burleson handled the prosecution in Lufkin. Like Alvin, they did a bang-up job. We got our second conviction. Faulder was once again sentenced to die. In two trials, twenty-four of his peers have unanimously found Stan Faulder guilty of cold-blooded murder, but yet, as of this writing, he still lives.

---

[22] At this writing, Alvin is the 124th District Court Judge. He is as good a judge as he was a prosecuting attorney.

Through the years Faulder has filed appeal after appeal. I can not begin to remember all of them, but here are a few. One complaint was that Jack Phillips should not have been allowed to pay for the special prosecutors. Never mind the fact that we citizens are paying for Faulder's defense team. That appeal did not fly. The appellate court found that, though Hill and Burleson worked on the case, Foster maintained control of the case through his assistant, James McCoy.

Our next problem was we had no jurisdiction. They tried to free him on a writ of habeas corpus, claiming that since Faulder was from Canada, the State of Texas had violated the Vienna Convention on Consular Relations. This treaty requires an arresting government to notify a foreign national of his right to contact his country's consulate for help. They put forth that it was fifteen years before the Canadian government knew that the State of Texas had Faulder. Also, for fifteen years no one in his family knew what had happened to him. They thought he was dead. Never mind that Faulder had explicitly forbidden his defense attorney, Vernon Solomon, from contacting the Canadian government about his family or his whereabouts. The Fifth U. S. Circuit Court of Appeals ruled that the failure to notify Canadian authorities in no way affected the ultimate conviction and death sentence. Strike two.

Another time he claimed that an incompetent attorney represented him. Let me tell you, I can think of very few attorneys I would rather have defending me than Vernon Solomon. The appeals court must have agreed, Faulder lost that appeal also. In fact, he has lost every one of his appeals. Maybe one of these days he will run out of things to appeal and lady justice will finally be served.[23]

Co-writer's note: Shortly after the arrest of Faulder and Summers, Inez Phillips' son, Jack, issued the following statement in the April 23, 1975, issued of the Gladewater Mirror:

"It is hard for me to completely express the feeling that my family and I share with our friends in hoping that we may soon find out what actually happened in my mother's home on that terrible night of July 8.

"We want to thank the entire community and our many friends for their compassion, their patience and the love they have so abundantly extended my family.

"We want to express our sincere appreciation for the many officers who so diligently worked on this case. We want to recognize the efforts of Police Chief Jay Banks and the Gladewater Police Department, the very fine master detective work of Captain Bill Roach and Gregg County Sheriff Tom Welch's department.

---

[23] At this writing, 1998, Faulder is still appealing and has been successful in getting the Secretary of State of the United States appealing for him.

"Our very special thanks to Ranger Glen[n] Elliott for his expertise as a law officer and 18 months of untiring efforts in the case. He is compassionate and has kept me informed at all times as to his progress. We are indeed fortunate to have Ranger Elliott stationed in our area and criminals should take note of this. We want to express our thanks to the Texas Rangers."

CHAPTER XI
HEADLESS IN THE SABINE

On Saturday, November 6, 1976, at 7:55 a.m., I was in my office when the phone rang. It was Johnnie Spradley, Sheriff of Panola County.

"Glenn, we've got a body in the Sabine River on Highway 43 between Tatum and Marshall. It's in the water, right at the bridge. Can you come down?"

"I'm on my way, Johnnie."

"Glenn."

"Yeah."

"We've got a body, but we don't have a head."

"I'll be right there."

I arrived at the scene at 8:30 and joined Spradley and Deputy Mack Cranford. Due to the early hour, and very little traffic, the crime scene was still intact.

At 6:45 that morning Edward Lowe had found the nude body floating, front side up, in the river. Ironically, Lowe, from Mesquite, Texas, was a Dallas police officer. Lowe and a neighbor had brought their sons to East Texas for a canoe float trip down the Sabine River to Logansport, Louisiana. Lowe's wife was from Logansport, which is located on the Texas-Louisiana border. The plan was for Mrs. Lowe to drop the men and boys at the river while she went on to Logansport to visit her family.

You can imagine their shock when they started to launch their canoe and saw a totally nude, headless body floating a few feet away. Lowe contacted the Panola County Sheriff's office, and then Sheriff Spradley called me.

About one hundred feet from the riverbank we found a large amount of blood stains. From the vast amount of blood, and its freshness, this was un-doubtedly the murder scene. From the footprints and scuff marks we could tell that the body had been carried to the river and dumped in. Clearly the killer had assumed that the current would carry the body downstream. I guess he thought it would wash all the way to the Gulf of Mexico and no one would ever find the body. Who knows, it might have worked if the river had been up. But it wasn't.

In November things are usually dry in Texas. November, 1976, was no exception. The Sabine was down—way down. In Panola County you could wade the river at almost any point. So, when the body was dumped into the river, it did not go anywhere. We were unable to find the head. It had either flowed off, or been disposed of somewhere else. Units from the Carthage and Henderson Fire Departments began searching for the head and any other evidence that might have been dumped into the river.

Panola County Judge Buck Davis conducted an inquest at the scene. We could find no identification of any kind. Any jewelry, if there had been any, had been removed and every stitch of clothing had been taken off. The body was covered with tattoos—flowers and a shark on the left arm, a five pointed star in the palm of the left hand, birds on the right arm, a coiled cobra above the right knee, "Louie 67" on the left knee, and a swastika, also on the left leg. I would have bet that this guy was a real winner.

I fingerprinted the body and we took pictures. I made some superb plaster of Paris from the several excellent tire tracks at the scene. The only physical evidence at the scene was a comb and an eight-track tape player. What little evidence we had, plus the fingerprint cards and pictures, was submitted to the DPS laboratory in Austin for assistance in making a positive identification. The body was sent to the Dallas County Crime Laboratory for an autopsy.

While still at the scene I was approached by John Morris of Beckville, Texas. The night before, Morris and Roy Dupree, along with their wives, were returning to their homes in Beckville from a high school football game in Jefferson. They had stopped along the way for a late supper in Marshall, and as they were crossing the river at about midnight a pickup suddenly pulled out in front of them from the road leading down to the river. Not happy with being cut off, they had paid particularly close attention to the truck. It was a 1965, three-quarter-ton, faded blue Chevrolet, with what appeared to be green homemade cattle-type sideboards. Even more conspicuous was the Nevada license plate. You don't see a lot of Nevada vehicles on the back roads of East Texas at midnight.

After five hours of searching we still had not found the victim's head, but my personal attention was no longer needed. I decided to follow the hearse to Dallas. I wanted to stay on top of this as much as possible. I wanted whatever information the autopsy revealed. The trail was still hot, and I did not want to give it any chance to cool off.

Hawthorne Funeral Home in Carthage was in charge of delivering the body to Dallas. I followed behind the hearse. We had just about reached the Smith County line when word was radioed to me that the head had been recovered. I radioed the ambulance and told the driver to go on to Dallas; I was going back to the crime scene and would meet him at the lab.

After hours of searching, the Henderson Rescue Unit had found the head approximately five hundred feet downstream from the body. The face was heavily bearded, with still another tattoo on it. There were also three small-caliber bullet holes in it. Two of the bullets had passed completely through the head; the third was recovered during the autopsy. One of the shots, near the left side of the nose, had been fired at extremely close range.

I put some plastic in the back floorboard of my car, put the head on it, and headed for Dallas. While driving I radioed Tyler and requested that what few facts we had be put on the NCIC computer. At the end of the message, I added, "There could be a blue pickup with homemade sideboards and Nevada plates involved." Maybe I would get lucky and make a hit.

I arrived at the Dallas Police Lab about the same time as the ambulance carrying the body.[1] After depositing the victim's head with an attendant, I learned that the Flagstaff, Arizona, Police Department had made an inquiry, from the NCIC broadcast, concerning the blue pickup.

I called the Flagstaff Police Department and talked to M. E. Eickmeyer. On November 3, they had received a call of a burglary in progress in their city. Though the thief had gotten away before they could arrive, a positive identification of the pickup had been made. It was a 1965 blue Chevrolet, three-quarter ton, with sideboards. They had also secured its license number: WE-0731, Nevada. The reporting officer, Byron Allen, had run a trace on the truck and found out that it belonged to Winfield Bowers of Reno, Nevada. They told me that they had called Reno two or three times with no response.

On Monday, November 8, I contacted the Reno Police Department personally. I told the Reno officer that the pickup in question might have been used in a murder. Would he please send someone to check out Bowers for me. He agreed. About an hour later he called back. He had sent a man to the Bowers home. He reported that Bowers did not have the truck. His son, Gerald,[2] had borrowed the truck several days before to go to Sacramento, California, and he had not seen his son or the truck since.

I asked, "Did Mr. Bowers know if anyone had gone with his son when he left?"

Reply: "I don't know, we didn't ask."

"When did he leave?"

"Well, we didn't ask."

I must admit I was getting a little exasperated. I asked if there was a detective on duty.

"Yeah. I got one on duty."

---

[1] The ambulance driver drove at the 55-mph speed limit. As has been said before, Glenn was well known for his fast driving. As he has said over and over, "I was always in such a hurry. I was always trying to catch up."

[2] Full name, Gerald Allan Bowers. Nickname, Jerry.

"Could I please speak to him?"

Detective Sergeant Morgan came to the phone. I explained to him what we had and asked if he would go back and speak to Bowers.

"Sure. Be happy to."

He called back and reported that he had talked with both Mr. Bowers and Gerald's wife, Frankie. She had not seen her husband since Saturday, October 30. They had been having trouble, and after a fight he had borrowed his father's pickup and left town for parts unknown. She had neither seen nor heard from him since. The only other thing she knew was that when he left, a man she knew only as Nathan accompanied him.

Mr. Bowers confirmed that his son had indeed borrowed his truck, claiming that he and a friend were going to Sacramento. When questioned as to any link Gerald had to East Texas, he said that when Gerald was in the Army, he had been stationed near Leesville, Louisiana, at Fort Pope. He loved to deer hunt and had wanted to return to the area. It would not surprise him if he had gone to the area. He also gave Sergeant Morgan the name of a close friend Gerald had in Shreveport—Charles Dunmoyer.

Sergeant Morgan had called me on a Monday night. The next morning I called Ben Kitchens of the Caddo Parish Sheriff's office. I asked him to look up Bowers' friend and find out what he could. I also gave him a description of Bowers' pickup and asked if he would look around for it. I got the same answer I got every single time I asked for help from the Caddo Parish Sheriff's office: "No problem. Consider it done."

Things continued to move swiftly. On Tuesday, November 9, Danny Carter, from the DPS Laboratory in Austin, made a positive identification of the body. He was Nathan James Koon, twenty-eight years old, last known address, Reno, Nevada.

Not surprisingly, he was currently on parole and had a rap sheet that would reach almost from Longview to Reno. I contacted his parole officer in Reno—Karen Smith. She provided me with Koon's next of kin. His father, Jessie Koon, lived in Florida. Mr. Koon was contacted for disposition of the body. The city of Dallas cremated the remains.

A picture of Koon was sent to the Reno Police Department. Sergeant Morgan again visited Frankie Bowers. She confirmed that the man in the picture was in fact the man who had accompanied her husband when he departed Reno.

Given this evidence, Panola County Judge W. B. Bush issued a capital murder warrant for the arrest of Gerald Allan Bowers. We put out an all-states pickup on Bowers and his truck.

Two days later, November 11, Deputy Ben Kitchens, of Caddo Parish, Louisiana, called. As we suspected, Bowers had been in Shreveport for the last several days. We were close. He was booked on the Delta Airlines 1:30

p.m. flight to Reno that very afternoon. Unfortunately it was already well past 1:30. Hoping the flight might be running late, we checked with the airline, but the plane had already left Shreveport. But Lady Luck might still be with us. The flight had a scheduled stop in Dallas. If we were lucky, we might catch Bowers in Dallas. If we were successful it would save us many problems—mainly, no extradition from Nevada. Unfortunately, Lady Luck was not with us. The flight had already departed Dallas. Before arriving in Reno, the plane had to make a stop in Las Vegas. Currently it was still in the air between Dallas and Las Vegas. Wasting no time, we contacted the Reno Police Department and requested that Bowers be detained when he got off the plane.

Bowers got quite a surprise when he stepped off the plane at the Reno Airport. The Reno Police Department arrested him. When he checked in at Shreveport's airport, he had checked a .22 caliber rifle through to Reno. In true airline tradition, they lost the rifle. Fortunately, it was later found.

Meanwhile, back in Shreveport, Ben Kitchens called and told me they had located and impounded Bowers' pickup at the airport. They had towed it to their impound yard and would keep it there until I could get back to Shreveport. I love those Louisiana boys.

The next morning, Friday, I hooked 'em to Shreveport. Deputy Kitchens and I had depositions to get from Bowers' friends—Charles Dunmoyer, Rose Ann Fountain, and Larry Smith. Fortunately for them, their stories were consistent.

Bowers had shown up, unannounced, in Shreveport at about three o'clock the morning of Saturday, November 6. He had been extremely nervous about something that had happened in the Sabine River bottom, but would not say what.

He made arrangements with Smith and Fountain to stay with them until he could get a job. Smith felt that getting a job would be no problem. He was working at a service station and could arrange a job.

Thereafter, every day he would buy the local paper and hastily go through it, but whenever the local news came on television, he would leave the room. They claimed that he never gave any explanation. He showed his friends a Smith and Wesson .357 Magnum[3] and some jewelry he admitted he had stolen.

The day before, November 10, Bowers told Dunmoyer that he had to go back to Reno. He had called his mother, and she told him he was in a lot of

---

[3] It turned out that this pistol had been stolen from the car of James Young. Young and his family had been vacationing in Idaho. They had stopped for the night in Sparks (a Reno suburb), Nevada. During the night someone broke into the Young car and stole, among other things, the .357. Young was a California highway patrolman.

trouble. The police had been around and they had a warrant for his arrest. According to Dunmoyer, Bowers talked to a Reno policeman and was told he had better come on back to Reno.

He immediately booked passage with Delta Airlines for a flight to Reno the next day. He had checked a .22 rifle through to Reno, but he had left the jewelry and pistol in Shreveport. When we left, we took the jewels and pistol with us.

Completing the depositions, Ben and I went to the impound yard to go over the pickup. Jim Hood[4] of the Caddo Sheriff's office was in charge of collection of evidence. We dusted the truck from top to bottom for fingerprints; dirt samples were removed from each wheel well; blood-stains from the seat and back bed were removed; all the contents of the truck were removed, marked and examined; ink impressions and plaster of paris casts were made of the tires. Of course, photographs of every angle were made.

We had enough evidence for probable cause. Sheriff Spradley and I made arrangements to fly to Reno to question Bowers, and we hoped to return him to Carthage without having to go through extradition proceedings.

On Monday, November 15, Spradley and I flew to Reno for the questioning. Arriving in Reno, we were assisted by Detective W. D. Walen of the Reno Police Department. After turning over the evidence recovered in Shreveport that concerned the Reno burglary, we checked into a motel. We would visit Bowers the following morning.

When Spradley and I arrived at the police station the following morning, Bowers and an attorney that he had hired, Sam Francouich, were waiting for us. At first Bowers and Francouich indicated that he would not waive extradition.

While we were sitting there I explained to Bowers and Francouich that we had enough evidence to take him back to Texas. I had established that Koon was heavily into drugs, was a homosexual, and had even tried to form a cult on the campus of the local college in Reno.

I told Bowers, "You know you're going to be tried for this case in Texas. I promise you that. The Governor is going to issue a warrant for you and the Governor of Nevada is going to honor it. We're going to bring you back to Texas and we're going to try you. This guy was sorry that you killed. But you know, the more expense you cause for us, the more time it's going to cost you in the long run."

He did not say anything, so Spradley and I, along with Francouich, left. Johnnie and I were going to go to the motel to freshen up, then go get some-

---

[4] Jim Hood did not work in the field, but if you needed someone identified, there was no one better than Jim. Jim has since passed away. I was privileged to attend his funeral in Louisiana.

thing to eat. Just as we reached the door the jailer called and said, "This boy wants to talk to that Ranger again."

I went back to talk to Bowers. He waived his right for his lawyer to be present, saying, "I don't want him. I'm going to sit here and tell you about it. I want to go back to Texas and get whatever punishment I'm going to get."

Sitting there in the jail I took a sworn affidavit. He admitted killing Koon and said he would waive extradition the next morning in court. By this time Francouich had returned and he tried his best to talk Bowers out of going back to Texas, but Bowers had made up his mind and he ignored Francouich.

On Thursday, November 18, Bowers appeared before Judge Peter Breen and made the following statement, "Your Honor, I committed this crime and I'm going back to Texas and face the music."

The Judge said, "Well this is unusual, but you've already said you weren't pleased with your attorney and you don't want another one. I can't do anything but let you go if that's what you want."

With that, he ended the session. As I was leaving, Judge Breen called me over to the side bench. "You better get him out of Nevada pretty quick."

I needed no further urging. We went straight to the airport and caught the next plane to Texas.

Bowers explained that he and Koon had been arguing ever since they had left Reno over just about everything. Koon had made three or four passes at him. Being straight, Bowers was not interested. The night of the killing, they had stopped under the Sabine River Bridge to get some sleep. They had no sooner stopped than Koon started coming on to Bowers, this time real strong. Claiming that he had had enough of Koon and was afraid for his life, he pulled out his .22 pistol and shot Koon three times in the head.

When asked why he severed Koon's head, Bowers explained, "I took his clothes off; there was identification in them, and I threw them in the river." We never did recover any of the clothing. Continuing, he said, "I thought, well, I could cut his head off and nobody would ever be able to identify him."

He reasoned that with the head and body severed, at least one would float down the river until one and hopefully both, reached the Gulf of Mexico. Then Koon would be lost forever. He wrongly assumed that even if one part of the body was found, without the other, positive identification could not be made.

Bowers accompanied us to the crime scene and showed us where he had thrown the .22 pistol he had shot Koon with, and the knife he used to sever the head, into the river. Divers from the Henderson Rescue Unit recovered the knife, but the pistol was never recovered. While at the scene he made another statement, confirming the first statement, regarding the murder.

On June 9, 1977, before 123rd District Court in Carthage, Texas, Gerald Bowers pled guilty and was sentenced to twenty years in prison.

CHAPTER XII
KENTUCKY FRIED CHICKEN NOTES

The week of September 19, 1983, had been a long week. I had just returned from my hometown where I had spent my fifth straight Friday watching the Windom National Bank. We had completed a profile on a male and female bank robbery team that always hit on a Friday and during school hours. We believed that it was a husband-wife team who had children in school. Later events would prove the profile correct. We knew it was about time for them strike again. We teamed with local officers and FBI agents and watched seventeen banks for several Fridays in a row. My duty was at Windom, an area I was, of course, very familiar with.

Watching the bank from a room in a house beside the bank was the most rest I had received all week. As was typical with me, I had been in a dead run all week. I had been in Henderson attending court; over to Carthage helping officers from the Baton Rouge, Louisiana, Police Department with a theft investigation in which we recovered $40,000 in stolen property; back to court in Longview; then over to Carthage to assist the Louisiana boys take statements in their case. No sooner had I finished in Carthage than I had to hurry back to Longview and Kilgore to support visiting Georgia police officers investigating a theft that had happened in Brook County, Georgia. We recovered and returned $45,000 in stolen property to some happy folks in Georgia.

Little did I realize on that Saturday morning when Kilgore Police Officer, Danny Pirtle, called at about eight o'clock I had spent my last Friday sitting on the bank in Windom.[1] When I answered the phone I started down the road of the most frustrating case I worked on in my entire thirty-eight year career. Until the day I retired four years later, there would hardly be a day, let alone a week, that passed that I did not work on the Kentucky Fried Chicken Murders.

Today,[2] Craig Eye Associates is located at 800 North Henderson Street

---

[1] Three weeks later robbers did hit the bank in Windom. They were apprehended and sentenced. Unfortunately I was not there. I was still knee-deep in the KFC murders.

[2] 1998.

209

(Highway 259), directly across the street from the Community Inn Motel in Kilgore. You could not ask for a more peaceful-looking place. And it is— today. But on Friday night, September 24, 1983, it was the most violent location in America. Three twenty-year-old Kilgore College boys and two middle-aged women, all but one employees of the local Kentucky Fried Chicken, were abducted after closing the restaurant, taken about fifteen miles south of town to a lonely oil well lease, and murdered.

On Friday night, at approximately 11:00 o'clock, Kim Miller reported to the Kilgore police that her mother, Mary Tyler, was missing from the Kentucky Fried Chicken Restaurant. Ms. Miller, 17, herself an employee of the restaurant, had gotten off work at nine o'clock. As usual she went home to await her mother who normally arrived about 10:30. When 10:30 came and her mother still had not arrived, she called the restaurant. Alarmed when she failed to receive an answer, she drove to the restaurant. Finding the normally locked back door standing open she rushed into the restaurant. When she saw blood on the floor she became scared. Jumping into her car she rushed to Kilgore's Laird Memorial Hospital frantically searching for her mother. Learning that neither her mother nor any of her co-workers had been to the emergency room, she headed for the police department. After listening to Ms. Miller's report, an officer was dispatched to the restaurant to investigate.

Foul play was a definite possibility when Ms. Miller's claim of the unlocked door and blood on the floor was confirmed. An officer was ordered to guard the building until investigators could arrive. When I arrived at 8:30 the following morning, the crime scene investigation had not yet begun.

We discovered that not only Mrs. Tyler was missing, but fellow employees Ms. Opie Hughes, Joey Johnson, David Maxwell, and Monte Landers (a friend of Johnson and Maxwell) were also missing. The Hughes, Johnson, and Tyler vehicles were still in the parking lot.

We knew nothing out of the ordinary had happened at closing time. A fellow employee, Lanetta Wilson, 16, had gotten off work at ten o'clock. As she was leaving the restaurant, she remembered seeing Mary Tyler, 37, emptying the trash. Opie Hughes, 39, had been getting ice cream. Joey Johnson had been moving things in the kitchen. David Maxwell was sitting in back talking with Johnson as he worked. Monte Landers had been sitting up front waiting for his friends, Johnson and Maxwell. She knew all but Landers.

Ms. Wilson had been very lucky that night. If she had lingered any at all there would have been six victims.

Inside the restaurant it was obvious that something sinister had taken place. A pool of blood nine inches in diameter was found near the cash register; more blood was in the office and on what we learned was the filing cabinet where the money was kept; and there was a small trail of blood between the two. Being an establishment where blood was not uncommon, we could not at first be sure the blood was human. In fact, one investigator did a quick spot analysis and reported it as animal blood, and it was so reported in the local newspapers. But after laboratory analysis it was proven to be human. We later determined that it belonged to Mary Tyler. We believed that she put up a struggle, or possibly identified one of the robbers, and was struck by one of the assailants.

One of the first people interviewed was Lean Killingsworth, the store manager. She reported that two thousand dollars had been stolen. Normally there was not that much money kept on the premises, but they had inadvertently failed to make their normal afternoon bank deposit.

By midmorning, other than having five missing persons, we did not have much. We had a baseball cap that we could not definitely tie to anyone, and footprints near the back door that had been smudged and were never able to be positively identified. There was not any evidence that any firearms had been discharged. All we knew for sure was that the abduction had taken place between the time Ms. Wilson got off work at ten o'clock and the time Ms. Miller called the restaurant searching for her mother at 10:30. Because of the blood we knew someone had probably been hurt, and we knew two thousand dollars was missing.

I have often been asked if during the morning I thought that the missing people were dead or alive. Of course, I had no way of knowing for sure, but I suspected the worst. When you have been in this business as long as I have and when your gut talks to you, I have found it is seldom wrong. On this day my gut feelings told me the worst had happened. I just could not see anyone being able to hold five people from 10:30 the previous night until now, without someone getting loose. Regretfully, my feeling of doom was valid. At about 10:30 a.m. we received a call from the Rusk County Sheriff's Office. At 10:20 a.m. a Henderson Clay Products employee, Arthur Warlick, had found our missing persons on the company's oil well lease in Rusk County. All were dead.

Rusk County was assigned to Ranger Stuart Dowell, but Stuart was doing weekend National Guard duty so I immediately made preparations to head for the murder site.

The Tyler Police Department had the best crime laboratory in the area. At the beginning of the crime scene investigation, Kilgore's Chief of Police, R. C. Headen, had called them and asked if they would send their lab team to Kilgore. By the time we received word of the discoveries of the bodies, the Captain-In-Charge, Doug Collard, and his team had arrived from Tyler, so even though there was much yet to be done, I was able to leave.

The murder site, a grassy, fenced-in area of a few acres surrounded by woods, is located a few hundred yards east of State Highway 323 on the Walker King Road, in the Pleasant Hill Community, seventeen miles south of Kilgore and seven miles north of Henderson. The only entrance into the area was through a locked gate over a cattle guard.

Every morning Warlick checked the well to make sure it was operating properly. Oil field workers are well known for being rough and rowdy at work and play. When Warlick first saw the bodies he thought some of his buddies were playing a joke on him, but when he saw the blood he knew this was no hoax. Getting on his pickup's two-way radio, he excitedly told his dispatcher what he had found and to call the police. Unfortunately every roughneck in the area heard Warlick's call and rushed to the scene. By the time the Sheriff's Department arrived, there was already a sizable crowd at the scene. All investigators will tell you that they do not want anything, no matter how minute or seemingly insufficient, disturbed at a crime scene. But be that as it may, there was a large well-intended crowd there, and we were left with no choice but to work the site the best way we could.

It would be wrong to describe what we found at the lease as a murder scene—it wasn't a murder scene; it looked more like an outdoor St. Valentine's Massacre. The bodies of Johnson, Landers, Maxwell, and Tyler were lying side by side, face down. Hughes' body was about forty yards north of the others, also face down. All had been shot at least once in the back of the head.

Being a place where five murders had just taken place, it would be natural to think the scene would have been bloody, but it wasn't. Each had been slain in what can only be described as an almost professional manner. Hughes, Landers, and Maxwell had each been shot twice in the back of the head. Tyler had been shot once in the back of the head and once in the back. Johnson had bullet wounds in the back of the head, back of the neck, and in his back on the right side. You will notice the common denominator for each of the victims is "in the back."

There was no evidence then, or later, that any of the victims had been physically mistreated in any way, with the exception of the already-mentioned Mary Tyler. Although there was no visible marks on Johnson's body, unlike his cohorts he had been shot three times.

Investigation of the bodies showed that eleven shots had been fired. With the exclusion of Joey Johnson, all the victims had been shot twice. Gunshots are noisy, and several neighbors heard the shots. James Atkinson, who lived near the site, said he heard screams and told his wife so. She was watching *MASH* on television and said she had not heard anything. She thought it was probably kids making noise after the local Friday night football game. Another neighbor, Preston Crim, heard gunfire at about 11:00 o'clock, but did not think anything about it. Night hunting is not unusual in East Texas.

Whenever the conversation turns to the KFC murders, I can usually count on three questions. Did the victims know their killers? Why were they taken to the Pleasant Hill Community? Was there more than one shooter? I think

212

so. I do not know. Yes.

I believed then, and I believe now, that the only way the killers could have controlled five people for as long as they did was for the victims to have known and trusted, at least to a certain degree, their abductors. I believe the killers knew they had been recognized, but assured the helpless people that they were only going to take them somewhere a long way from a phone, tie them up, and let them go. If this scenario is correct, as I believe it to be, it would have given the victims hope. If you were scared half to death and looking for the slimmest straw to cling to, it would have made sense. By the time they got loose and to a phone, the abductors would have safely made their getaway. If this was not correct, they would have known their situation was hopeless and surely they would have attempted to escape.

Why were they taken to the Pleasant Hill Community? I do not know. Did they go from Kilgore through New London and then on to Pleasant Hill, or did they travel down Highway 259 toward Henderson and then cut across to Pleasant Hill? Again, I do not know. But obviously, whoever was running the show had to know something about the oil field and the miles and miles of twisting and turning oil roads that crisscross the oil patch.

Was there more than one shooter? I believe there was. As I have already said, I do not believe one person could have possibly controlled five people who thought they were in mortal danger for more than a few minutes at the most. Also, when we recovered the bullets we knew for sure that at least two guns had been used in the executions, one a .38 special, the other a .357 Magnum. All the bodies, except Opie Hughes, were lying in a straight line. Ms. Hughes made a run for it; the others had moved hardly at all. I do not think one shooter could have fired fast enough, and accurately enough, to kill all four without more than Ms. Hughes running for her life. As for Ms. Hughes, I believe that she realized what was going to happen, or more likely what was happening, and she made a break for it. Tragically, she was not fast enough. She was chased down, forced to the ground and shot.

As I stated earlier, Rusk County was assigned to Stuart Dowell. As a courtesy and knowing I could use a good hand, I called Captain G. W. Burks in Dallas and asked him to contact Stuart at the National Guard Armory in Terrell, Texas. After being contacted, Stuart headed for Rusk County. Before he arrived, we finished with the bodies and Billy Crawford and his employees of the Crawford-Crim Funeral Home bagged the bodies and moved them to his funeral home in Henderson until the proper paperwork was completed. Once completed, he, along with Rusk County Deputy Doyle Williams and Stuart, who had just arrived from Terrell, transported the bodies to the Dallas Parkland Hospital[3] for an autopsy. Meanwhile, William Brown of the Rusk

---

[3] This is the same Parkland Hospital that President John F. Kennedy and Governor John Connally were transported to on that fatal day in November, 1963.

County District Attorney's Office, Officer Danny Pirtle and I completed the crime scene investigation at the murder location.

Stunned, outraged, scared, mad, confused—all describe the feelings of the citizens of Kilgore and the whole area. Sure, Kilgore had witnessed more than its share of violence during the last fifty-odd years. In 1930, when Dad Joiner discovered the massive East Texas Oil Field, Kilgore had been a tiny community of seven hundred folks. Within weeks it exploded to a population in excess of seven thousand. Violence had certainly been no stranger to Kilgore. But there was something different and terribly wrong with someone taking two hardworking, middle-aged women, and three young men barely past boyhood, out to a lonely oil well site, and shooting them like you would a rabid dog.

Understandably they wanted answers and a conviction—and they wanted it right now. The press was constantly pushing for details, and I had no problem with that—to a point. The public has a right to know how an investigation is going only to the extent that it does not jeopardize the investigation. And that is exactly what we did, we told everything we could—without going too far. But one area newspaper, the *Longview Daily News*, felt we were not doing enough, and said so editorially. According to the newspaper we lacked leadership, and what we needed to solve the case was a "specialized unit" from the Department of Public Safety that could put a "new perspective" on things. Continuing, through insinuation, they claimed, the case was not being handled in a professional manner. I have to admit this upset me. For the only time in my career I responded to a newspaper editorial:

Editor:
I have read many of your editorials in the past, agreed with some and disagreed with others, but always tried in my own mind to understand your viewpoint.
Your editorial dated 12-10-84, regarding the two unsolved multiple murders in Rusk and Gregg counties should have had more mature research before publication.
I myself have explained to your staff the role played by the Texas Department of Public Safety in cases such as these. We are the outside agency called to assist. We in the Texas Ranger service have specialized training plus years of experience and numerous contacts inside and out of law enforcement. Our agency receives calls on a regular basis to assist in training other officers in these areas. Our work on a daily basis places us side by side with well trained officers and beginners. This association and sharing of knowledge and experience enhances our ability and theirs to do a job. To insinuate that these cases are not being investigated in a professional manner is an insult to our profession.
Your writer suggests that some other motive other than robbery was the reason for these murders. Please relate to this officer some

214

reliable evidence to support that conclusion.

Your editorial indicates that no one is in charge. Well let me assure you that our profession is made up of some professional people. We are not so childish that if we are not in charge we won't play on the team. This investigation has been a team working together, sharing and exchanging information with all agencies, yes praying to Almighty God for strength in our field in order to bring these cases to a proper conclusion. Also asking for patience to withstand pitfalls placed in our path by those who seem to know everything.

I accept my responsibility to the people of this community and this state; please accept yours.

Glenn Elliott
Texas Ranger

I got the response from the editor I expected—none.

The editor's insinuation that there were motives other than robbery came from two rumors—one of the victims had a formula for making dope, and it was this formula that the killers were after; or, one of the victims was either selling dope or owed one of the attackers dope money—the rumormongers never made clear which one was the "real" motive. I never believed, then or now, that the killers were after drugs or a delinquent drug bill. I believe it was a simple act of robbery by druggies looking for cash to buy drugs. Fate turned an unkind face on five innocent people when she allowed some lowlifes to stumble onto an establishment that had two thousand dollars in daily receipts in a filing cabinet.

Usually when I meet anyone from this area for the first time the first question I receive concerns the KFC Murders and was if Jimmy Mankins, Jr. was the killer. At the time of this writing the case is still pending and all I can say is what is already public knowledge.

Anyone we could find who had been to the KFC that night, we questioned. We located and questioned the last nine customers to visit the restaurant that night. We interviewed employees, friends, relatives, passersby—anyone who might have had the tiniest bit of knowledge. It was exhausting. During the immediate months following the murders we questioned over two thousand people. Try to realize that these people did not just show up and volunteer information. Some did, but many had to be located and brought in for questioning.

Obviously one group we really zeroed in on was the dopers. You have to understand dopers; they like to brag among themselves. I think almost every doper in the area bragged to one another that they had done the KFC killings. They wanted to portray a "wanna-be tough guy" image to their peers.

Citizens and businesses in the Kilgore area, several who were my personal friends, did what they could; they put their money where their mouth was. They got together and put up a $50,000 reward for the arrest and convic-

215

tion of the killers. This brought all the lowlifes out of the woodworks. Dopers claiming that old so-and-so was the killer were deluging us—give me the $50,000. Of course we checked each lead, but they all proved false. But one name kept coming up over and over — Jimmy Mankins, Jr.

We started gathering up for questioning every doper and so-called bad person we could get our hands on. We asked the standard questions regarding whether they had any knowledge of the crime, but unbeknown to anyone, we were looking for something in particular—a broken fingernail.

While the pathologist and his assistants were removing Joey Johnson's clothes in preparation for an autopsy, a fingernail was discovered lodged between his pants and tucked-in shirt, at the beltline. This fingernail was going to lead us down many roads. Dr. I. C. Stone of the Dallas County Forensic Science Laboratory told us that the striations[4] in a person's fingernail are as unique as fingerprints. If the striations match, there can be no mistake. I worked with a lot of pathologists over the years, but I assure you I have never worked with one better than Dr. Stone.

In a general sweep of the area for known drug users and sellers and known offenders, Mankins was picked up. I was in Henderson interviewing, and Mankins was about the eighteenth or nineteenth person I interviewed. As each person, male or female, came in, I told each the same thing, "Lay your hands up on the table and let's see if you've got any scars or marks on your hands." When Mankins laid his hands on the table the nail on the right ring finger was broken off. I went all the way through the interview without ever mentioning the nail, but as we wrapped up I asked him was how he had broken his fingernail. He claimed that while on the way to our interview he had noticed the fingernail was cracked, and he had torn it on off and thrown it away. At this point we were not quite ready to make a big issue of a missing fingernail.

Dr. Stone had already told us that if we found anyone with a broken fingernail we needed to take a cast of the nail area. I asked Mankins if we could take a cast of his finger and he agreed. Sheriff Strong contacted a dentist friend of his who furnished a solution used to make molds for your teeth. The Sheriff sent a deputy to the dentist's office for the solution. When he returned we made a cast of Mankins finger, which we sent to Dr. Stone in Dallas.

To be sure Dr. Stone requested more clippings of Mankins' nails and a blood sample. Shortly thereafter Mankins gave me what I needed, without argument. I marked the blood sample and ten separate fingernail clippings and sent them to Dallas. Shortly, we got our answer back—it was a perfect match; the nail belonged to Jimmy Mankins, Jr.

---

[4] Striations are the tiny ridges and grooves in your fingernails and toenails.

Many think an arrest should have been made at this point, but for whatever reason the Rusk County District Attorney, Bill Ferguson, felt we did not have a strong enough case and we needed more. Being a positive thinker, it was my thought that with our foot in the door, more evidence would follow.

For the next twelve years the KFC killings remained in limbo. Finally in mid-1995, eight years after my retirement, the Attorney General of the State of Texas, Dan Morales, decided to go for an indictment against Mankins. Those of us who had worked closely on the investigation were called to testify before the grand jury. Rumors had it that there was going to be a change of venue to Beaumont. You could feel a sense of relief sweep over Kilgore. For twelve years the question had been asked over and over; why wasn't Jimmy Mankins arrested and put on trial? Now it was finally going to happen—Jimmy Mankins was going to stand trial.

Yes, it looked like he was going to stand trial, but I did not feel good about what was happening, a feeling I shared with others. I felt the trial was being done for all the wrong reasons, mainly politics. And there was one thing most people either did not know, or chose to overlook—in 1995, we did not have one shred of evidence that we did not have in 1983.

On Monday, December 13, 1995, a bomb exploded. All charges against Jimmy Mankins, Jr., were dropped. Everyone, from the people on the street to the news media, demanded, "How could this happen?" Easy. The Attorney General got his cart in front of his horse.

This was the second highly publicized case the Attorney General's office has been involved in East Texas. A short time before Morales decided to indict Mankins, Kelly Wilson, a teenage girl had mysteriously disappeared in Gilmer, Texas never to be heard from again.[5] Like the KFC killings, the people demanded answers. And like the KFC case, the Attorney General charged in, arrested a bunch of people, led everyone to believe that the case would go to trial in the near future, and then dropped all charges.

In 1983, DNA testing was in its infancy. In 1995, the infamous fingernail was sent to Washington for analysis, but after the indictment had been announced. The result was devastating to the prosecution. Tests did not show, conclusively, that the fingernail belonged to Mankins, neither did they show it didn't. But the damage was done, and that was that—case dismissed.

Attorney General Morales' intentions could have been more than political—I do not know—but regardless, things went astray in both cases. One thing I do give him credit for: at least both cases were brought to a public hearing.

Those of us in law enforcement have to rely on the forensic labs, and I know there are none better than ours. I also know no one is a better forensic

---

[5] At least as of the date of this writing, 1998.

scientism that Dr. I. C. Stone. The only way I would believe he made a mistake was if he came to me and said, "Glenn, I made a mistake." But that has never happened.

CHAPTER XIII
THE KILLERS

In my nearly four decades in law enforcement I was involved in far too many cases to cover in this book, but some were so interesting, or special, that I can not in good conscience omit them. Without going into very much detail, I would like to briefly revisit a few of these cases.

MARTHA "VICKIE" CROWDER

Not long ago I, like the rest of the world, was stunned while watching the evening news when Nancy Smith's two babies were pulled out of a pond in North Carolina. For days we had watched and sympathized as a heartbroken Ms. Smith told how a black man had kidnapped her precious children. At the same time, I began to get a sinking feeling in the pit of my stomach. It brought back a flood of memories from 1964.

During my thirty-eight years as a lawman, if I ever worked a harder case, emotionally, than the Rickie Dale Crowder case, I don't have a clue what it was. Even though I was barely involved with the case, it was a nightmare. Rickie Crowder lived only twenty-two months, and from the evidence, his short life was not a happy one. Rickie's father was Rex Crowder of Longview. In 1966, Crowder was in the Air Force, stationed at Clark Field in the Philippines. The woman who brought little Rickie into this world was Martha "Vickie" Crowder. Originally from Pineville, Louisiana, her mother and brother were living in Longview, and she had been living with them since Rex had gone to Manila.

Shortly after 8:00 p.m. on Sunday, October 4, Crowder reported to the Longview Police that her twenty-two month old son, Rickie Dale, had been taken from her 1964 Falcon while it was parked at the Earlee Shopping Center[1] in Longview. She was going to Fuller's Walgreen Drug Store, but

---

[1] The Earlee Shopping Center is located at the southwest corner intersection of High & Whaley Street in Longview.

because the parking lot was so crowded, she claimed that she had to park the car some distance from the drug store. She said she walked to the store, bought some supplies, and when she returned to the car, Little Rickie Dale was missing. Her memory was terribly fuzzy, but she seemed to remember two black men had been sitting in a 1950 Ford car right beside where she parked.

The news hit the community like a thunderbolt: "Lost Child!" The Gregg County Sheriff's Department and the FBI joined the Longview Police Department. Longview Chief of Police Robert Tutt requested my assistance. I wish I could say that I was instrumental in the solving of the case, but I wasn't. Longview Detective Earl Claxton broke the case on Wednesday, October 7. But I am getting ahead of myself.

When news of the kidnapping hit the community, several people called the police station reporting some of Vickie Crowder's activities, and what kind of mother she was. The information was consistent, and not good. The Crowders had two boys: Rex, Jr., five years old, and twenty-two-month-old Rickie Dale.

One neighbor reported that she had heard Crowder state she was going to send the boys to their father in Manila. She was twenty-five and they interfered with her personal life too much. One way or another, she was going to rid herself of the boys. The neighbor also noted that she had heard from mutual friends that it was not unusual for Crowder to beat the children.

It did not take long to establish a few facts about the case. We knew that she had hired H. L. and Hazel Miller of Gladewater to babysit. At two o'clock on the day of the kidnapping, she had dropped Rickie off with the Millers. She had returned at five o'clock the same afternoon, paid the Millers one dollar and fifty cents for babysitting, and left their home at approximately 5:30.

When asked if she would go to Tyler to take a polygraph test, she agreed after much deliberation. After signing the necessary papers, she along with her mother accompanied Longview Detectives Bob Connell and Travis Puckett to Tyler to take the polygraph test. Robert Deaton, of the Tyler Police Department, administered two separate tests. She failed both tests miserably. Test results showed that she knew a lot more about the kidnapping than she was revealing. The only reason we could figure as to why she agreed to take the test in the first place was because of her mother being present. If she had refused, it would have looked bad. Of course, that's only conjecture on my part.

When questioned further about her whereabouts and activities that afternoon, Crowder became extremely hostile to the investigating officers. They caught her in lie after lie. The more lies they caught her in, the more hostile she became. Her reply was always the same—her personal affairs were none

220

of their business and had nothing to do with getting her child back. She had told them all they needed to know, and her word ought to be good enough for them. An example of how malicious she was: a picture of Rickie Dale was needed so that posters could be put out for the boy—officers had to almost forcibly take a picture from her.

She continued to lie and dig herself deeper and deeper into a hole. The very afternoon she was in Tyler taking the polygraph test, I was in Henderson interviewing one of her boyfriends at length. He was anxious to tell me everything he knew about Crowder; he wanted to put as much distance as he could between himself and her. He admitted that he had started going with Crowder about the time her husband had gone overseas. They had first met at the Palms Lounge on West Marshall Avenue in Longview. She was a barmaid, and came on to him like ". . . she did with most men, a runaway freight train." She asked him to wait for her until she got off work at midnight. He did. That night and during the ensuing weeks, they had a real good time. He said she always had plenty of money, and was very "sexy," to put it mildly. He also said that she was not a person to say no to, she had a volcanic temper.

On the day of the kidnapping she had called him and wanted to meet him that afternoon at the Horseshoe Lounge in Longview. They met at two o'clock, left in his car, and returned about 4:30. Dropping her off, he returned to Henderson. Even though he had not seen her since, he had talked to her. The day after the disappearance, she called him and told him about the kidnapping. Considering the circumstances, he was amazed at her calmness and that she seemed not the least bit upset. During the conversation she continuously assured him that he was not involved in any way, and that she would not mention his name. That was the last contact he had with her. I had the distinct impression that he wished he had never heard of her.

Her brother, Curtis Felter, added additional light to her character when he was questioned by Deputies W. H. Owen and Clyde Arthur. In Felter's statement, he said that his sister had moved in with him and their mother in Longview on August 4, 1964, when her husband left for Manila. He was upset that his sister spent precious little time at home, and had left the children for their mother to take of. Although her husband, Rex, Sr., was sending her five hundred dollars a month for his family's upkeep, she wasn't spending it where it was intended. Felter was bitter that in her letters to Rex, she said she had to keep both her mother and brother up. According to her, after paying all the bills she barely had money left to feed the kids. Felter said the truth of the matter was, the whole time she had been living with them, she had contributed a grand total of fifteen dollars toward groceries and the well-being of her sons.

Other horror stories continued to come in. It seemed that a few years earlier almost the exact same thing had happened to Crowder and her other son, Rex, Jr., in Pineville, Louisiana. Fortunately, the tot was found safe and sound.

Whoever said that knowing someone is guilty, and proving it, are two very different things, knew what he was talking about. It was obvious that this gal was lying like a dog, and the evidence continued to mount. But knowing and proving. . . .

On Wednesday, October 7, another acquaintance of Crowder, N. N. Brewer, told us that Crowder had borrowed his vacuum cleaner. She had used it to go over her car from one end to the other. Mr. Brewer gave Deputy Clyde Arthur and me the vacuum bag. I sent the contents of the bag to the DPS lab in Austin. They proved to be negative.

But the jig was about up for Vickie Crowder. Later that same day, Detective Claxton broke the case. That Wednesday morning, Claxton returned to the Felter home. Upon arriving he found Crowder, her mother and brother at home. After being invited in, he sat down on the couch and asked her how she was feeling. "Fine," she said.

She told him that her five-year-old son, Rex, had earlier in the morning told her that he could see his brother crying on a hill. Her brother, Curtis, spoke up and said that was true. The boy had awakened him at two o'clock that morning. He had been dreaming, and in the dream he could see his brother crying.

Earl asked where the boy was. She said he was in school. He told her that he would go get the boy and take them anywhere they wanted to go if it could help find Rickie Dale. She said that would be fine, but first she had to see Foster Fort, a reporter for the *Longview News,* at eleven o'clock. Aggravated at her priorities, Earl had no choice but to agree to wait until after the interview before beginning the search. He agreed to pick up Vickie, Rex, Jr., Mrs. Felter, and Curtis Felter at one o'clock that afternoon.

Returning at the appointed hour, he was just in time to meet Crowder, Rex, Jr., and Curtis Felter pulling into the driveway. Obviously Crowder was very upset about something. He asked Felter what the trouble was. Felter replied that shortly after Earl had left, a lady from the church had come by. When she heard about the boy's vision she offered to take them to the spot the older brother had seen in his vision. Crowder, the boy, and Felter had loaded into the woman's car and Rex, Jr., directed them to a place off Spring Hill Road, where he told them to stop. I suppose the church lady had second thoughts. She remembered a sick mother she had to check on, and she did not want to be involved in this affair. Crowder overheard the lady, took it the wrong way, and pitched a "raving fit." She refused to ride back with the lady. Felter rode back home, and had no sooner arrived when he got a call from his sister asking him to pick up her and Rex, Jr., at a liquor store on Spring Hill Road and Marshall Avenue. He did so, and as they pulled back into their driveway, they met Detective Claxton.

Earl asked Felter to take him to the place where Rex, Jr., had just taken them. He took them to a location in Northwest Hills. After taking a quick glance at the wooded area, he decided to have it searched later.

Earl and Felter returned to the Felter home at 1024 West Marshall. He again talked to Crowder, and she acted as if nothing had happened. When asked if she was ready, she said yes. Earl, Vickie Crowder, Rex, Jr., and Felter loaded into Earl's car and started driving, following the boy's directions.

Going as the boy directed, they turned off Loop 281 onto a dirt road. They continued to a deadend. Less than a mile and a half from Loop 281 and McCann Road, they stopped at a destitute area. I know it's hard to believe today, but in October 1964, Loop 281 was brand-new and had very little traffic and virtually no businesses on it.

Getting out of the car, Earl said he would search the creek bed at the bottom of the hill for the boy. Crowder got out of the car, saying that she would help. They had gone only a short distance when he heard her scream, "Oh, my baby, my baby!" and she started to run to the bottom of the hill where a lifeless body lay.

Earl intercepted her, and started her back toward the car. Crowder fainted. (I don't know if she really did, or if she was just a good actress. Personally, I suspect the latter.) Regardless, Earl picked her up and called her brother to come and help. But Felter was in a state of shock, having seen his tiny nephew at the bottom of the hill. Earl managed to get Crowder, Felter, and little Rex back to the car. He called for help from his squad car.

The boy was dead. A more appalling sight I have never seen. The baby had died of exposure less than twenty-four hours before being found. I can not begin to imagine the terror that a twenty-two-month old baby must have felt wandering around lost for a whole day and two nights. Tired, cold, hungry, thirsty, terrified, and mystified. God only knows what must have gone through that tiny, innocent little boy's mind.

I wish that had of been the end of my involvement, but it wasn't—there was still the autopsy. I have sat through a lot of autopsies, but this was far and away the worst. Watching the gruesome work, I could not imagine how anyone, let alone a parent, could be heartless.

We indicted her on murder charges. Her attorney felt she could not possibly get a fair trial in Longview. He asked for and was granted a change of venue to Quitman, Texas. She was tried, and this piece of human garbage was sentenced to twenty years in prison. And an innocent twenty-two-month old baby whose only crime was interfering with his mother's partying was sentenced to an eternity in a premature grave.

JOHN DOROUGH

One of my most often-asked questions is: "Who was the coldest, meanest person you ever met?" If I ever ran across anyone colder or meaner than John Melvin Dorough, Jr., of Longview, I don't know who it would have been. Like Vickie Crowder, I had very little to do with his case, but I will never forget it.

On September 29, 1977, I got a strange phone call from Frank Odom of the Gregg County DA's office. He had gotten a call from the Mental Health and Retardation Center in Longview. Odom said the doctor wanted someone from law enforcement to visit him. He had just had a patient who told him a chilling story. Before I go any further, I want to emphasize that the Center was a State-run operation. The State of Texas paid the doctors; thus there was no doctor-patient privilege.

I met Captain Bill Roach of the Gregg County Sheriff's Office and we proceeded to the Retardation Center. The doctor told us a gruesome story. John Dorough had visited his office and disclosed to the doctor that he was having a variety of mental problems. He had told the doctor that he had only recently gotten out of the Army[2] and returned to Longview from his duty station at Fort Bliss in El Paso.

Shortly before his discharge, on a dark, moonless night, he had gone out in the desert on the outskirts of El Paso where young lovers often parked. Then he waited. He didn't have long to wait before a car containing young lovers parked. As soon as the young couple stopped, Dorough assaulted the couple with a .22 magnum derringer. After getting the teenagers out of their car, he made the young man get into the car's trunk. Then he turned his attention to the girl. He forced her to lie down on the backseat of the car and raped her.

Once finished with the girl, he intended to put her in the trunk as well, but he made a mistake. He should have made the girl get into the trunk immediately, but he didn't. When he opened the trunk, he shot and killed the young man. I suppose he thought she would just patiently wait until he was finished killing her boyfriend and then meekly allow him to murder her. But she didn't play the game as he planned. With Dorough's attention focused on murdering her boyfriend, she made a break for the desert and miraculously made it. Once there, she went to ground. Peeking around the welcome tumbleweed, she watched as Dorough searched for her frantically. All the while he searched,

---

[2] Dorough was discharged on September 15, 1977.

he screamed for her to come out. He assured her that hiding would only make matters worse. She was terrified, but not stupid. She wasn't buying into that for one second and she had enough of her wits not to move a muscle. He finally gave up on finding her and disappeared into the night.

Staggering through the blackness of the desert night, she finally reached a house and was able to call for help. The El Paso Sheriff's Department worked hard on the case for weeks, but they had been unable to develop any solid leads into the murder and rape.

Then Bill and I heard the doctor's story. We returned to the courthouse, and called the El Paso County Sheriff's Office, and were immediately put through to Detective Wallace "Eddie" Brown. As we related the doctor's story, we could tell that he was becoming very excited. When we finished the doctor's report, Brown said, "Man, y'all are telling me things about this case that have never been made public. This has got to be right."

The El Paso officers went to nearby Fort Bliss and secured Dorough's Company picture. The girl had said that while she was being raped, her attacker had left the car door open and the dome light was on. She had gotten a good look at the rapist, and assured the police it was a face she would remember until the day she died. When presented with the Company picture, she immediately picked out Dorough. This was the type of lineup identification that you dream of, with everyone dressed exactly alike, standing exactly the same, and all with the same expression on their faces. As far as picture line-ups go, it would never get any better than this.

On October 1, I received a call from Detective Brown informing me that warrants had been issued on Dorough on two counts of aggravated kidnapping, one count of aggravated rape, and one count of capital murder. The warrants would be in my possession shortly. He asked if we would locate Dorough and, if possible, arrest him.

While waiting on word from El Paso, we learned that Dorough's mother, Dorothy, was living at 519 Buchanan, in Longview. There was no question that this man was extremely dangerous, so we laid our plans accordingly.

We secured a warrant, and, besides me, the arresting team would consist of Gregg County Sheriff Tom Welch, Deputies Ken Hartley, Bill Roach, Joe Money, and the investigator from the Gregg County DA's Office, Frank Odom. Our plan also required the help of the Sheriff's dispatcher. In fact, she was the key ingredient in our plan. Once we were in position, she was to call the Dorough home and say she was the long-distance operator from El Paso, and had a person-to-person call for John Dorough. If he came to the phone she was to tell him to stand by, the calling party had to deposit money on the other end. While she had him on hold, she would radio us and we would go in — and go in fast. We were sure that if he answered the phone, we could take him without any shooting. It would be very unlikely that he would have a gun in one hand and a phone in the other, especially in his mother's home. Sheriff Welch, Deputy Hartley, and I would go in the front door, while Deputies Roach and Money guarded the back door. Frank Odom was to remain in contact with the dispatcher and signal us if Dorough answered the phone.

It worked like a charm. His mother answered the phone. "Long distance for John Dorough."

"Yes, he's here. Just a minute."

Dorough answered, and the dispatcher-"operator" put him on hold and relayed to Odom that he was on the phone. In the front door Welsh, Hartley, and I went. And there stood Dorough, with nothing in his hands except the phone. He knew we had him cold-handed and did not offer the least bit of resistance. He remained calm and quiet as Sheriff Welch put the handcuffs on him and took him out the front door to jail.

After they left with her son, Hartley and I stayed behind to talk to Mrs. Dorough. She was a nice, hardworking woman who did not deserve the problems her son handed her. I told her why we had arrested him, the circumstances around the murder, and, an outline of how it had all come down. Needless to say, she was distraught—not panicky, but distraught.

I remember it was a Saturday and she was frying chicken. She cut the stove off, sat the chicken aside, and all three of us sat down at the kitchen table. I told her what I was looking for—a 22 pistol. She said, "Yeah, he's got one in there in the top drawer."

I proceeded to explain to her in detail that, "We can't seize it without you giving us permission to search. I've got a consent to search form in my car." I went to the car, got the form, brought it in, filled it out, and explained it to her, again in minute detail.

Before signing, she asked, "What happens if I don't sign this?"

I explained, "I'll leave here and go to a Justice of the Peace and try to convince him that I've got probable cause to get a search warrant. If I do, I'll come back with the search warrant and then we'll legally search your house." And I added, "Of course, I'll leave this officer outside to make sure that nobody leaves here with any property, but I don't think you'd do that."

She said, ".. there is no need to go to all that trouble . . ." and she signed the form.

I found the .22 derringer right where she said it was. Ballistics proved it to be the murder weapon.

On Tuesday, October 4, Detective Brown and Sergeant Booker of the El Paso Sheriff's Office arrived in Longview to escort Dorough back to El Paso. We were talking while waiting for their prisoner to be prepared for the long trip back. One of the El Paso officers[3] said, "Well, there's a belt buckle the

---

[3] I don't remember which officer it was.

girl described that he had on and I bet it's out there at Dorough's house too." They had not told us about that, but I remembered seeing the belt buckle while searching for the pistol. I told them to delay their departure so that we could go before a judge and secure a search warrant for the Dorough house. Along with Hartley and the El Paso officers, we returned to Dorothy Dorough's house, presented the search warrant, and found the belt buckle right where I remembered seeing it.

Well, the case went before this old liberal judge in El Paso, and he threw out the pistol as evidence even though ballistic experts had positively identified it as the murder weapon. By the time Dorothy Dorough got on the stand, her son's attorney had had time to work on her. She testified that she was so distraught and upset sitting at the kitchen table, she didn't really know what she was signing. She hadn't really wanted to sign the form, but claimed she was afraid of me and what I would do to her if she didn't sign. The judge ruled the consent to search inadmissible and agreed with Dorough's attorney that I had coerced her into signing.

I promise you, I have never been more courteous to anyone in my life than I was to Mrs. Dorough. I went to great length to explain, in detail, what the consent to search form was. I guarantee you; she understood perfectly what she was signing. Naturally she was upset. Who wouldn't have been if her son had just been arrested for kidnapping, rape, and murder. But she was in control and never—and I mean never—did she once show any concern that Ken Hartley or I was the least bit aggressive towards her.

But even with the judge refusing this key evidence, he could not deny the victim's dead-bang identification. The jury agreed. Dorough was given a life sentence.[4]

DENNIS WHITE

On Tuesday, July 6, 1965, I received a call from Harrison County Sheriff Earl Franklin requesting assistance in the investigation of an unidentified body found near the Scottsville area. At the time, Interstate 20 was under construction. Near the intersection of I-20 and FM-2199[5] was a pond from which the road builder[6] hauled water they were using in the construction of the highway. Since late Saturday, one of the drivers hauling the water, Tillman

---

[4] On December 5, 1996, Dorough became eligible for parole, but did not make it.

[5] In Texas some roads are designated Farm to Market—FM.

[6] Howard Brothers Construction Company, Paris, Texas.

Harting,[7] had smelled an odor of something dead that grew worse with each passing hour. You have to have survived the incredible heat and humidity of an East Texas summer to understand why the quickly-worsening smell did not at first evoke any suspicions. But by Monday afternoon, July 5, the odor had become so wretched that Harting and another construction worker, S. D. Winn,[8] investigated.

Climbing to the top of the pond's earthen dam and looking down the rear side, they were greeted with a ghastly sight—something that had once been a human being. But the blazing hot sun of a Texas summer had bloated the human remains into a grotesque form beyond any possible recognition by the human eye alone.

Grotesque is not a strong enough word to describe what we saw, but grotesque or not, we had a job to do. Once we completed the crime scene investigation, the body was removed to Sullivan's Funeral Home in Marshall. Arriving at Sullivan's the next day, I was joined by Harrison County District Attorney Charles Allen, Marshall pathologist Dr. Mildred Cariker, Sullivan's employee A. D. Wall, and the DPS lab team; Chemist Charles Bearsley, Fingerprint Expert Billy Weir, and Photographer Wallace Nelson.

Because of the horrendous odor the decaying body emitted, Sullivan had thankfully arranged a temporary morgue in his garage—complete with a large fan to blow the gagging odor through the open garage door. We had identified the body as that of a white male, with a small bullet hole completely through the head. But that was as far as we had gotten. The body was in such an advanced state of deterioration that we were not able to fingerprint it. This could only be accomplished with the proper equipment from the lab in Austin. I assisted the lab boys in removing the victim's hands and lower jaw. (And you thought being a Texas Ranger was just fighting it out, with the bad guys, and also always winning, and of course, always winning the girl, just like they do on TV!)

After completion of the autopsy I questioned Mr. Harting. He remembered seeing two men fishing in the pond the day he first started smelling the body, Saturday. It only took a short time checking the neighborhood before we identified the fishermen as R. D. Hays, a local Marshall man, and his friend James Case from Nacogdoches, Texas. We contacted them and asked them to come to the Sheriff's office. Arriving in short order, they confirmed they had been fishing at the pond the previous Saturday, and had smelled something dead. They had assumed that it was a dead animal of some kind. The possibility that the odor was from a decaying human never entered their minds. They had found a Czechoslovakian blank-firing starter pistol, and a

---

[7] From Detroit, Texas.
[8] From Paris, Texas.

steel hunting knife at the pond, but they assumed someone had simply lost them.

The next day, July 7, I received a call from Joel Tinsdale, head of the DPS lab in Austin. The body had been positively identified as twenty-seven-year old Airman First Class William Travis Martin, Jr. Currently he was stationed at Keasler Field,[9] Mississippi. He lived off base in the nearby town of Ocean Springs. The Ocean Springs Police Department had reported him missing on July 4. I contacted their Chief of Police, W. T. Broom. He reported that Martin had left Ocean Springs at six o'clock on the afternoon of July 2, intending to pick up his mother in Fort Worth, Texas, and had not been seen since. It had been confirmed that he left driving a blue-green, 1964, International pickup, with a Wyoming license plate. He was also reported to be carrying a white leather bag containing his personal items, fifteen dollars in cash, and a Standard courtesy credit card his landlady, Mrs. M. St. John, had loaned him.

I asked why he was driving a pickup registered in Wyoming. He had just been transferred to Keasler Air Force Base from F. E. Warren Air Force Base, in Wyoming and had not yet re-licensed in Mississippi.

We did not know it at the time, but the following day, Thursday, July 8, we broke the case. Actually an on-his-toes DPS dispatcher in Tyler, Hiram Watson, helped break the case.

After positive identification had been made, I had contacted the DPS radio operator in Tyler and requested that they broadcast a message to all points regarding the vehicle in question. The following morning while enroute from Longview to Marshall, I again called the DPS radio office in Tyler and asked Watson if he would rebroadcast my request. Hiram had not been on duty when the All Points Bulletin had first been broadcast. After reading the message, he radioed me and asked me to call him on the phone[10] regarding a relating message between El Dorado, Arkansas, and Lufkin, Texas.

As soon as I got to Marshall I called Hiram. He said he had picked up a radio message from the Lufkin Police Department to the El Dorado Police Department inquiring if they had an unsolved murder in their area, where a small caliber pistol was used.

The law enforcement business is like any other—you have to work together. If Watson had not been on his toes and put two and two together—an inquiry into a possible small caliber killing in Arkansas, and our small caliber murder—this case might not have been solved. Maybe I'm prejudiced, being an old radio operator, but this is a classic example of people doing their job, and seldom being noticed.

---

[9] Near Gulfport, Mississippi.

[10] There were police scanners even then. This was very important information and Hiram did not want it to be picked up by anyone but me.

I immediately contacted Chief Billy McKnight of the Lufkin Police Department. He advised me that he had Dennis Richard White in custody on a charge of rape. His victim reported that while being held by White, he had flashed a pistol and bragged that he had killed a man in Arkansas, and if she did not do exactly as instructed he would kill her too.

I asked what kind of transportation White was using when he was arrested. Chief McKnight told me that White had been arrested by three of his officers[11] in the local bus station with a ticket to Monterrey, Mexico, in his possession. They had assumed he did not have a vehicle. I asked the Chief to inquire from the victim if she had seen White driving a vehicle. She replied that she had indeed seen him driving a blue pickup.

Chief McKnight told me that he, the victim, and White were just leaving for Houston to run each on the polygraph, and asked if I would like to join them. I told him I certainly would, and arranged to meet them in Houston. I contacted Sheriff Franklin and asked if he would like to accompany me to Houston. He did. I also called Charlie Neal, the polygraph operator in Houston. I briefed Charlie—who would later be a Texas Ranger—on the details of our murder case in Scottsville, and requested that he question White about Martin's murder while running him on the polygraph. I also requested that a Houston Ranger, John Hoyt, sit in on the test until I could get there.

About 2:00 p.m. while enroute to Houston I received a radio call from Neal advising me that White had admitted that he had killed a man in East Texas, stolen his pickup, and later abandoned it at the parking lot of the Angelina Hotel in Lufkin. He also named fifteen-year-old Ronnie Kay as his accomplice. Furthermore, White made a written statement in his own handwriting admitting the murder.

I called Marshall and asked the Harrison County Assistant District Attorney, R. P. Watson, to contact Chief Deputy Robby Robinson, per Sheriff Franklin's request, and for the Chief Deputy to sign murder complaints on both White and Kay. I then called the DPS lab in Austin and asked Joel Tinsdale if he could furnish assistance in processing the victim's pickup for evidence. By then we were in Lufkin, so we stopped to investigate the pickup.

Flying one of the DPS helicopters, the lab crew arrived in Lufkin at 4:15 p.m. We went over that pickup from one end to the other with the proverbial fine-toothed comb. We found bloody rags, cut up seat covers, one unfired .22 caliber long rifle bullet, an empty billfold, and other papers. By 6:00 p.m. we were finished and the lab boys had the evidence bagged, and headed back to Austin.

Meanwhile, White had been returned to Lufkin, arraigned before Judge Homer Greenville, and booked for rape and carrying a concealed weapon—a

---

[11] Kenneth Birdsong, Leonard Chandler, and C. R. Stanley.

seven-shot Harrington-Richardson .22 caliber revolver, loaded with regular and hollow point ammunition. When arrested he had a bus station locker key. When we opened the locker it contained a white leather bag that matched the bag reportedly carried by Airman Martin.

Under questioning by Sheriff Franklin and me, White said that he and Ronnie Kay were from Rockford, Illinois. At Lufkin he and Kay had parted company. Kay had called his mother for money so that he could go home. She had wired him the money and he had left, via bus, for Rockford earlier in the day.

I went to the local Western Union office in Lufkin and requested a copy of Kay's telegram. I was told it was Western Union's policy not to give copies of telegrams without a court order. Okay, if that's the way they wanted to do it, we'd get it that way. The following day, July 9, I went before Judge O. L. Hubbard, of Lufkin, and obtained a letter from the court giving Western Union the authority to give us the requested information. Armed with the letter, we went back to the Western Union office, and got a copy of the telegram. By this time I also had arrest warrants for both White and Kay for murder.

We contacted the Rockford, Illinois, Police Department and relayed the warrant numbers and information regarding the case. I told them that the necessary paperwork was on its way, and asked if they would please go to Kay's mother's home; if Kay showed up, I asked if they would detain him until the warrants arrived. They offered their cooperation to assist in any way possible. It was police departments like Rockford's that made my job so enjoyable.

On Friday, July 9, Sheriff Franklin, White, and I left Lufkin headed for Marshall. Before delivering White to the Harrison County Jail, he directed us to the spot on Highway 80 east of Marshall where he shot Airman Martin. Then he took us to the spot on the pond where he and Kay had dumped the body.

Late that afternoon we took White before Harrison County Justice of the Peace J. G. Stauts for arraignment. A lot of time was spent warning him of all his rights before the law. He understood and agreed to give a voluntary statement to Assistant District Attorney Watson.

The following day, we received a call from the Rockford, Illinois, Police Department. They had Ronnie Kay in custody. Furthermore, he had signed a waiver to return to Texas, and had made a statement admitting his part in the murder.

On Sunday, July 11, Sheriff Franklin and I left Marshall headed for Rockford, Illinois, to pick up Mr. Kay. We arrived in Rockford the following afternoon. We immediately went into conference with Kay's attorney, P. A. Nicolosi. Mr. Nicolosi requested that we wait until the following day before starting extradition proceedings. We agreed. The next morning, Kay, in open court, signed consent papers to return to Texas. We loaded him into our car and left Rockford immediately and arrived back in Marshall the following day, Wednesday, July 14.

In Marshall, Kay gave a detailed statement admitting his part in the murder. His facts were almost identical to the statement given by White.

This murder was about as senseless as they come. It seems that White was soon to go on trial in his hometown of Galena, Illinois, for rape, and he wanted to get out of town, fast. Though only fifteen years old, Ronnie Kay was already a wanderer. He had only returned to Galena from Arizona a few days before. He had been back but a few days before he realized he had made a mistake—tiny Galena was still boring and could never provide the adventure and excitement he yearned for. When he teamed up with Dennis White he got more action than he bargained for. But that was still in the unknown future.

Before leaving Galena they had to overcome two problems: money and a car, of which, they had neither. They managed to rake up a few bucks between them. As for the car, that was no problem. On June 29, White stole a 1957 Oldsmobile 98 from John Deery's used car lot in Galena and headed south toward Jackson, Mississippi, to visit a would-be girlfriend.

They got as far as Marked Tree, Arkansas, before a blowout forced them to abandon the Olds. From Marked Tree, after much frustration, they managed to hitchhike to Jackson. Finally arriving in Jackson, they made a beeline for the girl White thought would welcome him with open arms. They were in for quite a shock. The "girlfriend" made it extremely plain that they were about as welcome as the plague, and told them in no uncertain words to hit the road. On the road again without any money or a vehicle, White stated to Kay that he had a .22 pistol that belonged to his father, and one way or another ". . . he was going to get some money."

Around midnight, July 2, they were thumbing it on westbound Highway 80 in Jackson when Airman Martin stopped to give them a ride. As they drove westward they visited and made small talk. About 4:40 in the morning they stopped at a truck stop in Shreveport, Louisiana, and ate breakfast, which Martin paid for. Leaving the truck stop Martin asked White if he had a driver's license. White said he did, and Martin asked him to drive so that he could get a few hours of badly needed sleep. Martin, sitting at the passenger door, and Kay, in the middle, were soon asleep.

Shreveport is located near the Louisiana-Texas border, and they had only gotten about five miles into Texas when White slapped Kay on the back of the head and told him to lean forward. Half asleep, Kay did as he was instructed. No sooner had he leaned forward than White drew the revolver he was carrying, stretched his arm across Kay, put the pistol next to Martin's head, and fired. The sound of the .22 going off in the small confines of the pickup cab was like a cannon. Kay, suddenly wide awake, bolted straight up in the seat. White yelled at Kay, "Get down, you fool." Still reaching across Kay, he pressed the pistol against Martin's head and pulled the trigger again. This time the bullet misfired. Undaunted, White thumbed the hammer again. This time there was no misfire, and another bullet ripped into Martin's head. Not satisfied, White fired yet a third time. After the first shot, Kay said that Martin reached out as if grasping for something. After the second shot, Martin slumped down in the seat. Even after the third shot, Martin was not dead, but started moaning.

Kay cried out to White, "What have you done?"

White's only reply was, "We've got to get rid of the body."

"He's not dead!"

"He will be in a few minutes. With three bullet holes in his head, he'll die."

Stopping the pickup beside a pond, White jumped out of the truck, ran around to the passenger door, yanked it open, and with the pistol still in his hand, ordered Kay to ". . . get out here and help me." They drug Martin to the top of the pond dam, where White went through his pockets, emptied them, removed all of nineteen dollars that Martin had on him, and stole the wristwatch off Martin's arm. White then put his foot under Martin and shoved him onto the backside of the dam.

Returning to the pickup they started south again. White ordered Kay to throw all of Martin's personal effects out the window and clean up all the blood he could. What he could not clean up, he was to take a hunting knife that was in the cab and cut away the bloody section of seat cover and throw it away. Reaching Lufkin they stopped. White went his way, and Kay his. It was at this point that Kay wired his mother for thirty-five dollars so he could return to Galena, Illinois. White bought a bus ticket to Mexico.

Since he had awhile to wait on the bus, White decided to cruise Lufkin. Somehow he picked up a local girl, and quickly reverted to his true self—he raped her. Like many criminals, he must have thought he was invincible. He was a picture of unconcern and innocence sitting in the bus station when the Lufkin police arrested him for the rape.

Dennis Richard White was tried in the 71st District Court in Marshall, Texas, on December 16, 1965, and found guilty of murder. He was sentenced to life imprisonment.

Ronald Eugene Kay, being a fifteen-year-old minor at the time of the crime, and because he turned state's evidence, was paroled.

HENRY LEE LUCAS

On January 19, 1984, Ranger Stuart Dowell and I heard the confession of one of the worst serial killers that every stalked an innocent victim: Henry Lee Lucas. From 1975 until his arrest on June 11, 1983, Lucas and his partner, Ottis Toole,[12] claimed to have killed more than six hundred people from one end of the country to the other.[13] When he started confessing, Lucas confessed to every unsolved murder in the last eight years in every corner of the country. Many of the killings he claimed would be proven conclusively not to have been committed by the gruesome duo.

Of the six hundred people Lucas claimed he and Toole had killed, though they preferred young, white females, they didn't hesitate to kill black women. They also killed many older women and young children. While preferring women, they did not hesitate to kill men. But they usually only killed men during an armed robbery or when a man was with the female victim they had chosen. They were also responsible for the slaying of more than one homosexual.

Lucas' and Toole's M.O. varied little. They did not stalk their victims for long. They would pick someone out and move quickly on them. They used various come-ons, from the standard pickup to the more exotic—Toole was known to dress in drag.

Nor did they discriminate as to how they killed. Some they beat to death; others they stabbed; strangulation was another favorite; but for most, there was always the old reliable method of shooting. They also liked mutilation; they dissected, decapitated, and lacerated. Lucas was very fond of this; he was known to have carried various body parts in a bag around the country with him.[14]

Lucas never claimed to have been sent by God to avenge some wrong. In fact, he never tried to justify his actions in any way. The closest he ever came to an explanation for the majority of the killings was his inability to satisfy his sexual needs with a "live" partner. Several of his proven victims suffered the added indignity of having perverted sex performed on them—after they were dead.

---

[12] By 1983 Toole was already doing time in Florida. Earlier Toole and Lucas had wandered back to their base, Jacksonville, Florida. While there, Ottis Toole had been arrested and sent to prison. He died while incarcerated.

[13] Lucas and Toole were suspected of killings in Arkansas, California, Colorado, Florida, Georgia, Kansas, Kentucky, Louisiana, Maryland, Missouri, Nebraska, Nevada, New Jersey, North Carolina, Oklahoma, South Carolina, Texas, Virginia, and Wisconsin.

[14] He killed an unknown male in Plainview, Texas. The victim's head was found in Scottsdale, Arizona, more than seven hundred miles from Plainview.

234

Of course, when captured and charged, his attorneys went for the "innocent, by reason of insanity" defense, but that did not fly. Before going to trial Lucas was examined by a battery of psychologists and psychiatrists. Their conclusions were the same: he had a strong personality disorder, but he was sane. Lucas was a sociopath[15] of the worst kind. He would kill anyone, without the least bit of remorse or misgiving. His first known killing was in 1960—he spent ten years in a Michigan prison for killing his own mother. She was a prostitute, and he claimed that he hated her because she lied, mainly about his alcoholic father.

Lucas could be used as a textbook case to prove that rehabilitation seldom works. He was released from the Michigan State Penitentiary on August 22, 1975. A few days later it was confirmed that he and Ottis Toole killed Curby Reeves in Smith County, Texas, on September 9, 1975.

One of his earliest known serial killings was eighteen year old Lilly Darty of Marshall, Texas, and she was not one of his false claims. There is absolutely no doubt in my mind that Lucas and Toole killed the young lady. Here is how it happened.

On November 1, 1977, Toole and Lucas were in Marshall. They had stopped at the Fast Food Service Store located just north of I-20 on Highway 59 in Marshall. When Miss Darty walked outside the store, Lucas engaged her in conversation. With a little coaxing she agreed to ride around with Lucas and Toole. They drove about half a mile north of Marshall's city limits on Highway 59 and at random turned onto a country road. They parked and walked about a hundred feet into some woods to a deer stand. There, they drank, smoked marijuana, and had sex. Finishing with the girl, Lucas shot her twice in the head with a .32-caliber pistol, once in the right temple and once in the back of the head. Then Lucas and Toole got in their car, and drove off.

Miss Darty's father reported her missing the same day, Monday, November 1, 1977, but the girl's body was not found until Tuesday, December 20, 1977, almost eight weeks later. Deer season was in and some hunters had stumbled upon a gruesome sight, a human skull. They immediately contacted the Harrison County Sheriff's Office. Sheriff Fletcher Shivers[16] contacted me asking for my assistance. The following day I joined Sheriff Shivers at the courthouse and drove to the murder scene. About fifty feet from the skull we found what was left of the body. I do not want to offend, but between the August heat and the varmints, there was little left. We did find the orange pantsuit, wedge shoes, and a ring she had been reported to have been wearing.[17]

---

[15] Sociopath. A person without conscience, or feelings.

[16] This is the same Fletcher Shivers I worked with in the Judge Roe murder in Uncertain, Texas that was discussed earlier.

[17] Her father positively identified these articles as belonging to his daughter.

Doctor Robert Palmer performed an autopsy. He confirmed that the two bullet wounds to the head caused her death. Small lead fragments were also removed from the inner skull, but there was not enough of the bullets left to make any kind of identification.

I wish I could say I had a lot to do with bringing Lucas to justice, but I didn't. Mike Cox[18] has written a book about Lucas and the law enforcement people who brought Lucas down, so I am not going to get into that.

When Lucas started confessing, he was sent all over the area to clear up supposed murders he had committed. On January 14, 1984, I drove to Tyler and met Ranger Stuart Dowell.[19] We picked up Lucas and headed for several places where Lucas claimed to have slaughtered his victims. To be honest, I thought he was nothing but a blowhard, and all he would do was lead us on a wild-goose chase. Needless to say, my anticipated results of this trip were skeptical at best. But when we headed back to Tyler later that same day, there was zero doubt in my mind that Lucas had murdered Lilly Darty.

Nearing Marshall, Lucas instructed us to exit off I-20 and head north on Highway 59. Although there were many convenience stores along Highway 59 in Marshall, as we passed the Fast Food Service Store, Lucas pointed it out saying that was where he and Toole had picked up Miss Darty. I was mildly surprised that he had pointed to the correct convenience store, but it proved nothing, he could have read about that in a newspaper. Lucas was known to have a photographic memory. As we continued driving, Lucas described the clothing Miss Darty had been wearing, but this too could have come from a newspaper. Following his directions, we continued north on Highway 59, heading toward what he claimed to be the crime scene. There was no doubt in my mind that we had caught him in a lie; we were headed in a direction I did not think would take us anywhere near the murder scene.

We had to be careful with this guy; he was extremely smart. We already knew that he would watch the driver real close. He would pounce upon the slightest inconsistency. If you slowed down and looked, or even glanced at the crime scene, as often as not this was all he needed. Seeing the slow down and the glance he would say, "This is the place." Remember, he was admitting to every murder that was placed before him. Needless to say, Stuart and I were using extra precaution not to tip Lucas off.

Continuing north on Highway 59, he suddenly directed us to turn left and head down a small country road. I knew we had him in a lie. We traveled only a short distance when he said, "Stop," and pointed in the exact area

---

[18] Mike is the DPS's Chief of Media Relations in the Public Information Office.

[19] Stuart had transferred to Tyler from Dallas after Bob Mitchell made Sergeant and transferred to Waco.

where the body had been found. We got out of the car and walked only a brief distance into the woods until he stopped us again, saying, "This is where it happened." And it was.

What had confused me was the direction in which Lucas had led us to the murder scene. In 1977, at the time of the murder and in all the subsequent trips to the murder scene, I had left from the courthouse and gone directly through town to the murder scene. When you are getting a confession from a suspect, you do things differently. You don't simply drive to the scene and say, "Is this where you killed the girl?" A fool stunt like that would last in a courtroom about two seconds. You follow the suspect's directions, without any—and I mean any—coaxing. Lucas took us to the scene the way he and Toole had gone, and a way that I was unaware of.

I have already said it once, but there is absolutely no doubt whatsoever in my mind that Henry Lee Lucas and Ottis Toole murdered Lilly Darty. The 71st District Judge in Harrison County agreed. He sentenced Lucas to sixty years in prison.

For all the murders that Lucas committed, as of this writing[20] he is still sitting on Death Row in Huntsville.

DERAL CLARK

Of course I didn't know it at the time, but this was it—my last murder case.

At 10:30 on Thursday morning, November 6, 1986, a citizen reported to the Harrison County Sheriff's Office an abandoned Lincoln Continental at the Highway 59 Sabine River Bridge on the Harrison-Panola county line. Deputies Danny Lovett and John Wix responded to the call, but since the vehicle was on the Panola County side (south) of the river, they notified the Panola County Sheriff's office.

Panola County Deputies J. B. Jones and Gary Hale checked the car. They found no outward signs of wrongdoing, but they did run a check of the license plate. The owner of the vehicle, Bethel Lilly Connor, of Avinger, Texas, had not reported the vehicle stolen. The car was on a dirt road and it had rained heavily the night before. Whoever had pulled down the narrow dirt road had gotten stuck in the mud. It was reasonable to believe that the owner had simply gone for help.

---

[20] 1998.

The following afternoon, Panola County Lieutenant John DePresca, observed the vehicle still parked at the same location, but like the previous day, the car had not been reported stolen. Since Avinger is in Marion County, he requested that its sheriff's department contact the owner, Mrs. Connor, and find out why her car was abandoned in the middle of a Panola County dirt road.

Marion County Sheriff Walter Thomas responded that Beth Connor had been dead for about a year, but her husband, Charles, normally drove the car. Sheriff Thomas also said it was common knowledge that Connor was known to carry large amounts of cash. He dispatched Sergeant Eddie Hindsman to the Connor residence to question Mr. Connor.

Sergeant Hindsman asked Constable Charlie Gibson to accompany him to the Connor home. Arriving there, they found no one home. With no one home, and his car abandoned in Panola County, they were naturally suspicious of wrongdoing, so they entered the house. It had been ransacked. Sergeant Hindsman notified Sheriff Thomas, who advised him to secure the residence for fingerprinting. He then notified Panola County of his deputy's discovery.

Armed with this information Lieutenant DePresca immediately returned to the abandoned vehicle. Suspecting foul play, he asked Justice of the Peace Buddy Harris, Constable J. D. McGuire, and Investigator Kevin Jones of his office to accompany him. He also summoned a tow truck to pull the car out of the mud. Waiting for the tow truck, a thorough investigation of the riverbank and surrounding area was conducted, with negative results.

Once the tow truck pulled the car out of the mud and onto dry ground, DePresca and Jones removed the back seat so they could see into the trunk of the car. Peering into the trunk, Jones saw what appeared to be a human foot. DePresca ordered the trunk lock removed and the lid opened. With the trunk lid opened, they were greeted with the sight of a man's bullet riddled corpse. Wasting no time, Judge Bell held an inquest on the spot. Completing the inquest he called Hawthorn's Funeral Home[21] personnel to take the body to the Southwest Forensic Institute in Dallas.

The following morning, November 8, 1986, I got a call from Panola County Deputy Kevin Jones.[22] "Glenn, we've just found the body of a Marion County resident, Charles Connor, in the trunk of his car. Could you come over?"

The next day, November 9, we got our break. Rae Lyn Seagraves, the

---

[21] The Hawthorne Funeral Home is in Carthage, Texas.

[22] I worked throughout this case with Kevin. At one point I told him, "You can't get any work done sitting on your butt. Let's go. I've solved more cases spinning my wheels than by setting on my butt." Later his wife told me he had paid me one of the finest compliments anyone ever paid me in my life. He told his wife, "I'm sure glad I didn't have to work with Mr. Elliott when he was young."

owner of McConnell's Grocery Store in Marshall, told us a woman had approached her husband, Jerrill Wayne May, to cash a thirteen hundred and some few dollars check that was made out to Charles Connor. The woman offered Connor's driver's license as identification of handwriting to prove the signature on the check was genuine. She also promised to make it worth Wayne's time if he would cash the check. Recognizing the woman as a waitress at the local El Chico's Restaurant, he did not take the offer. Instead he called his wife over, and presented the check and driver's license to her. Ms. Seagraves told the woman that if she did cash the check, she would have to hold the check for thirty to sixty days to make sure Connor did not stop payment on it. She told Seagraves that she did not have to worry about the check clearing; " . . . the guy is my boyfriend's uncle, and he died last night." Ms. Seagraves told the woman she would not cash the check.

Ms. Seagraves' husband told us that during their conversation he had asked the woman if she still worked at El Chico's. "No, I'm working at What-A-Burger now." He remembered that the check had been drawn on the Republic Bank in Dallas. He also said that even though he did not know her name, he could make an identification from a photograph.

By the following day, November 10, Detective Jones and I had identified the woman as Patricia Burns Bullock Prather. We immediately contacted her and later the same day we interviewed her at the Sheriff's Office in Marshall. From this point, things happened quickly.

Prather, in her sworn statement, said that at about three o'clock Wednesday afternoon, November 5, a man she knew only as Mark came to her house in Marshall looking for her boyfriend, Deral Clark. She told Mark that Clark was asleep. He said that did not matter he needed to see Deral right then. He went into the bedroom and awoke Clark. She did not hear what they discussed, but in a few minutes, Clark got out of bed, got dressed, and left with Mark.

Clark returned to Prather's house about five o'clock, ate supper, then watched some TV. Between seven and seven-thirty, Clark said he had to leave, but added, "I'll be back in a little while." He got in his Dodge pickup and drove off. About ten o'clock she saw Clark turn into her driveway and pull his pickup behind her house. Following closely behind the pickup was a Lincoln Continental.

Clark entered the house and asked Prather, "Do you know where I can cash a check?"

She asked, "Is it good?"

"Yeah, it's good," he said.

"Maybe the grocery store where I get groceries will cash it," she said.

"Okay," he said, "I'll be back later."

Clark got into his pickup, and with whoever was driving the Continental following closely behind, pulled into the street, and headed in the direction of Highway 59.

At four o'clock the following morning, Clark returned to Prather's house. She said he acted real nervous and sat on the edge of the bed for awhile holding his head like he had a headache. She asked him what was wrong, to which he replied, "Nothing."

At two o'clock that afternoon, Clark drove Prather to McConnell's Store. According to Prather, Clark did not show her the check, or the driver's license, until they pulled into the McConnell's parking lot. Also according to her, she asked her boyfriend where he had gotten the check and license.

"My uncle gave it to me to get some tires, rims, and battery to fix up my truck."

She asked, "Why doesn't your uncle cash it?"

"Because he's dead," he replied.

Seemingly satisfied with Clark's blunt answer, she got out of the pickup and entered the store, and as previously described, attempted to cash the check.

By the time we questioned Prather, she said that Clark had left to visit his mother in Longview, but would return the next day.

Investigator Jones and I continued our investigation and soon uncovered some interesting facts. We identified "Mark" as Andrew Henry "Andy" Thomas. We learned that Connor was not Clark's uncle, but did know him quite well and had for a long time. We also discovered that one of Connor's neighbors, Jackie Hall, reported that she had seen a white pickup parked in front of the Connor house on November 5 sometime between the hours of 8:00 p.m. and 9:00 p.m.

We felt we had enough to make an arrest, so later the same day, November 12, we got an arrest warrant issued in Carthage.[23] While all of this was going on, we had located Clark at his mother's home in Longview. Arriving at her house, he submitted quietly.

Under questioning, Clark admitted his involvement in the check-cashing scheme, but refused to admit having anything to do with Connor's death. He said that he had gone to the Marshall I-Trend Tire Store and convinced the store owner that his uncle was Charles Connor. His uncle, Clark explained to the storeowner, was in Colorado hunting, and as soon as he got the pickup fixed up he intended to join him. He claimed that before leaving for Colorado, his uncle had left his nephew his driver's license and a check in the amount of $1,341.93 to get four new tires and rims on the truck. Still spinning his tale, he said that his uncle was in a hurry to get to Colorado, and since this was only his hunting truck, his favorite nephew, Derel, could take care of the details and, when completed, bring the truck to him.

---

[23] Carthage is the county seat of Panola County.

There are certain things about this tire purchase story that I still find puzzling. Why would Connor travel a thousand miles from Marshall without his driver's license? If he wanted new tires and rims for his hunting truck in Colorado, obviously he was driving, and I know for a fact that a driver's license is required in Colorado. And why had he not cashed the check before he left? It was dated long before the date of the tire sale, November 8, 1986. Be that as it may, Clark must have been pretty convincing—the store owner bought his story. After deducting the cost of the sale, $541.13, Clark received the balance of $800.80 in cash.

The day after we arrested Clark, Marshall attorney Vernon Solomon[24] contacted me. His client, Andy Thomas, wanted to talk to me. Solomon called me and said, "The boy wants to tell his part of the Connor killing." I had never talked to Thomas. It seems that as Kevin Jones and I passed his house, by pure chance Thomas saw and recognized me, and assumed the worst. He spooked and called Vernon Solomon. The next day, November 14, Jones and I talked to him, with Solomon present, and he confessed to his part in the crime; but by then we already had the whole sorry story.

The previous day, the 13th, Clark had confessed the whole story to Jones and I naming his accomplices, Andy Thomas and Dennis Fincher.

He, Andy Thomas, and a friend of Thomas' whom he did not know (Dennis Fincher) had been riding around in Clark's pickup. Their wandering and drinking took them by the Crestwood Club near Lake of the Pines. Passing the Connor home they saw his Continental sitting in the driveway. Clark told his companions that the man who lived there was his uncle and he always had a lot of money around. As we have already seen, Connor was not related to Clark in any way. According to Thomas, Clark had earlier discussed robbing a man he claimed was his uncle. Whether Thomas or Fincher knew Clark was lying about his kinship with Connor is immaterial. They all agreed that robbing Connor would be an easy way to get some quick cash.

They planned accordingly. In the cab of the pickup Clark had a .38 revolver and a twelve gauge, sawed off shotgun. Arming himself with the pistol, he gave the shotgun to Thomas; Fincher was unarmed. They drove to a Gibson's Discount Store near Lone Star where they purchased three ski masks and two pair of gloves.[25] Completing their purchases they drove back to the Connor's, parking the pickup about fifty yards from the house.

Knowing Connor would not open the door to anybody wearing a ski mask and realizing he would be instantly recognized, he convinced Thomas to knock on the door, without the benefit of a mask. The plan was for Thomas to hold the shotgun at his side, out of sight, and when Connor answered the

---

[24] This is the same Vernon Solomon who defended Stan Faulder, Inez Phillips' killer.
[25] Clark already had a pair of gloves.

door he was to tell him he had car trouble and ask if he could use the phone. Before he could reply, the masked Clark would rush the open door and gain entry before Connor could shut it. The third robber, Fincher, was to stay in the pickup until his partners had gained entry into the house, then he was to join them in the house. The plan worked like a charm, almost.

When Connor opened the door, the hoodlums rushed into the house. Inside Clark pointed his .38 at Connor and told him to ". . . lay down!"

Clark's masquerade failed to fool Connor. "Well, if it isn't Deral Clark."

Clark again ordered, "Get in the house and lay down."

Clearly, Connor knew Clark, but just as clearly, he took him seriously. He retreated into the living room and stretched out in the floor.[26]

Here the Clark and Thomas statements differ. According to Clark, Thomas started cussing Connor and threatening him if he did not tell where the money was hidden. Not so, said Thomas and Fincher. In their statements they said that Clark began beating on Connor, threatening him, sticking the barrel of his pistol in Connor's mouth and up against his nose trying to get him to tell where he had his concealed money. Finally Connor said he would cooperate. Connor led him into a bedroom, whereupon he gave Clark three hundred dollars in cash he had hidden. Ransacking the bedroom, Clark found Connor's driver's license and a check for $1,341.93. Giving his victim no choice, Clark made Connor endorse the check. He handed the cash to Thomas and tied Connor's hands behind his back with a belt.

Meanwhile, Thomas and Fincher continued turning the rest of the house upside down looking for more money. They came up empty-handed. After forty-five minutes of ransacking, they realized they had gotten all they were going to get. They forced the still-bound Connor into the trunk of his car. Closing the trunk, Clark said he would drive the Lincoln, and he ordered Thomas and Fincher to follow him into Marshall. Following instructions, Thomas got behind the wheel of the pickup and followed Clark. Along the way Fincher threw the twelve gauge out the window.

Arriving in Marshall, they stopped at a Church's Fried Chicken and ordered some food. Thomas paid the bill and handed the balance of the money to Clark. He gave Fincher ninety dollars and Thomas one hundred twenty-five dollars, pocketing the balance. Leaving Church's they went by Thomas's house so that Fincher could get his car. Leaving his two friends, Dennis Fincher's role in the crime ended at this point. Clark and Thomas were only beginning.

Arriving at Patricia Prather's, Clark and Thomas stayed only about ten

---

[26] Clark and Thomas's statements differ on this point. The incident just described is Thomas' version. Clark claimed that when Connor opened the door, Thomas charged him, knocking him down, causing Connor to hit his head on a table, and causing a minor wound.

minutes. After talking privately with Prather, Clark called Thomas outside. In private he told Thomas ". . . they had to do something with him." Getting back into the Lincoln, with Thomas following in Clark's pickup, they headed south on Highway 59. Crossing the Sabine River Bridge, Clark turned left onto a small dirt road intending to drive the car into the river. Earlier it had rained heavily and Clark did not get far before he high-centered the vehicle. Getting out of the car, he walked back to Thomas and said, "I got it stuck. I'm gonna have to do something." Walking back to the Lincoln he reached into the glove box and pressed the trunk release button.

With the .38[27] in one hand, he opened the trunk lid with the other. As the trunk lid rose, Connor made his bid for freedom. He tried to strike out at Clark, but was not quick enough. Clark fired three times, hitting Connor in the right temple, the left eye, and in the back.

Closing the trunk, Clark and Thomas wasted little time heading back to Marshall. In his confession Clark told us he had thrown the murder weapon into a creek. Harrison County Deputies Frank Garrett and Carmon Pigg, following Clark's instructions, went to the 500 block of Blanche Street in Marshall and recovered the pistol.

On November 17, Fincher, in the presence of his attorney, confessed to his part in the crime.

At their trials in 1987, Deral Edward Clark entered a plea of guilty for murder and was sentenced to life imprisonment. He also pled guilty to aggravated kidnapping and was sentenced to forty years in the state penitentiary for that crime. Andrew Henry Thomas pled guilty to kidnapping and was sentenced to twenty years in prison. Dennis Ray Fincher took a plea of aggravated robbery and was given a sentence of ten years.

Every peace officer has certain crimes he enjoys working on more than others. Some like vice, others robberies, etc. I always liked working homicide cases. Of course, I did not know it then, but that was it—my last murder case. For every case, murder or otherwise, I have discussed in this book, I could have related a dozen more.

---

[27] The pistol was a .38 caliber Arminius Titen Tiger revolver.

HOMER GARRISON, JR.
Director
JOE S. FLETCHER
Assistant Director

Commission
TOM R. HICKMAN, SR.
Chairman
W. E. DYCHE, JR.
C. T. McLAUGHLIN
Commissioners

TEXAS DEPARTMENT OF PUBLIC SAFETY

5805 N. LAMAR BLVD.
BOX 4087, NORTH AUSTIN STATION
AUSTIN

April 3, 1962

Mr. Glenn Elliott
Texas Ranger, Company "B"
Box 10
Marshall, Texas

Dear Glenn:

I have just looked over your Criminal Offense Report
(MO #91544) detailing an account of the investigation
of the burglary of the Bloomburg State Bank which occurred on the night of March 16, 1962.

This is certainly a very comprehensive report and indicates an excellent investigation.

With best wishes, I am

Sincerely yours,

Homer Garrison, Jr.
Director

HGJr/gh
cc: Captain R. A. Crowder

CHAPTER XIV
AND OTHER LOW LIFES

THE BLOOMBURG BANK BURGLARY

Often when I was in Dallas I visited a roundtable meeting of police officers from the Metroplex area. These officers were from nearly every branch of law enforcement: Rangers, Highway Patrol, sheriff's departments, numerous local police departments, and federal agencies including the FBI. Over lunch they discussed various crimes and criminals that concerned their area. The first thing that struck me was the way they shared their information, just the way police officers should. By comparing notes as to who was operating in the area, and their methods, there is no telling how many criminals ended up in prison because of these meetings. Unquestionably, I saw the advantage of such a meeting in my area, and determined to create a similar organization. Thus was born the Ark-La-Tex Peace Officers Meeting. The way I visualized the organization was that, and the way it turned out, it would be an unofficial organization with no president, secretary, or any other officers. We started, and remained, simply a group of peace officers getting together once a month to discuss common problems.

I shared my idea with Gregg County Sheriff Noble Crawford and he agreed that we needed to copy the Dallas effort. On April 6, 1970, I wrote a letter, which Noble and I both signed, and sent it to police departments all over the area. I contacted fellow state, local, and federal officers in western Louisiana, southwestern Arkansas, and, of course, East Texas. I was amazed at the turnout we had at our first meeting at the Downtown Motor Inn,[1] in Longview on April 23. Looking back, I should not have been. I don't care that the news media and movies love to portray the police as being nothing but a bunch of on-the-take, crooked drunks, and just plain no-goods. Maybe there is a minuscule number of officers like that, but believe me, their numbers are infinitesimal. If you look, what you will find is countless thousands upon thousands of overworked and underpaid officers out there doing the best

---

[1] The Downtown Motor Inn was originally a Hilton Hotel. After serving briefly as a dormitory for LeTourneau College, it was razed in the mid-1990s.

they know how every day.

Like any organization, it took a lot of work to keep the Ark-La-Tex Peace Officers Meeting going. Once a month I made sure that I contacted all the different departments in the area and reminded them of our meeting. By doing this I was able to keep a good attendance until the day I retired. You can easily see the pride I took in our meeting. It was a well-placed pride, and I can truthfully say that many cases that might have gone unsolved were brought to a successful conclusion through the sharing of information with other officers over lunch.

A police officer's first and only reason for existence is to serve and protect the public. And you do that by working together. There is no accomplishment that I achieved during my thirty-eight-year career that I am prouder of than having a reputation of working with my fellow officers—all officers: local, state, and federal.

Even though the case described below happened more than seven years before the of the birth of the Ark-La-Tex Police Officers Meeting, few cases exemplify police agencies working together better than my first major felony case as a Ranger—the Bloomburg, Texas, bank burglary in early 1962. I worked hand-in-hand with Texas and Louisiana sheriff departments, city police departments, a juvenile delinquent officer, a probation officer, and the FBI. This was truly an example of police working together to protect and serve.

Ever since the first bank opened I suppose someone has tried to rob it. The Bloomburg State Bank offered an enticing target. Many factors made it ideal for thieves and burglars. Besides being a small bank with little or no security, in a town that had no local law enforcement, it is located smack up against the borders of Arkansas, Louisiana, and Texas which was ideal for thieves to make their getaway.

At approximately eleven o'clock, on a freezing cold Friday night, March 16, 1962, unknown persons broke into the Bloomburg State Bank. Using an acetylene torch they cut the combination out of the bank's vault door, forced out the vault locks by hand, and entered the vault. Inside the vault was a Mosler safe. We found the knob from the safe on the floor, where the thieves had tried to gain entry, but since it was equipped with a time-lock they were unsuccessful at opening it. The dial can't open a time lock until the appointed time has arrived. But these were determined, and experienced, bank burglaries and they had an answer to a time lock—take the whole safe. The Mosler measured 34 inches by 22 inches, and was freestanding. They placed several large books on the floor and placed the safe on it. Attaching a cable from a wench truck they had stolen in Atlanta, Texas, they pulled it out the west rear door of the bank and onto the sidewalk. Once outside they loaded the safe on the bed of the wench truck and calmly drove out of town. Like I said, they were experienced and well-prepared.

The burglars had gotten off with $28,323.50 in cash—both coin and paper—plus an additional $5,000 in money orders and U. S. Government series "E" bonds.

No matter what era people live in, they always fondly remember "the good old days." Invariably things were better "then"; people cared more "then"; and they definitely got involved "then." And the smaller the community, the better things were "back then." Small communities cared much more for their neighbors "back then," and in "Mayberry" where everyone knew everybody, they did not hesitate to get involved, "back then." Oh, really? In 1962 Bloomburg was, and still is, a small rural community in the northeastern Texas county of Cass. Its population on a busy week was only a few hundred people. During the burglary the thieves made no attempt at secrecy. Several citizens heard the burglars banging away in the bank. One man lived in the bank building directly over the vault and admitted, as did several citizens, hearing the burglars between the hours of 11:00 p.m. and 1:00 a.m. Some even acknowledged not only hearing, but looking out their window and seeing the wench truck in action. Not one person reported anything to the authorities. So much for how much more people were involved in the "good old days."

The following morning at 7:30 I received a call from Sheriff Bill Dowd asking if I would assist in the investigation. Bloomburg is about seventy-five miles from Longview, so I did not arrive at the crime scene until 8:45. I have investigated countless crime scenes, but I have never seen one more filthy. There was tobacco juice all over the floor. But that didn't stop us, and over the weekend Sheriff Dowd and I investigated not only the bank, but also the immediate area around Bloomburg, asking questions and looking for evidence.

We also broadcast the description of the burglary throughout the country. As professional as this job had been, there was little doubt in our minds that this was not the thieves' first job. By comparing notes with other departments we could put together a pattern. And once we had a pattern, we could narrow the field as to who we were looking for.

I surveyed the bank employees as to whether any questionable-acting person had been in or around the bank the last few days. The bank manager, E. D. Simmons, reported that an unknown man, about thirty-five years old, and acting very suspiciously, had indeed been in the bank about a week before asking to change a ten-dollar bill. Also, on the previous Wednesday, March 14, an unknown female had inquired about opening a savings account. People living in urban areas may find it strange that bank employees remembered two unknown people being in the bank. Bloomburg is a typical small, southern Mayberry—strangers entering their bank would be noticed.

We discovered that the wrecker that had been used to hoist the safe, a 1947 three-quarter-ton pickup with a wench, had been stolen the night of the burglary from Atlanta, Texas. We located a site about one mile from the bank where the burglars had unsuccessfully attempted to move the safe from the wench truck to another vehicle. Also, a 1956 Chevrolet pulpwood truck had been stolen in Bloomburg the night of the burglary, but it had been abandoned where the transfer had been attempted. It had apparently been stolen to obtain its gasoline. A hole had been punched in the bottom of the gas tank.

On Monday, March 19, Sheriff Dowd and I drove from Bloomburg to Hosston, Louisiana, forty miles away. We had contacted all the police departments in the surrounding area and made them aware of the burglary and the methods used. Consequently, when a stolen wench truck was recovered about a mile and a half from the Red River bridge between the Louisiana communities of Hosston and Plain Dealing by Bossier Parish Deputy Frank Goodman, we were contacted immediately.

We were looking for a 1947 one-half ton Chevrolet; this was a 1946 Dodge, two and one-half ton wench truck, stolen in nearby Bradley, Arkansas, the night before from a Carl Baker. Without a doubt, this was not the wrecker used in Bloomburg on Friday night, but we were sure our thieves had used it. Paint samples taken from the back of the wrecker matched the color of the missing safe.

On Tuesday I again traveled to Shreveport to visit Homer Bryant, Chief of the Criminal Division of the Caddo Parish Sheriff's Department. I brought Chief Bryant up-to-date on the case. Listening attentively until I finished, he gave me several names of people then known to be in the Shreveport area whom he thought capable of having pulled the burglary. One was familiar— Ivey Lee Umphries. Ivey Lee had already been convicted twice in Texas for burglary, and was currently free on bond for safe burglary and armed robbery in Louisiana.

Reportedly he was living with this girlfriend, also a suspect in the bank burglary. But when shown pictures of Umphries and his girlfriend, the bank's employees were unable to make a positive identification.

On Thursday, March 22, I returned to Shreveport. After gathering information from the Shreveport Police Department concerning Umphries, I went on to Shreveport's sister city—Bossier City—to visit with its police. They had information that Umphries worked for a company in Minden, Louisiana. This company had furnished the money for his bond for the above-mentioned burglary case.

Leaving Bossier City I met Bossier Parish Deputies Frank Goodman and Roy Bain, and Sheriff Bill Dowd at the Highway 2 bridge where it crosses the Red River. Deputies Goodman and Bain had found a spot under the bridge where something had been buried. We believed our missing safe had been temporarily deposited here.

Checking the area around the bridge we found tire tracks that matched those of the stolen Bradley wench truck which had been recovered only about a mile and a half away. The deputies had also discovered the footprints of several men and one woman (who had worn eight inch, spiked heels) several pieces of rope, a clipboard with the name of a Minden, Louisiana company written on the top, several pieces of chain, and numerous paint scrapings from several nearby small, low-hanging tree branches.

It was not hard to piece together what had happened. The burglars were running out of darkness and they had to stash their cache until it would be safe to travel with it. After all, it would have been rather obvious that something was amiss if they had been seen driving down the highway with a safe sitting on the back of a wrecker. They had stolen the Bradley wrecker to lift the safe into another vehicle. Finishing with the wrecker they had driven it a short distance away and dumped it.

Early morning travelers had seen the wrecker sitting close to the bridge, but had thought nothing about it. This region is known as the Big Thicket because of the heavy growth of pine trees. One of our biggest industries is logging; therefore it was common to see logging equipment—and a wench truck is a common logging tool—early in the morning. Loggers are a lot like farmers; it's seldom that the rising sun does not find them in the fields.

We left the river location and went to Minden, Louisiana, where we contacted Webster Parish Deputy Buster Atkins and asked for his help in locating the owners of the company whose name we found on the clipboard. Atkins informed us that they had moved to Monroe, Louisiana.

Checking further, we learned from Haynesville, Louisiana, Probation Officer Kendrix[2] that the brothers had been on probation, but their time had expired. We also found that they were reportedly in deep financial trouble.

In the ensuing weeks we continued to gather information. We learned from the FBI that bank burglaries in Nash, Oklahoma; Lena, Mississippi; and Bernard, Kansas, matched the M.O. of the Bloomburg Bank burglary. On May 15 the Bloomburg safe was recovered near Cotton Valley, Louisiana, about seventy-five miles from Bloomburg, in the Dorcheat Bayou at a place called Uncle Ralph's Fishing Camp. It had been opened, but we recovered no evidence that would help us with the case.

But by this time we felt we had sufficient cause to request warrants for Ivey Lee Umphries and the owners of the Minden, Louisiana company. We went to Queen City, Texas—you never know when you leave Atlanta and enter Queen City—and secured from Cass County Judge John Hanes arrest warrants for all three.

We sent a message to the owners of the company that we had a warrant for them and it would be best if they came in voluntarily. They contacted us and agreed to meet Sheriff Dowd and me in Longview, and at the appointed

---

[2] I do not remember, if I ever knew, Officer Kendrix's first name.

time they showed up. We wasted no time and quickly started questioning them. Three hours later both still denied any guilt or knowledge of the burglary. They went so far as to agree to take a polygraph test in Dallas.

On Thursday, March 29, the brothers, Sheriff Dowd, and I traveled to Dallas. Results of the polygraph showed that neither had been present when the safe was stolen, but both did show a strong reaction when Bloomburg was mentioned. Both claimed under further interrogation that they had thought of Bloomington, Illinois, when Bloomburg was mentioned. Maybe so—that is where they were arrested after escaping from the Mississippi state penitentiary where they were being held on a three-year sentence for burglary. After completing the polygraphs, both were returned to Longview, where they had left their car, and allowed to return to Louisiana.

On Monday, April 2, I received a call from Bossier Parish Juvenile Officer Otis Allen. On Saturday, March 31, Sergeant Daniels, of the Shreveport Police Department, had brought in for questioning sixteen-year-old boy who was the son of one of the owners of the company in Minden. He had been going to different stores with a black, wooden box filled with almost two hundred dollars in coins, trying to exchange the coins for paper bills. Becoming suspicious, one of the clerks notified the police. All weekend he had been questioned. At first the boy claimed that he had found the money under a bridge, but when taken to the bridge, they found there had been no evidence of any activity for a long time. As he would do several times, he changed his story.

The following day found me again in Louisiana. Happy Ewing, also from the Bossier Parish Juvenile Department, questioned the young man for three hours. All he ever admitted was that he had gotten the money from someone close to him, and if he talked he would be in trouble, so he would not talk.

It's funny what you remember about events. The thing I remember most about the questioning was the large plug of tobacco the boy chewed. Just as we began the interrogation the young man put a huge wad of tobacco in his mouth. I have always had little regard for chewing tobacco; if there is a nastier habit, I don't know what it is. Before he put the wad in his mouth I reminded him that we had no spittoon and he would not be allowed to spit on the floor, and since I never have liked seeing someone spit into a cup, so just where did he plan on spitting? In his best, "I'm a real he-man" tone of voice, he said, "I don't need anything to spit into, I swallow."

So we let him chew and swallow. Three hours later he was greener than fresh spring grass. Looking at me with the sickest eyes you have ever seen, he mumbled in a feeble little voice, "I'm sick. I gotta go to the bathroom." Considering the amount of tobacco juice in his stomach, I was amazed he had survived as long as he did. I have to give it to the boy; he was tough—he never did own up to where he got the money.

250

I left Louisiana and returned to Marshall to question Ivie Lee Umphries. Since the burglary, he had dropped out of sight and we had been unable to locate him. But it turned out we didn't have to, he dropped himself right into our laps. He had been in Henderson shacked up with some old gal. But enough fun is enough. He figured he better get his girlfriend's car back to her before she caught him with another woman. Leaving Henderson in a drunken stupor he got nearly to Marshall before running off the road. Investigating the accident, the Harrison County sheriff's department arrested him for DWI, carrying a pistol, and operating a motor vehicle without a license.

Under questioning he, not surprisingly, denied any knowledge of the Bloomburg burglary. He also refused to take a polygraph test. I was confident we had the right man, and I knew that he was not going anywhere; too many people wanted the pleasure of his company. Cass County, Texas, wanted him, as did Caddo Parish, Louisiana. Ivie Lee must have felt he was playing against a stacked deck; even his bondsman had filed to be relieved of his obligation on Ivie Lee's bond.

I knew I had my man, but I just could not find the undeniable piece of evidence that would put him away. We could not charge him, and he eventually found another bondsman and hit the street again. But old Ivie Lee just could not stay straight.

On December 7, 1962, Sheriff Dowd, Ranger Red Arnold, FBI agent Sam Cotton, and I drove to Hot Springs, Arkansas, to pick up Ivie Lee. At the time of the burglary we had broadcast the serial numbers of the money orders throughout the region. In Hot Springs, Ivie Lee had passed one of the stolen hundred dollar Republic Express money orders renting a room at Dan's Courts. Before he could get very comfortable, the Hot Springs Police had him in custody. When arrested he also had on his person seven additional one hundred dollar and two fifty-dollar Republic Express money orders—all from Bloomburg.

He was returned to Texas to stand trial for the Bloomburg State Bank burglary. He denied any involvement and proclaimed his innocence throughout his trial, but the jury was not buying. He was found guilty and sent to prison.

This case is a classic example of departments working together for the citizens: Texas Rangers, county and parish sheriff's offices, the FBI, local police departments, probation department, and even the juvenile department.

Postscript. I have always enjoyed visiting with senior citizens in nursing homes. A few years ago I was visiting in a local nursing home in Longview when I saw a familiar name on one of the doors, Ivie Lee Umphries. I stopped in to say hello. I'm afraid Ivie Lee was suffering from Alzheimer's Disease. He no longer knew anything or anybody. He died shortly thereafter.

HOMER GARRISON, JR.
Director
JOE S. FLETCHER
Deputy Director

TEXAS RANGERS
TEXAS DEPARTMENT OF PUBLIC SAFETY
5805 N. LAMAR BLVD.
BOX 4087, NORTH AUSTIN STATION
AUSTIN

Commission
C. T. McLAUGHLIN
Chairman
HOXIE H. THOMPSON
TOM HICKMAN
Commissioners

April 11, 1962

Homer Garrison, Jr., Director
Texas Department of Public Safety
Box 4087, North Austin Station
Austin, Texas

Dear Colonel:

I have just received and reviewed a progress report of the investigation of the burglary of the Bloomburg State Bank, Bloomburg, Texas which occurred March 16, 1962, as submitted by Ranger Glenn Elliott of Marshall, Texas, same being hereto attached and self-explanatory.

In my opinion, this report is one of the best ever submitted on the progress of an investigation, being detailed day by day as he made the investigation. I think that Ranger Elliott should be commended for the excellent manner in which he has found and preserved evidence at the various locations in order that it might be used at the proper time. It will be noted that he has preserved and marked all evidence and made proper notes to accompany them, which to me is a must in conducting an investigation.

You will note also that Ranger Elliott has had fine cooperation from many local officers, both in Texas and the State of Louisiana, as well as agents of the F.B.I.

All in all, I believe, since this is the first major case that Ranger Elliott has worked on, this report shows he is sincere in his work and has taken advantage of the things that were taught him in the schools he has attended and takes advantage of every opportunity to better himself by counseling with officers who have had more experience and it is my belief that he will make one of the best Texas Rangers in the entire state.

Respectfully,

R. A. Crowder, Captain
Commanding Company "B"
Texas Rangers

RAC:bas
Attachment

bc: Ranger Glenn Elliott

You can imagine the pride this rookie Ranger felt when
I received this letter from Captain Crowder.

252

THE LONGVIEW SCHOOL BUS BOMBING

Throughout America, and especially the south, racial problems were at the forefront during the sixties and seventies. Longview was no exception. Around midnight, July 4, 1970, I was awakened by Longview Police Detective Clifford Felts calling. During the next seven days I worked one hundred fourteen hours, drove five hundred forty-five miles, and flew another one hundred seventy-five miles. By the time we finished this investigation, I have to admit I was tired.

While on routine patrol, Longview Police Officer Ross Rosbrough was passing near the Longview Independent School Bus storage area at 1111 East Young Street when a final Fourth of July explosion suddenly lighted the area. Unfortunately, this display of fireworks was not done in a spirit of celebration, but rather in a spirit of hatred.

From one end of the country to the other, integration was the order of the day. The most hated of all the means of accomplishing this was busing. In some places it was accepted peacefully, in others violently. Regretfully, on July 4, 1970, some local residents resisted violently. Demonstrating their displeasure with busing, someone cut through the chain link fence surrounding the Longview ISD's[3] school bus yard and planted explosives under several of the buses.

I arrived at the scene a few minutes past midnight, and joined Felts, Longview Chief of Police Roy Stone,[4] Assistant Chief Robert Tutt, and FBI Agent Charles Brown. Our investigation revealed that twenty-seven explosive charges had been planted, and of the thirty-six buses parked at the facility, three-three were damaged to one degree or another. Estimates of damage were not immediately available, but it was thought that each bus had suffered approximately one thousand dollars in damage.

We established that entry into the yard had been gained by cutting, at ground level, a thirteen by seventeen-inch hole in the eight-foot chain link fence surrounding the yard. The hole was cut behind the fourth bus from the west end of the yard. Once inside the yard, the bombers placed the dynamite on the pavement under and beside the buses, with none attached to the vehicles. All the charges were connected with a twenty-two-foot safety fuse cord. We also found a two-cent box of Fire Chief Matches in the same area.

---

[3] ISD, Independent School District.
[4] This is the same Roy Stone who had assisted me arresting Mose Swidan when he killed Nick Georgepul in downtown Longview in 1950.

Most valuable of all, we recovered one Atlas dynamite box designed to hold fifty, one and one-quarter inch, by eight-inch sticks of dynamite. We also found two set of footprints and tracked them from the hole in the fence to the rear of Gillespie Paint Manufacturers at 211 Gum Springs Road.

Willard Pratt, an explosive expert from Marshall, was summoned to the scene. Mr. Pratt estimated that the twenty-two foot safety fuse cord would have burned for at least fourteen minutes before reaching the detonating fuse. Pratt explained that even though Officer Rosbrough reported hearing one explosion, there had in fact been twenty-seven explosions. The prima string cord, which is a detonator itself, burned at a rate of twenty-two thousand feet per second, thus making it sound like one massive explosion. Pratt also advised that he doubted if we would find any fingerprints, because the bomber undoubtedly wore gloves. Any explosive with nitro in it will seep through the pores of unprotected skin and give the user an extreme headache. One thing was evident; the bomber knew what he was doing. And just as unmistakably, he had not meant to totally destroy the buses; he had done the amount of damage he wanted to do.

A few days earlier, on June 25, a bomb had been thrown into a house at 1901 Leona Street in Longview. The resulting blast had blown a large hole in the house's side. The house, located in a white neighborhood, was offered for sale by J. G. London, and had been purchased earlier in the day by Magnolia Jackson, a black female. Ms. Jackson's house had burned earlier and she was looking for one to replace it. When she found the house on Leona, she bought it with the intention of moving it to her lot. We speculated that the bombers did not know this and were trying to stop Ms. Jackson from moving into "their" neighborhood. Eyewitnesses saw two white men drive by the house moments before the explosion. We suspected the bombers were the same people.

We were not without suspects. For those of you who were not around, or not old enough to remember, racial problems were real bad in the 60s. We had been tracking racial bigots for several years and had a list of questionable characters. At the top of this list was the owner of the Land-of-the-Lakes Catering Service, one Fred Hayes of Longview. We considered Hayes, a balding forty-three year old, to be extremely dangerous as far as racial problems were concerned. Thought to be associated with only one national group, the John Birch Society, he had at one time or another been involved with several radical local groups such as the Minutemen, and the Raiders.

You would think the Klan would have been heavily involved, but they were not. The only time I had anything to do with the KKK was when I got a call from a prominent local farmer.

"Glenn, there's a cross in the yard of a black church in our community. It was put there last night and it's still sitting there." Without ever pausing for breath he continued, "It didn't catch fire, but it's a Klan cross I can tell you.

We just don't know what to do." I told him to stay calm; I would be there in a few minutes.

When I arrived at the church, I parked my car, walked over to the cross, tore it down, and put it in the back of my car. I carried it down the road a short distance to a desolate area and threw it in a ditch. That is the only Klan problem I ever had, and I'm not sure it was the Klan, only some wanna-be trying to imitate them.

Hayes did not consider the groups he had been running with passionate enough in their beliefs, so he and some extremist followers, whom he apparently had control over, broke away and formed their own group. We knew Hayes was printing material and recruiting heavily, neither of which was against the law. We also believed he was probably making homemade bombs and other weapons. This was illegal, but we had not yet been able to prove it.

It took money to finance these activities, and his business seemed to be relatively successful. He delivered food and drinks to many of the businesses and manufacturers throughout the area, thus allowing him to move around and make contacts without raising suspicions.

From the evidence left at the scene we knew that the brand name of the dynamite used was Atlas. We started checking the area to find who had bought this brand in the last few months. Chief Stone and I discovered that Southwest Pipe and Supply Company in Shreveport was the nearest outlet of Atlas Dynamite. The relationship I had worked so hard to develop with other police departments in the area once again paid off. Going to Louisiana presented absolutely no problem, and of course the Shreveport Police Department offered Chief Stone and me any assistance we needed.

Fortunately we didn't need any help; Southwest Pipe cooperated completely. Their records showed that one of Hayes' closest associates, James Woodall, had purchased the type of dynamite we were looking for on three different occasions in the last four months: March 6, March 20, and May 29.

The next day, Wednesday, July 8, we questioned Woodall. He admitted that he had purchased fifty units of dynamite, prima cord, fuses, and blasting caps for Hayes. The same day another Hayes conspirator, Robert Sparks, admitted that he had helped manufacture two bombs consisting of four, one-half sticks of dynamite, placing them in hand lights and transporting them to Nacogdoches in the company of Hayes and two other accomplices. At the time Nacogdoches had civil rights demonstrations taking place and they wanted to stop them. Their plan was to place the hand lights on a busy corner in the black section of town. These lights were the kind that required a large battery to power them. They replaced the battery with dynamite wired to go off when someone turned the switch on. With that much dynamite, and at that range—point-blank—they were not designed to scare or hurt. They were meant to kill; and being in a busy area, they were meant to kill a lot of people. Thankfully, neither bomb went off.

Sparks also admitted transporting four sticks of dynamite to Hayes the same day that Ms. Jackson's house was blasted, but he disavowed taking part in the construction of the bombs or the bombings. Furthermore, he acknowledged that he and Hayes had one time planned to bomb the school buses in Longview, going so far as to set off some charges at Robert Stone's farm in Harrison County to test what would happen under certain conditions. But on the night of the bombing he and his wife were in Huntsville, Alabama, and had no part in the execution of the plan.

When he started talking, Sparks was a fountain of information. Hayes was beginning to get nervous with all the law around and the day before, July 7, Hayes had instructed him to destroy any remaining evidence. Sparks gathered all the remaining dynamite, went to Stone's farm, and detonated the explosives.

Hayes had not always been nervous. Within hours of the explosion Longview was crawling with FBI agents. There must have been twenty or twenty-five agents here. The word had literally come down from the mountain, Washington, to get some convictions—and fast. You would think this many FBI agents would make a suspect go to ground.

If Hayes was anything, he was bold. When they arrived in Longview, the FBI headquartered at the Contessa Inn in the western part of town. One night most of them were in the lounge when the waitress came over to them and said the gentleman in the corner had bought this round of drinks. "The gentleman in the corner" was none other than Fred Hayes. The Agent-In-Charge was unhappy, to say the least. Not only did they refuse Hayes' offer, but also the Agent-In-Charge ordered his men out of the Contessa Inn and to the Holiday Inn, then on Highway 80 on the other side of Longview. The Agent-In-Charge asked me what I was going to do now that Hayes knew all of us were there. He must have thought I would at the least go into hiding, surfacing only when surrounded by fellow officers. He was astounded when I told him I was not going to do anything out of the ordinary. I told him I had lived at 317 Ruthlyn for about twenty years (still do) and that my phone was listed (still is). If Hayes wanted to, he could call me. So while the FBI was moving, I went home and went to bed.

Early on Friday, July 9, Tyler FBI Agent Bob Stevens and I gathered up Sparks and went to Robert Stone's farm near the Harleton community. Stone gave us written permission to visit his farm. Stone joined us as Sparks directed us to a large hole in the ground where he had destroyed the dynamite. Sparks admitted that he had acted alone and was solely responsible for the destruction of the explosives.

Another close associate of Hayes, Glenn Parker, was questioned on Sat-

256

Federal Bureau of Investigation
United States Department of Justice
Washington, D. C.

July 28, 1970

Mr. Glenn Elliot
Company B
The Texas Rangers
Post Office Box 774
Longview, Texas 75601

Dear Mr. Elliot:

I have been advised of the outstanding coopera-

tion you afforded our Dallas Office in connection with the

recent investigation involving the bombing of school buses in

Longview. Your professional assistance and the long hours

of your own time so selflessly devoted to this matter contrib-

uted immeasurably to the successful results achieved. We in

the FBI are indeed appreciative.

Sincerely yours,

J. Edgar Hoover

I think anyone would be proud to get a letter like this from J. Edgar Hoover.

urday, July 11, by Agent Stevens.[5] Parker admitted assisting Hayes in the bombing of Ms. Jackson's house. He had driven the car while Hayes planted the bomb. He had also gone with Hayes to the Stone farm to pick up two boxes of dynamite, Cardo prima cord, caps, and several other items to be used in bombing the buses. He was to return to Hayes' house after supper to assist in making the bombs, but decided this would undoubtedly bring down more heat than he wanted to deal with, so he didn't go back.

Undoubtedly Hayes didn't hold any hard feelings. He discussed the bombing in detail with Parker, telling him that he and Kenneth McMaster went to the school bus depot and set the bombs. Hayes' wife, Clarita, was to pick them up, but a police car "spooked" her, and she abandoned them, thus forcing them to walk home.

The next day, Sunday, July 12, Parker took Agent Stevens and me to his father's farm in Harrison County and showed us where Hayes had stashed his equipment. We found the boots worn by Hayes the night of the explosion. He explained that Hayes had read in the *Longview News* that footprints had been found at the rear of the parking lot and this was the reason for hiding the boots. We also found a large amount of ammunition, an automatic rifle, a homemade shotgun, more explosives, and literature published by Hayes.

The Justice Department was so heated up about this case that they brought in a special prosecutor from Washington. They didn't need to do that; we had a first-class prosecutor in Tyler named Robby Hadden who could have handled the case just fine. But they didn't ask me. Hayes was found guilty in Federal court on four cases of illegal weapons and for bombings and was sentenced to the Federal Penitentiary.

As for me personally, I am proud to say that I got a letter of commendation from J. Edgar Hoover himself for my work on this case.

VAN ADAMS AND ASA STINE, JR.

Until you work in it every day, you have no idea how many low-life human beings there are in this old world. One of the most repulsive is a rapist.

I worked a lot of gruesome assaults and rape cases in my career, but none worse than the one I want to tell you about now. About ten o'clock one night a teenage couple[6] went parking. Nothing unusual about that. Kids have

---

[5] I never worked with a finer officer, FBI or otherwise, than Bob Stevens.

[6] The names of the victims and the location of the crime have been intentionally deleted. These people suffered enough indignation for one lifetime, without me bringing their names forth again.

been doing that since the invention of the automobile. But unlike most parkers, they would suffer an unholy hell for the next three hours. They were attacked, beaten repeatedly, the girl raped over and over, and both totally and completely stripped of their dignity by two real low-lifes, Asa Stine, Jr., and Van Edward Adams.

About seven o'clock one warm summer evening, Stine and Adams left their hometown, and traveled to a neighboring town where they bought beer and wine. After cruising around a short time, they stopped at a beer hall to play pool. Tiring of pool, they went looking for women. They left the beer hall about 10:30 p.m., drove to a nearby town, and stopped to visit a female friend. They spent about an hour at the girl's house before leaving to look for another girl that Adams knew. Before they could reach the second girl's house, they met her driving down the road. Adams was driving and he started blinking his car lights for the woman to stop. She pulled over onto the shoulder of the road. Adams left his car and joined the woman in her car. He was with the woman about five minutes when he got out of her car and walked toward the waiting Stine to tell him he was going with the woman. Obviously the newfound girlfriend wanted nothing to do with Adams, or his friend. As Adams walked back to his car the woman took off, fast. By the time Adams and Stine got cranked up the woman had disappeared from sight.

Between the two, they did not have a clue where the woman had gone, so one road was as good as the next. They turned into the first road they came upon. There they found the teenagers parked in the boy's car. Adams and Stine drove slowly past the teenager's car, stopped for a moment, then backed up. They got out of their car and walked to the teenagers' vehicle. Adams asked if they had seen a blue car go by. The boy first answered no, then said a pickup and a car had gone by. Adams said he was looking for his wife, who was out running around with some "dude."

Adams then started back for his car when he met Stine coming towards the teenagers with a jackhandle in his hand. As they passed each other Stine said to Adams he was going to take whatever money the boy had. By holding the jackhandle behind his back the boy in the car thought it was a gun. When he got to the teenager's car, Stine told the boy to get out ". . . if he wanted to live." Still thinking Stine held a gun, the boy got out of the car. Stine demanded that the boy give him all the money he had. Without argument, the boy took all the money he had, seventy dollars, from his billfold and handed the money to Stine, and replaced the wallet in his back pocket.

Stine and Adams retreated for a few moments, conferring. Stine said to Adams, "Say man, let's have some fun," at which point Adams said, "Wait a minute, let's just scare the crap out of them." Stine was having none of that. He meant to do more than scare them — a lot more.

The next three hours was a living hell for the young couple. The boy was outside the car, but the girl was still sitting in the car. Adams ordered the girl to get out of the car. In the following three hours, Stine and Adams repeatedly raped the girl. She was forced to commit unnatural sexual acts on her attackers. Not satisfied with their own perversion, they forced the boy to commit equally unnatural acts on the girl. With his perversion still not satisfied, Stine took the jackhandle and used it as a sexual tool on the girl. All the while Stine and Adams continuously cursed and beat both kids.

This nightmare had started at about ten o'clock. By one in the morning the attackers had satisfied their perverted minds. They stole the boy's billfold, car keys, two rings from the girl, and the clothes of both, leaving them in the country totally naked and afoot.

You can only try to imagine the helplessness that this young couple felt. Here they were, out in the country, naked, no vehicle, and having been brutally assaulted for three hours. They had little choice; they had to get help as quickly as possible. The girl was in desperate need of medical help. Naked, they walked into town, found a house, and secured clothing. The boy went to the Sheriff's office; the girl was rushed to the hospital.

Early the following morning I got a call from the Sheriff asking for my help. Arriving at the his office I asked if I could interview either of the victims. As soon as I was with the young man, I asked if he would take us to the spot of the assault. He guided us to a side street in town. He claimed they had been parked directly under a street light. I told him I could understand his fears, but for us to help him, he had to be completely truthful with us. We both knew this was not where the attack happened. He admitted this was not the place where the crime had been committed. He did not want the girl's parents, or his, to know they had been parked. I assured him that both sets of parents had once been young and they would understand. Right now all anyone wanted was to put behind bars the animals that had violated them. He apologized for misleading us and took us to the actual scene.

Before leaving the crime scene, Stine wanted to make sure they had left no fingerprints. He made the girl take the boy's shirt and wipe the car down. I guess they thought they were being smart, but as is the case with most criminals of their stature, they were dumber than a stump. Stine did not remember the boy, but the boy remembered him—they had once worked together.

The boy told us he thought he recognized one of the attackers. We rode out to the job where both had worked, and sure enough the boy made a positive ID on Stine from the personnel pictures. Regretfully, he did not have any idea who the second attacker was.

We put out an APB[7] on Stine, but we were unable to locate him for several days. Our break came a couple of days after the attack. A worker for

---

[7] All Points Bulletin.

Fort Worth Pipe and Supply had mulled all day with what his nephew had bragged about the night before. Finally, he decided, nephew or not, he had to tell someone of the outrage his nephew had boasted about. He went to his boss and told him that one of his nephews from East Texas and a friend of his had spent the previous night with him. They had all gotten drunk and the boys had bragged about having raped a woman back in East Texas. He was particularly disgusted by the way they laughed and bragged about some of the things that they had put the couple through. The boss listened until the man finished, and then he called the Ranger office in Dallas and talked to my sergeant, Lester Robertson. I had already called Lester and briefed him about the crime before sending him my report.

Lester called me and told me what had just been reported to him. Stine was at the Big Tex Apartments in Fort Worth. He asked, "Do you want us to go over there and talk to him?"

"No," I said. "Why don't you just let the Sheriff and me come on up there and talk to him."

"Okay."

I called Ranger Tom Arnold,[8] picked up the Sheriff and headed for Fort Worth. We arrived at Tom's office at about eleven o'clock in the evening. Tom was unfamiliar with the Big Tex Apartment area, so we decided to wait until the next morning and interview the uncle when he showed up for work.

By six o'clock the next morning we were at Fort Worth Pipe and Supply waiting. At a quarter to seven the uncle showed up. We asked him if his nephew was still at his apartment. Yes he was, but his friend had returned to East Texas. He gave us his key and a detailed layout of the apartment. The Sheriff, Tom Arnold, and I headed for the apartment house.

It was still early morning when we arrived at the apartment. I took the key and, as quietly as possible, unlocked the door and entered the living room. The apartment was exactly as the uncle had described. Looking into the bedroom I could see Stine laying in bed, buck naked and sound asleep. I slipped my .45 out of its holster and eased up beside the bed. I took the barrel of the pistol and lightly tapped him on the temple. I didn't tap him hard enough to awaken him the first time, so I tapped a little harder the next time. If you have ever heard the term "bug-eyed," that would describe Stine when he opened his eyes and all he could see was the business end of my Colt .45 automatic. I never had a more peaceful arrest. He literally was shaking lying on the bed as I read him his Miranda warning. When I finished Mirandizing him, we made him get up and dress. Tom Arnold went back to the uncle to get his sworn statement.

Even though we had a warrant for Stine's arrest, in Texas you still have

---

[8] Tom was the Ranger stationed in Fort Worth.

to take a suspect before a magistrate so he can again have his rights read to him. So the Sheriff and I loaded Stine in our car and headed for the nearest magistrate, Judge W. W. Mathews in Fort Worth. Before the judge Stine admitted to the charges and named Van Adams as his accomplice. After completing all the proper paperwork, we headed for East Texas.

Arriving in East Texas we quickly locked Stine up and secured a warrant for Adams. By ten o'clock that night both attackers were in jail. The next day word had spread all over town as to the sheer brutalities committed by Adams and Stine against two of their youngsters. I was uneasy. The town was in a nasty mood, so I stayed at the jail the second night as additional security. Thankfully, my fears were unfounded and the night passed peacefully.

In the ensuing trial both Asa Stine and Van Adams were found guilty of robbery against the boy and each was sentenced to forty-five years in the state penitentiary. On the charge of rape against the girl, both were once again found guilty and each was sentenced to life in prison.

SECTION 4

End of
the Line

Texas Ranger Company "B"
350 W. Interstate 30
Garland, Texas 75043
June 08, 1987

JAMES B. ADAMS
DIRECTOR

LEO E. GOSSETT
ASST. DIRECTOR

COMMISSION
RUBEN R. CARDENAS
CHAIRMAN
JOHN W. FAINTER, JR.
CALVIN R. GUEST
COMMISSIONERS

Leo E. Gossett, Director
Texas Department of Public Safety
P. O. Box 4087
Austin, Texas 78773

Dear Sir:

In my last official letter to the Director's office, it is with pride that I address a DPS classmate as Director. As you will remember, in April 1949 we were accepted into one of the finest organizations in the world. After 38 years of service, I feel that I have met the obligation I agreed to accept.

I respectfully request that my retirement day be at the end of the working day August 31, 1987.

The Department of Public Safety and the citizens of this fine state have been good to my family and myself. I shall always be indebted to both.

Sincerely,

Glenn Elliott, Texas Ranger
Company "B", Longview, Texas

GE:lw

cc: H. R. Block, Senior Captain
    James Wright, Captain Company "B"

1856-1986
COURTESY • SERVICE • PROTECTION

This says it all.

STATE OF TEXAS
OFFICE OF THE GOVERNOR
AUSTIN, TEXAS 78711

WILLIAM P. CLEMENTS, JR.
GOVERNOR

Ranger Glenn Elliott:

It is with sadness that I note your retirement from the ranks of
the Texas Rangers. I know that a similar feeling of loss and
sadness is reflected among many of your fellow Rangers as well.

You have touched many lives during the twenty-four years you
have spent as a Texas Ranger in Marshall and Longview. To those
on the wrong side of the law, that touch was certainly more
deserved than welcomed.

Being a Texas Ranger is not easy. It is hard to become a Texas
Ranger, of course, but it is also hard to uphold their ideals
and to live with the legend created by your predecessors. You
deserve credit for living up to the reputation and legend
established by the Texas Rangers.

Your interest in providing for the safety of the citizenry in
Texas -- and, indeed, the United States -- is commendable. It
began when you entered the U.S. Army in World War II. It continued when you joined the Highway Patrol in 1949. I know that
your interest in public safety will not end with your retirement.

Rita and I both appreciate your service to the State of Texas.
It will serve as an inspiration for future Texas Rangers.

Sincerely,

William P. Clements, Jr.
Governor

WPC/jr

266

CHAPTER XV
EPILOGUE

I had had my time. Like my friend, Lewis Rigler, I too was proud to have served my time as a Texas Ranger Private. Could I have been an officer? It was mine for the taking. All I had to do was reach out and take it. In the preceding pages you have heard me mention Jim Ray many times. There had been no Department of Public Safety until the reorganization in 1935 created it. One of the sections created was the CLE (Criminal Law Enforcement) to which the Rangers and the Highway Patrol answered. The Chief of the CLE answered only to the Colonel. No Ranger had ever come within smelling distance of being the Chief of the CLE. None, that is, until 1969. By then Jim had promoted to Sergeant and transferred from Tyler to Midland. He didn't stay there long before be became Captain of Company C in Lubbock. In 1969 Jim attained the highest rank any Ranger has achieved before or since. He became Chief of the CLE.

One of the first things he did after he became CLE Chief was try to get me to transfer to Austin and become a Sergeant. I really didn't want it, but Jim is not an easy man to say no to. So I went to Austin on his insistence and appeared before the Commission that chose the Sergeants. I had no more than entered the room before I realized that this was not for me. The politics in that room were so thick it didn't leave any room for oxygen. I came out of the room and kept on going straight to Longview—where I belonged.

Chief Jim Ray: When I first became the Chief of the Criminal Law Enforcement, I knew I needed some good men. I knew of none better than Glenn. I persuaded him to come to Austin to interview for a Sergeant's position. He interviewed, but being a Sergeant just wasn't for him. Glenn is one of the greatest, if not the greatest, field Ranger that has ever lived and looking back he made the right decision. But I assure you, if he had wanted the job, it was his for the taking. And I guarantee you one other thing, if he would have taken the job, I would have made him a Captain within a year. Make no mistake about it, I had the power to do it. And not only could I have done it, I would have done it!

Today, other than the questions about the Kentucky Fried Chicken mur-

267

ders, I guess the most-asked question I am asked is why I retired. I was only sixty-one years old and I suppose people thought the only way I would retire was to be drug out kicking and screaming. Honestly, there was not any one thing, but rather a combination of several. It wasn't something I had thought and agonized about for years. I never gave it a thought until about a year before I actually retired. Why should I? I could still do the job. But several things over a long period of time made me realize it was time to hang it up. Let's face it, we need some mature officers, but youth and endurance is a very important part of any group, especially law enforcement.

One factor was Ronny Griffith. Before becoming a Ranger he had been a Highway Patrolman in Kilgore. After he became a Ranger he was stationed in Amarillo, but I knew he and his wife Martha wanted to come back to Longview. Martha was from this area and Ronny was raised just up the road a bit in New Boston. About a year and a half before I retired an opening occurred in Dallas. I told Ronny that as it now stood I planned to retire in about a year. Amarillo is in Company C, and since transfers are easier within a Company I suggested that he apply for the opening in Dallas. If I did follow through with my plans to retire in 1987, it would be easier for him to make an intra-Company transfer from Dallas to Longview, than from Amarillo to Longview. He was successful with his requested transfer to Dallas.

Another thing that really rubbed me wrong was the time sheets. The state in its infinite wisdom had decided we should become clock punchers and work only forty hours a week. Imagine, a Texas Ranger having to fill out a time sheet. This was a burr under my saddle I just could not get rid of.

Also, and this was very important to me, Mother had left us in 1984 and Dad's health wasn't the best in the world. I knew I wasn't going to have him much longer and I wanted to spend as much time as I could with him. Dad left us in 1992, but those few short years were precious to me and to Dad. If for no other reason, this would have been enough.

But if I had to say what was the single most deciding factor it would be: I was worn flat-dab out. You don't work the hours I did, for as long as I did, without just plain old wearing out.

During a career with the Texas Department of Public Safety that spanned 1949 to 1987, I had six captains: J. Guy Smith, Glen Werner, Bob Crowder, Bill Wilson, G. W. Burks, and James Wright. Every one of them, without exception, told me that I did not have to work as hard as I did, but I only know one way to do anything, all out. Eighty- to one hundred-hour weeks, with over one thousand miles logged in my car, was not unusual. The people of Texas were paying me to do a job and I took that responsibility very, very seriously.

Do I have any regrets about the amount of time I put into my job. Catherine, Diane, and Dennis sacrificed the most for the job, but they understood I couldn't do it any other way. They know me better than anyone in the world and I don't think they would have respected me if I had been a slacker. So no, I have no regrets. If had it to do over, I would do it the same way.

PAUL HARVEY: Over my shoulder a backward glance. Paul Harvey was absent from this microphone for two days last week on assignment as they say. Or goofing off. Goofing off. With a long time friend, Richard Harvey, of East Texas, some mutual friends, we flew into the vastness of Ontario, north of International Falls.

As you fly north of north our land of lakes becomes a lake of islands. The tall trees start getting smaller again and it's sad to see the scars where the loggers intrude farther and deeper each year on the primitive wildness, especially since much of our forests are being ravaged to make lumber for Japan. But eventually our seaplane outdistanced the lumberjacks. We had three wonder-filled days on turquoise lakes under azure skies and nights listening to the cry of the loon and the ceaseless singing of a gentle nearby waterfall. Yes we did catch fish, all that we could eat and all they would let us bring home. Walleye and northern pike.

But these are occasions for feasting on reminisces around the lodge fireplace of an evening. With absolutely no access to newspapers, radio, or TV, we had time for the cross-pollination of ideas and some belly laughs. Otho Brand, the uncommon mayor of McAllen, Texas, the world's largest producer of some agricultural crops in our country and abroad. I'd have to live in Latin America as long as he has to glean his insight. Bob Adams who was the number two man in the FBI during some of its most turbulent years, a walking encyclopedia of information on law enforcement. Builder Lee O'Reed and car merchant Lem Barker and Texas Rangers Glenn Elliott and Bob Mitchell. What stories these men can share when there's time. And in the bush without distractions there's time. And the singing dentist from Tyler, Texas, Bob Nichols, making certain none of us took ourselves too seriously.

There's going to be a doing's later, later this day, today. Out on Caddo Lake in Marshall, Texas, when lawmen from all over converge for the retirement of Glenn Elliott, 38 years a lawman, and one of the best street cops ever anywhere.

I don't know what you know about the Texas Rangers, but they are an elite Corp of lawmen. Respected at all levels of law enforcement and revered in their home state. And if you had to pick one to represent the best of the best, that one would be Ranger Glenn Elliott. Today he's going to get some ap-

269

plause from his friends. There will be some leathery lawmen making jokes to hide tears, but any tears are for us who will have to make do without him. In war and peace, all of his adult years he has given to us. Now Ranger Glenn is going to have some years for his own family. But I'll tell you something, every rookie Ranger yet to be has a bright star to steer by.
Page Three.
*News Commentary by Paul Harvey
Recorded on August 26, 1987,
Regarding Texas Ranger Glenn Elliott's Retirement*

There's no question about it. The proudest moment of my professional career was my retirement party on Wednesday, August 26, 1987. I didn't get to hear Paul's broadcast that day. A whole slew of my dearest friends put together a retirement party at Rusty Howell's ranch between Marshall and Karnack that had to be seen to be believed. Over four hundred friends and fellow workers were there. But before describing the party I want to explain why Paul said the kind things about me.

A mutual friend of ours in Tyler, Richard Harvey—no relation to Paul— had a fishing camp in Canada that Paul used to go to regularly. Richard is a great friend of the Rangers and he often invited me and Bob Mitchell to join him at his camp. Several times Paul joined us. You have never experienced an evening until you have sat around a campfire listening to Paul Harvey tell one story after another. The week before I retired, Richard, Paul, and I, plus a few other close friends, had been to Richard's place in the far north. I don't think I have to explain the pride I felt when a man of Paul Harvey's stature salutes you before a worldwide audience. It is truly overwhelming.

But back to the party. They had set up a flatbed semi-trailer for a platform, and as I stood there as one after another of my friends rose to pay honor to me. I can't describe all my thoughts. They say that your whole life flashes before your eyes shortly before you die. I don't know if that's true or not, but I know all the good things that life has blessed me with swirled through my mind as I was standing there.

There is no man I have more respect or love for than Bob Mitchell. We're like brothers and so, not surprisingly, he paid me my greatest compliment of the day. Shortly before Bob came to Tyler as a Ranger, the State had told us we could start taking Saturdays off if we wanted to. One of the first things Bob asked me was if I was going to take off on Saturdays. I told him no; it was all I could do to finish in six days; there was no way I could get it done in five.

Also, by this time our written reports had changed dramatically—and for the better. When Jim Ray first became a Ranger in 1956, before taking the field at his duty station in Tyler, he had been assigned for a few weeks to work at the Headquarters Company in Austin. Bob Crowder was the Chief of Rangers at that time and he requested that Jim review the case reports and summarize his progress. What Jim found appalled him. Sketchy would not begin to describe what he found. Jim decided right then and there that his reports would be detailed. It didn't take long before Austin started demanding Jim Ray-type reports from all of her Rangers. Many complained and thought this was useless; after all, the current method had worked for a hundred and twenty-five years, hadn't it? From that point on our reports had to be detailed. Customarily I filled out my reports on Sunday afternoons.

Naturally, when Mitchell first came to Tyler as a Ranger I told him he could do his weekly reports on Sunday afternoons. He said he wanted to watch the Cowboys on Sundays. It drew a big laugh when he related that I had said he could do the reports during the commercials and half-time. Some who did not know me as well as most may have thought he was joking. Even though he told the story behind a laugh, he wasn't joking. And neither was I.

As I stood there my mind raced a million miles an hour. There was Slick Alfred, I remembered the day I picked him up his first day on duty as a Highway Patrolman back in 1956. It couldn't have been thirty-one years ago that I picked up that skinny kid at his house on Young Street—but it was. We rode together for five and a half years until I became a Ranger, and not once in all those years did we have a single cross word. There's a popular beer commercial going around that says it best: "Slick, I love ya man."

And there was Max. Words can never express my feelings for Max Womack. I have been graced with some great friends in my life, but none greater than Max. And I know Max feels the same way towards me.

And of course Jim Ray was there. I don't know of anything else to say about Jim that I haven't already said.

Predictably several of my officer friends from Louisiana were there and they too said some wonderful things. If I had not worn a Texas peace officer's badge, I would have been proud to have worn one from Louisiana.

But the highlight of the day came from my son Dennis. When he said he was proud of me, I almost lost it. What more could any father hope for than for his children to be proud of him.

The FBI was there; so were many of the sheriffs, district attorneys, district judges, and other friends from both law enforcement and simply friends of law enforcement. I can understand an entertainer accepting an award wanting to thank everyone and not miss anyone. No matter how hard you try, invariably you do, and so have I. But to all of you, I want to say thank you for being there. But mostly, thank all of you for allowing me to be your friend.

I can't close that remarkable day without mentioning one sad thought. I would have given anything if Lloyd Webb and Red Arnold could have been there. But they had passed on to the other side. Both have been gone a long time now, but I still miss them terribly.

There is one other group I owe the biggest thanks of all to: Thank you, citizens of Texas, for allowing me to be a part of the greatest law enforcement organization God ever graced the world with—The Texas Rangers.

Thank you.

LOOKING FOR A SOLUTION

The Ranger was doing his job
And looked very official in his white shirt
With a circle-star pinned to his pocket.
Like all Rangers he gave the impression
He was a solution waiting for a problem

—Author Unknown

Index

279

O

Oakwood Mobile Homes 78
O'Brien, Jack 166
Ocean Springs 229
Oden, Charles 188
Odessa, TX 164
Odom, Frank 179, 224, 225, 226
O'Holzappel, John 57
Oklahoma 163, 172, 175, 234
Old Betsy 14
Old Milwaukee Beer 167
Oliver, Brad 38
Oliver, Kenneth 38
Oliver's Store 26
Omaha, TX 106
"One Riot, One Ranger." 73, 89
O'Neil, Tip 5
Ontario 269
Ore City, TX 105, 109
O'Reed, Lee 269
Osaka Bay 24
Owen, W.H. 168, 169, 221

P

Pacific 21, 23
Palmer, Robert 236
Pan American Oil Company 85
Panola County
    64, 76, 197, 201, 202, 237, 238
Parish, Neal 19
Parker, Bonnie 62
Parker, Glenn 256, 258
Parkland Hospital 91
Parks, J.W. 125
Patton 24
Peoples, Clint 74
Perrin Air Force Base 86
Perry, Mann, Jr. 97
Philippines 23
Phillips, Inez 177, 178, 179, 180, 182,
    188, 194, 195, 196, 198, 199, 241
Phillips, Jack 180, 189, 198, 199
Phillips, Loyce 177
Phillips Oil Company 178, 180, 181

Pigg, Carmon 243
Pineville, LA 219, 222
Pirtle, Danny 209, 214
Pittsburg, TX 71, 106, 109, 110
Plain Dealing, LA 248
Plainview, Texas 234
Pleasant Hill Community 211, 212, 213
Pocatello, Idaho 13
Poore, L.F. 125
Port-a-Can 109
Prather, Patricia Burns Bullock 239,
    240, 242, 243
Pratt, Willard 254
Pritchard, June 73
Probst, Frank 134
Pruitt, J.W. 164
Pruitt's Lake 171
Puckett, Travis 220
Purple Heart 24

Q

Queen City, Texas 249
Quintana, R.Q. 125
Quitman, TX 223

R

R & D Cafe 19
Raiders 254
Ranch House Club 55
Ranger Company B 35
Ranger Well Service, Kilgore 183
Ray, Jerry James 185
Ray, Jim 56, 69, 70, 71, 73, 83, 84,
    89, 90, 136, 138, 155, 173, 181,
    182, 267, 271
Rayburn, Sam 5, 10, 17, 86, 87
REA (Rural Electric Association) 29
Reagan, Ronald 86
Red River 5, 248
Reed, Burl 98, 101
Reese, George 144
Reeves, Curby 235
Reno, Nevada 203, 204, 205, 206
Republic Bank, Dallas 239
Richardson, C.P. 125

282

T

Tales of the Texas Rangers 73
Tallerico, Domini 121
Tate, George 64
Tatum 96, 201
Temple, Shirley 25
Terrell, TX 55, 57, 213
Texarkana, Texas 163, 165, 168, 172
Texas Almanac 30
Texas Eastman 65
Texas Highway Patrol Training School 125
Texas Highway Patrolman 30, 36, 43, 77
Texas League 8
Texas Monthly 160
Texas Panhandle 13
Texas Ranger Hall of Fame & Museum, Waco, TX 9, 83, 105, 152
Texas-Oklahoma border 5
Thane, Elton 197
The Absent-Minded Professor 10
The Big Valley 96
The Cremo Cigar Company 8
The Henpecked Husband 10
The International Steelworkers 70
The Lone Ranger 8
The Rifleman 97
The Stars and Stripes 25
The United Plant Guard Workers of America 108, 112
The United Steel Workers of America 69
Thomas, Andrew Henry "Andy" 240, 241, 242, 243
Thomas, Jim 166
Thomas, Walter 238
Thompson, W.R. 125
Tigert, Norris 108
Tillman, Louie 25, 121
Tinsdale, Joel 229
Tisdale, Benjamin Thomas 189
Today show 73
Tommy Carlisle Wrecker Service 67
Toole, Ottis 234, 235, 237
Truman, Harry 24, 85, 86, 87

Tulsa, OK 188
Turner, Glen 96
Turner, Tom 185
Tutt, Robert 220, 253
Tyler Courier-Times 66
Tyler, Mary 210, 211, 212
Tyler, TX 38, 41, 69, 76, 83, 90, 103, 173, 194, 197, 203, 211, 220, 229, 236, 256, 258, 267, 269, 270, 271

U

Umphries, Ivey Lee 248
Uncertain, TX 93, 98, 235
Uncle Ralph's Fishing Camp 249
United Steelworkers of America Union 103
Upham, E. 125
Upshur County, TX 106, 109
USS Dashing Wave 23

V

Van Alstyne, TX 6
Varna, Emma 61
Virginia 234
Visage, Tommy 109

W

Waco, TX 35, 38, 74
Walen, W.D. 206
Walker, Kenneth 54, 130
Wall, A.D. 228
Ward, Betty 96
Ward, Tom 96
Warlick, Arthur 211, 212
Warner, Glen 55, 58
Washington, DC 5, 12, 86, 258
Washington State 22
Watson, Hiram 229, 231
Webb, Lloyd 39, 42, 43, 47, 50, 54, 56, 69, 78, 128, 129, 130, 131, 272
Weir, Billy 228
Welch, Tom 181, 194, 199, 225, 226
Werner, Glen 268
West Point 10
West Texas 90, 182

Western Hills Motel, Euless 187
Western Union 231
What's My Line? 73
Wheeler, Edward 62
Wheeler, Mrs. John I. 9
Wheeler., Mrs. Max 9
Whiskey Bend 63, 191
White, Dennis Richard 230, 231, 232, 233
White, H.A. 75, 134
White, Leo 106
White, Mark 157
White Oak, TX 197
Whitehead, R.L. 46
Wichita Falls Spudders 8
Wichita Falls, TX 15
Wiley College, Marshall, TX 144
Williams, Doyle 213
Willow Wild Cemetery 87
Wilson, Bill 134, 173, 268
Wilson, Dave 165, 166
Wilson, George 104, 107
Wilson, Lanetta 210, 211
Wilson, William W. 75
Wimberly, E.J. 69
Winchell, Walter 8
Winchester, Grandmother 8, 124
Winchester, Mary DeSpain 6
Winchester, Robert 6

Windom High School 9, 10, 117
Windom Methodist Church 8, 40
Windom National Bank 209
Windom, TX 5, 6, 7, 9, 15, 16, 17, 19, 22, 26, 27, 28, 30, 36, 38, 39, 61, 90, 115, 120, 209
Winn, S.D. 228
Winters, Dan 160
Wirasnik, C.J. 55, 56
Wisconsin 234
Wix, John 237
Womack, Max 137, 146, 150, 156, 174, 175, 181, 182, 271
Wood County 192
Wood, John 110, 185
Woodall, James 255
Worden McDavid Oldsmobile, Weatherford, TX 185
World War I 50
World War II 21, 25, 50, 87, 106
Wright, Carl 12
Wright, James 150, 268
Wright, Jim 5
Wyoming 229

Y

Yates, Ken 185
Young, James 205

ROBERT NIEMAN

Born in McLeansboro, Illinois, Robert and his wife, Donna, have lived in Longview since 1978. Together they operate their own business.

Robert's hobby is oral history as such was given the high honor of being named the oral historian for the retired Texas Rangers.

Robert is an honorary member of the Former Texas Rangers Association and proudly serves on the board-of-directors of the Texas Ranger Association Foundation.

Besides retired Texas Rangers, he has also recorded many hours with survivors of the terrible New London School Explosion of 1937 in which over 300 people, mostly children, were killed. He also proudly serves on the board-of-directors of the New London Museum.